The Practitioner's Guide to Child Art Therapy

Even in the face of challenging conditions, art therapy treatment offers meaningful opportunities for growth. It's not always easy, though, to navigate the complex interplay of art processes, relational states, and developmental theories. For any clinician looking for guidance on the ins and outs of using art therapy with children, there is no better resource than *The Practitioner's Guide to Child Art Therapy*. Both graduate students and professionals will find its pages replete with strategies for developing engaging and effective tools for understanding children's creative expression and applying this understanding towards treatment. Clinically relevant and theoretically sound, this book synthesizes the best of the literature on art development, art therapy, and child development, while emphasizing the powerful role of art media in fostering creativity and relational growth. Compelling case material and numerous art examples illustrate psychosocial, neurobiological, and attachment theories as well as practical applications, including working with attachment disruptions, anxiety, grief, parental conflict, economic poverty, chemical dependency, child abuse, and autistic spectrum disorders.

Annette Shore, MA, is an art therapist, supervisor, and a faculty member for Marylhurst University's Graduate Program in Art Therapy Counseling. She maintains a private practice in Portland, Oregon, and currently serves on the editorial review board for *Art Therapy*. With over 25 years of clinical experience, she has lectured and written about the creative process of art therapy from a developmental and relational perspective.

The Practitioner's Guide to Child Art Therapy

Fostering Creativity and Relational Growth

Annette Shore

Routledge
Taylor & Francis Group

NEW YORK AND LONDON

First published 2013
by Routledge
711 Third Avenue, New York, NY 10017

Simultaneously published in the UK
by Routledge
27 Church Road, Hove, East Sussex BN3 2FA

Routledge is an imprint of the Taylor & Francis Group, an informa business

Library of Congress Cataloging in Publication Data
Store Annette.
    The practitioner's guide to child art therapy :
    fostering creativity and relational growth Annette Shore.
    pages cm
    Includes bibliographical references and index.
    1. Art therapy for children. 2. Child psychotherapy.
    3. Art-Study and teaching. I. Title.
    RJ505.A7S5 2013
    616.89'1656—dc23
    2012045379

ISBN: 978–0–415–82902–1 (hbk)
ISBN: 978–0–415–82903–8 (pbk)
ISBN: 978–0–203–51756–7 (ebk)

Typeset in Minion
by Swales & Willis Ltd, Exeter, Devon

Printed and bound in the United States of America
by Edwards Brothers, Inc.

In memory of Siegfried Berthelsdorf and Laurie Perkin.

This book is dedicated to the visionary individuals who pioneered the field of art therapy and founded a life-affirming and meaningful form of therapy. Their efforts paved the way for generations of art therapists to follow.

Contents

Tables and Figures

Tables

Figures

Preface

As a child, the works of art that I saw in museums and those of my own creation filled me with a deep sense of meaning. I constantly drew pictures of girls, animals, and delicious foods. At school once a month, I painted on the easel in the back of the classroom. My pictures were of ballet dancers with tutus in rich muted colors, of girls eating ice cream cones and petting kittens. Creating artwork provided a way to experience pleasure, to express wishes, and to connect to feeling fully alive. As the youngest in my family, I often felt small and powerless. I remember drawing girls in the largest scale possible, perhaps as an attempt to counteract being the smallest. In doing so, I could feel like a big strong girl and also make sense of my relationship to others. The physicality and sensuality of art allowed me to represent both beauty and struggle through an eloquent language. Words, although very important, often fell short as a means of expression. These early art experiences later fueled my passion for the practice of art therapy—particularly in regard to its benefits for children. This book attempts to put into words the frequently nonverbal experiences of working with children in art therapy.

My philosophy of art therapy is founded on the notion that supporting development through creative and interpersonal connections strengthens both individuals and society. The theoretical basis is influenced by Erikson's psychosocial framework, which emphasizes relational engagement between individuals and society. Successful navigation through developmental struggles requires connections and support. The complexity of tailoring art therapy to individual developmental needs, preferences, culture, and personal style is explored in the chapters that follow. Studies of early relational development, as well as the contributions of dynamically oriented art therapists, offer a rich foundation for understanding and fostering growth within art therapy treatment.

Child art therapists embody a kind of interpersonal globalism, traversing between the realms of art, symbolic expression, nonverbal states, and theoretically based understanding. They enter both the magical and mysterious worlds of children and the intellectually complex arena in which the meaning of child behavior, emotion, and expression is conceptualized. An understanding of normal development versus degrees of disturbance allows for realistic expectations that respect each child's unique struggles. Playful and creative engagement, as well as a theoretical and conceptual framework, guide effective treatment and provide the basis for harnessing the propensities of each child.

Chapters 1 and 2 constitute Part I, "An Art-Based View of Child Development." The first chapter, "The Pictorial Language of Child Development: Theoretical Underpinnings," offers a historical context and a general introduction to theories of child development and art development. This fosters an understanding of the visual and relational language of art therapy treatment. In addition, summaries of studies of child art development by art educators and art therapists are included, as well as studies of child development that describe stage-related and relational growth in children.

The second chapter, titled "Artwork Tells the Story of Child Development," explores art expression as an interpersonal means of communication and developmental progression. Sequences of development are reviewed through case examples containing children's artwork with accompanying analyses that identify features of psychosocial, relational, and ego-developmental stages.

The progression of maturation as depicted in artworks serves as a foundation for assessing and responding to the needs of child art therapy clients. Thus, this chapter also provides tools for differentiating between normal stress and unhealthy disturbance, offering a pictorial and theoretical study of the continuum of art expression as related to developmental stages.

In Part II, "Interpersonal Developmental States: An Art-Based View," the focus, as the title indicates, turns to exploration of interpersonal development. It covers chapters 3 and 4. Chapter 3, "The Pictorial Language of Early Developmental States," describes interpersonal states in relation to both infant and toddler development and clinical art therapy with children. Personality development, as described by object relations theorists and neurobiological and attachment researchers, is explored in relation to child art therapy case vignettes. The emphasis is on the persistence of early developmental and relational experience and how this is assessed and addressed within the process of art therapy. Creativity and visual expression are a means for children to access and repair these states in art therapy sessions.

Chapter 4, "The Pictorial Language of Early Relational Trauma," addresses the experience of early relational trauma through relevant case vignettes that illustrate the effects of disrupted early attachment. The visual and creative language of attachment-disordered children's art is used to teach about the persistence of early relational states, therapeutic processes, and treatment goals.

Part III, "The Pictorial Language of Resilience and Vulnerability," begins with chapter 5, "Resilience: The Capacity to Struggle with Challenges." Here, the focus is on the concept of resilience as related to child development and art therapy treatment interventions. Identifying qualities of resilient children and building qualities of resilience within the treatment process are explored through case examples that illustrate the power of relational and creative art therapy. (In all case descriptions throughout the book identifying information and case material has been altered to protect client confidentiality.)

Chapter 6, "Vulnerability and Fluctuating Developmental States," is also included in Part 3. It explores implications for working with children who do not possess significant qualities of resilience. It includes art expression from several highly vulnerable children, illustrating their levels of fragility and related considerations for treatment. The emphasis is on integrating art observations with assessment of risk factors as the basis for developing interventions. The case material covers a range of presenting problems including organicity, low cognitive functioning, psychoses, and trauma-related disorders.

Part IV, "Tuning In to Children and Parents," begins with chapter 7, "Planning, Practical Matters, and Safety," which covers the initial framework for establishing effective treatment. Subject areas provide an overview relating to safety, containment, physical, logistical, and interpersonal factors. Case examples illustrate issues such as reducing anxiety (of both child and therapist), careful questioning of children, providing the right amount of structure (via art media and directives), and individualizing the treatment approach. Chapters 8 and 9 are contained in this part as well.

Chapter 8, "Engaging, Assessing, and Learning From Children," builds on chapter 7 and elaborates further on the theme of engaging children in art therapy activities during initial sessions. Case examples illustrate how to provide a structure that facilitates effective assessment and engagement through interventions that take into account individual and cultural treatment needs and preferences.

Chapter 9, "Engaging and Learning from Parents," addresses the fact that parents are an important and sometimes challenging presence within the process of initial assessment and ongoing treatment. This interface is explored with emphasis on constructively enlisting the strengths of parents in supporting the art therapy treatment process and the child's growth. Case examples illustrate what to say to parents, treatment dilemmas, and the potential impact of parents on the therapist. The interplay of parents, art therapist, and art processes are examined via case material that includes discussion of outcomes.

The final section, Part V, "Art-Based Attunement: Facilitating Repair," undertakes increasingly complex aspects of practice. Chapter 10, "Mentalization, Trauma, Attachment, and Art Therapy Narratives," explores *Mentalization*, an attachment-based developmental process, that involves interpersonal reflection, self-organization, and reciprocity. The art therapy experience is uniquely suited for helping children to mentalize overwhelming emotional states. Case studies explore art therapy technique and a theoretically oriented approach to mentalization, as a focus for therapy. The discussion differentiates treatment approaches relating to both complex and discrete trauma as well as disrupted attachment development. The case material refers to challenges such as dealing with secrecy, vicarious trauma and low levels of trust. The therapeutic approach incorporates art-based narratives with a focus on verbal and nonverbal relational experience. Mentalization functions enhance capacity to engage in reflective states and serves to reduce reactivity in children.

In chapter 11, "Building Sturdiness: Repairing Developmental Disruptions," case material addresses the concept of building developmental strengths and resilience within the process of longer-term child art therapy. A lengthy case study reviews and explores salient topics, including stages of therapy, art as therapy, gender, cultural factors, the therapist's reactions, and the function of grief.

The twelfth and last chapter, "Creativity, Containment, and the Therapist's Use of Self," is a tapestry of themes, exploring areas such as terminations; symbolic expression; behavior management; tolerating perceived therapeutic failures; and unanswered questions about the mysterious, the seemingly magical aspects of art therapy. The therapist's creative use of self is woven into each topic.

The book as a whole was developed with the goal of providing support to practitioners who work with children experiencing disturbance and chaos, frequently within conditions in which inhumanity and economic scarcity threaten to diminish the quality of treatment. An underlying premise throughout the following pages is the belief that even within difficult conditions, creativity, fluency in the language of art, and self-understanding are tools that assist practitioners in the dual processes of promoting growth in clients and finding meaning in their work.

Acknowledgments

I would like, first of all, to express my gratitude to the child art therapy clients and their parents, who not only have prompted and nourished the content of this book, but also have significantly facilitated my understanding of creativity, development, and relational growth. These individuals have allowed me to participate in mutual experiences of change and mastery. In addition, I wholeheartedly thank the students and supervisees whom I have been fortunate to work with. Their ideas and clinical work have significantly shaped my approach.

I am deeply grateful to Frances Kaplan who contributed her consultation, encouragement, and brilliant editorial skills as this book evolved. Christine Turner has been a patient, astute confidante and consultant regarding the structure and content of this book. A grant from Marylhurst University provided invaluable support that allowed me to complete this book.

I also wish to thank the following friends, family, and colleagues who generously lent support, understanding, and expertise at various stages of the book's development: Marion Burns, Ann Cole, Eleanor Koepke, Redmond Reams, Jean Shirkoff, Lee X Shore, Karl Urban, and Mark Urban. And I am grateful to the skilled Routledge editors George Zimmar, Anna Moore, and Marta Moldvai who supported this project and lent their expertise.

Part I

An Art-Based View of Child Development

1 The Pictorial Language of Child Development

Theoretical Underpinnings

Would any book of this nature be complete without reference to the saying "One picture is worth a thousand words"? Due to the fact that pictures are the primary language of child art therapy, these words are especially apt. Comprehension of the pictorial language of child development is an essential tool for effective child art therapy practice. This becomes the basis for understanding and engaging the wide variety of individual clients. For art therapists treating children, fluency in the language of art is a professional tool that is developed through personal art experiences and through the study of children's artwork. Such knowledge allows access to the inner world of children. It enables an understanding of emotional, interpersonal, and cognitive experiences at each stage of childhood. This fluency allows the art therapist access to the strengths, struggles, and motivations of child clients; it provides a compass for navigating the varied terrain of children's experiences, environments, and cultures. The art therapist's understanding of developmental stages, as related to the pictorial language of children, assists in developing understanding of the complexities of each child during the assessment and treatment processes.

In keeping with the focus on childhood of the book as a whole, this chapter explores the stages of visual art by children up to 12. Developmental theories and children's art are compared to revisit what it is like to be a child, progressing through age-related stages. This experience becomes the basis for entry into the creative and visual inner world of preadolescent children.

Artwork tells the story of a child's development and reflects each child's unique vision. This is one reason why child art is fascinating and delightful. Art expression reveals individual characteristics as well as aspects of child development that are universal. There are developmental sequences that all children go through, such as learning to walk or speak. Creativity and artistic expression also involve predictable developmental stages. It is the job of the art therapist treating children to study both the universal and the personal elements of development as a means of understanding creative expression and its relationship to functioning. An understanding of the interaction of creative and biological development can reveal various options for how to help children who experience disturbances as well as those who struggle with the challenges inherent in normal development.

Child Art Expression: A Snapshot of Child Development

Child artwork speaks eloquently about the child's perceptions, emotions, thoughts, and physical experiences. The nature of art is that it conveys something deeply meaningful about both individual and universal experiences. The viewer of artwork is invited to understand and empathize with the artist and to comprehend more broadly what it is to be human. Art expression has the potential to be satisfying and significant for both the artist and the audience.

It is difficult for most adults to remember what it felt like to be a small child. One way to be reminded is to look at art by young children. In doing so, one may remember the sense of playfulness and the joy of making silly pictures. For example, Figure 1.1 shows a drawing of an imaginary dinosaur by a 5-year-old boy. It reflects a time of intense curiosity and imagination that occurs prior to learning to read, write, and perform competitively. The large playful dinosaur is the center of attention in the scene, reflecting the imaginative innocence and egocentric qualities of a preschool child. The relative lack of fine motor control leads to a slightly clumsy but uninhibited and frolicking quality, unique to children at this stage of life. The capacity to freely imagine and to mix elements of fantasy and reality also speaks about the experience of the preschool child who is not yet firmly situated in reality. Through experiences, maturational processes, and the help of parents, the child develops an increasing capacity to become reality oriented. While playfulness is a universal experience for young children, in content and quality it always reflects the varied values, norms, and relational patterns derived from parents and the community at large (Golomb, 2011).

Figure 1.2 is a self-portrait by a 3-year-old girl. As in the previous example, the drawing reflects the bold simplicity inherent in the aesthetic and perceptual experience that is a feature of what Erik Erikson (1950) referred to as the play age. At this stage of development, children rarely depict groupings of people but usually portray isolated figures. This is generally not an expression of loneliness or isolation but is more likely attributable to a healthy level of egocentricity. This type of human figure, which includes a large head and no torso, is referred to as a "tadpole" figure (Golomb, 2003). (See chapter 2 for further discussion of the play age.)

During the elementary school years, however, children often depict groupings of people. Cooperative and competitive teamwork is a way of life for children by second

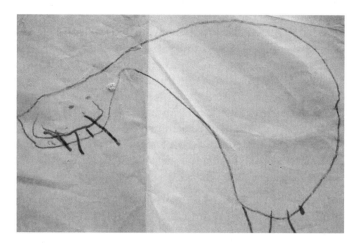

Figure 1.1 Dinosaur by 5-year-old-boy

Figure 1.2 Self-portrait by 3-year-old girl

or third grade, and their art reflects this. This is not to say that older children no longer depict large solitary figures, but in general, their experience and perceptions encompass more complex relationships as they mature interpersonally. Figure 1.3, a family portrait by an 8-year-old girl, illustrates many features of middle childhood: increased sense of reality; good fine-motor control; clear gender identity; awareness of one's role within a family, community, or peer group; and a high level of attention to detail. Also evident is the considerable presence of impulse control and frustration tolerance, which would be abnormal in a preschooler. While the characteristics of early art expression tend to

Figure 1.3 Family drawing by 8-year-old girl

be universal, western culture influences children to depict increasingly realistic representations as they mature. In many nonindustrialized cultures, artistic representation is characterized by symbolism and decoration (Golomb, 2011).

The above examples illustrate how the language of art encapsulates the fundamentals of child development. Rapid developmental gains are apparent in these drawings, which span just a few years. The first two illustrations reveal much about the playful innocence of the preschool years, while the third example illustrates the sense of order and conformity that develops gradually during the subsequent school years. Because art expression reveals much about individual and universal experiences, it provides not only the basis for understanding and empathizing with the individual child, but also the basis for understanding experiences of children in general. The study of child art expression provides a means for conceptualizing normal development as well as for detecting abnormal development. In other words, the art therapist is as concerned with signs of normality evident in artwork as with signs of failed maturation.

Importance of Developmental Theories

Developmental theories are based on rigorous and systematic observation of samples of people. They allow practitioners to be aware of generalities about how human beings function at various stages throughout the life cycle. Integration of developmental theories should be incorporated into practice, providing some objective measures for understanding both general and unique qualities of children. Clinical practice that is built upon developmental theory reduces the possibility of basing assessment and treatment exclusively on intuition or emotional reactions. This is not to say that art therapists should avoid using their intuition and emotional reactions as additional tools. Emotional reactions to art and interpersonal relationships are also key factors in conducting child art therapy. If emotional reactions were not part of the art therapist's tools, therapeutic relationships and processes would be meaningless. At the same time, knowledge of recent research and theory provides important objectivity that protects against mistaking supposition for fact.

There have been systematic studies of child development in a range of areas including physical, cognitive, psychosocial, psychosexual, and moral development. Developmental theories overlap, describing similar experiences from different angles. Likewise, children's art expressions provide snapshots of developmental stages, encompassing multiple aspects of development. Such snapshots provide eloquent material for a deep understanding of the sequences of child development. Winnicott (1971b) stated that a child therapist should have "in one's bones a theory of emotional development of the child" (p. 3). Studying children's art is a good way to enrich one's "bones." Art expression synthesizes so many areas of functioning that if one understands the language of art from a developmental perspective, it becomes a shortcut to understanding both child development and the essence of what it is like to be a child. This is a basis not only for sound clinical work but also for developing empathy, a crucial component of the treatment process.

The more one studies and observes, the more it becomes clear that art expression, speech, behavior, and perception are all very similar in their progression (Lindstrom, 1970). For example, children's speech begins with random sounds and eventually progresses to words, then sentences. Children's artwork has a similar evolution. It moves along a path that begins with manipulation of mashed bananas in the high chair, to making random scribbles, marks, and shapes on paper; to organization of forms; and eventually, to an organized and detailed visual narrative. In all areas of functioning, the increasingly complex grasp of reality is gradually developed through the child's own unique perspective, culminating in such functions as logic, abstract thought, ability to comprehend contradictory points of view, and ability to artistically portray perspective and gradation.

Expression of Destructive Feelings and Developmental Stages

Potentially destructive feelings, such as anger and envy, are part of the normal human experience. Preschoolers and older children with disturbances often demonstrate impaired ability to modulate such feelings. Because anger and destructive fantasies are normal, it is not unusual for artwork done by children who experience normal and pathological development to look somewhat similar. The degree and quality of such expression, as well as the age of the child, are factors to consider in evaluating the level of each child's adjustment.

For example, a 6-year-old boy, who had just spent some time in the presence of a baby, completed the drawing in Figure 1.4. He attempted to depict his perception of the

Figure 1.4 Baby by 6-year-old boy

helpless, incontinent state of this infant, perhaps as a way to reinforce to his own mastery of bodily functions and to reconcile both envy and repulsion in response to the baby's extreme level of dependency and helplessness. Several reactions including humor, fascination, and repulsion are included in this child's artistic portrayal, which exaggerates the baby's lack of body control and seemingly disgusting tendencies. It is normal for young children to react to a baby with envy and repulsion, a means of regression that solidifies their own developmental accomplishments.

Six-year-old children have not fully mastered the ability to control impulses. They still cause accidental messes and experience lapses in impulse or bodily control. Consequently, their art may include themes or an artistic style that reflects loss of control along with the intent to regain control. At one moment 6-year-olds can seem very grownup, and at the next, the composure falls apart; the child is reduced to tears or lashes out.

It is interesting to compare Figure 1.5, an impulsively executed drawing by a troubled preadolescent, to the 6-year-old boy's depiction of a baby, as they have some similarities. The boy who completed Figure 1.5 experienced abuse and instability throughout his childhood. His drawing depicts a provocative sexualized alien and was completed within an art therapy group in a school setting. This boy was anxious and disruptive. Both his behavior and his artwork reflected qualities of an earlier developmental stage, but with added features of strong preadolescent sexual and aggressive feelings. Preschool children

Figure 1.5 Sexualized alien by 12-year-old boy

are not likely to depict vulgar sexual content. Although preadolescents may depict sexualized content, this particular drawing, which was done in an attention-seeking manner, contains several concerning features, namely, hostile and frightening sexual imagery. Preadolescents experience a host of bodily and emotional challenges that are difficult to manage. Children who are maltreated are at risk for failing to build the foundation necessary to manage these confusing and potentially overwhelming feelings of later childhood. In this case, it is evident that the 12-year-old who drew the alien demonstrated a level of impulse control and emotional regulation more like that of a young child. He had extreme difficulty managing preadolescent developmental tasks and experienced poor regulation due to the stress of having been abused.

The above example provides an introduction to the complex study of normal versus disturbed development and illustrates one way the features of earlier development can appear in a drawing by an older child. There are numerous possible variations on this theme. In this particular comparison, an important distinction between the two drawings is that 6-year-old children normally have relatively weak impulse control, while older children are expected to have fairly good impulse control and a higher level of inhibition. In this case, however, the preadolescent boy's art expression contains features of earlier behavioral and artistic developmental stages due to his response to a history of maltreatment and to the challenge of impending puberty. Theories of artistic and psychological developmental stages furnish many guidelines for understanding this type of material. Each case must be considered individually, taking into account normal developmental sequences, environment, culture, current and past influences, present functioning, and artistic ability.

Artistic Development: Important Theorists

Studies that evaluate formal qualities of child art facilitate understanding of stage-related generalities. This type of study is helpful to art therapists in providing cues regarding healthy development versus indications of intellectual, emotional, organic, or physiological difficulties. There are several theorists who have made major contributions to the field of art therapy through their study of artistic development, a few of which are mentioned here. These contributors include representatives from the field of art education, psychology, and art therapy.

Lowenfeld: Art Educator and Researcher

Viktor Lowenfeld's (Lowenfeld & Brittain, 1987) research has been widely cited and relied upon by art therapists. Although Lowenfeld's stages may be overly simple for the purposes of art therapy evaluation, they do provide a sort of shorthand that has become an essential and widely used tool of child art therapy assessment and treatment. Lowenfeld (Lowenfeld & Brittain, 1987) collected and studied large samples of children's artwork. His study of graphic development continues to provide a clear and useful map of creative and mental growth. Although Lowenfeld was not a therapist, he classified numerous samples of child and adolescent artworks, identifying age-related features based on observation of organization, content, form, color usage, thematic content, and stylistic qualities. The stages Lowenfeld classified emphasize the progression towards increasing realism, beginning with the *Scribbling* stage of toddlers and early preschool-aged children. These early marks become more controlled, intentional and realistic, culminating in the stage associated with 4- to 7-year-old children, the *Preschematic* stage. During this period, children begin to attribute reality-based meaning to their often randomly placed early representational depictions that do not yet incorporate realistic use of color. The *Schematic* stage, characteristic of children aged 7–9, involves a more orderly approach to color and rendering of forms, employing geometric shapes and practiced schema for depicting subject matter such as baselines, skylines, and human figures. *Dawning Realism* also called the *Gang Age,* a period to which 9- to 11-year-old children may progress (if interested in art), involves increased depiction of detail and depth, as well as decreased reliance on the flat simple forms associated with the Schematic stage. Later stages, *Pseudorealism* and the *Period of Decision,* are associated with increasingly realistic adult-like art that includes skillful use of style, shading, and personal expression. Lowenfeld's classification system has been useful to art therapists because it provides a simple and widely understood tool for conceptualizing graphic development. At the same time, art therapists meaningfully apply this tool only when they have a complex understanding of developmental processes, disorders of childhood, and visual language.

Lowenfeld (Lowenfeld & Brittain, 1987) was an advocate for quality art education; he emphasized the need for schools to offer art education that encouraged individual creative work in a developmentally appropriate manner. He maintained that art is a means of learning as opposed to something to be learned. The methods he recommended required that art educators have an in-depth understanding of developmental stages and associated levels of creativity (which is not often emphasized for teachers). This approach overlaps with some of the fundamental principles that child art therapists employ because art therapy also seeks to promote maturation through creative experiences. Art therapists, however, add to Lowenfeld's approach an understanding of clinical factors and focus on children who are at risk and experience a range of treatment needs.

Lowenfeld's System Compared to Other Systems

For better or worse, Lowenfeld's (Lowenfeld & Brittain, 1987) research has become the "gold standard" for art therapists' classification of child art development. Lowenfeld's studies incorporated stages that provide a user-friendly shorthand for classifying graphic development. As with any classification system, Lowenfeld's work is most useful when it is applied with a spirit of inquiry that is integrated with contextual understanding of each child's experience, aesthetic preferences, efforts, and interests. Authors such as Golomb (2003) and Cox (2005) have developed complex theories of child art development that integrate perceptual, cognitive, philosophical, and aesthetic inquiry. Respect for the simplicity of form and the complexity of children's invention of meaning characterizes Golomb's theory. Cox's approach considers art forms as well as cultural, historical, and sociological variations and generalities. Complex approaches such as these embody a cognitive developmental perspective as well as a philosophy of children's art, emphasizing the meaningfulness of form as a pictorial language of experience, perception, cognition, emotion, and aesthetic sensibility.

Systems that emphasize complexity and highly individualized aspects of art development are less user-friendly than Lowenfeld's (Lowenfeld & Brittain, 1987) system. Although they more adequately match the need to be cautious in arriving at judgments and conclusions regarding individuals and groups of children, they do not lend themselves to being used as a simple classification system. Other researchers such as Koppitz (1968) and Di Leo (1977) have developed helpful child art developmental theories, but they are not as widely used for a variety of reasons including lack of extensive research data and limited applicability regarding normal as well as cross-cultural developmental sequences. Kellogg (1970), on the other hand, classified the marks that evolve into specific forms in drawings by young children, integrating a Jungian approach in which belief in the significance of the *mandala* (a symmetrical design within a circle) was interjected into assumptions about the universality of children's art.

Rubin: Art Therapist and Psychologist

Whereas Lowenfeld (Lowenfeld & Brittain, 1987) researched stages of graphic development, Judith Rubin (2005), a highly influential pioneer art therapist, categorized stages of artistic development. Graphic development, as conceptualized by Lowenfeld, is more often (although not exclusively) applied to observation of two-dimensional artwork. Rubin's system for understanding artistic development encompasses both two- and three-dimensional artwork with an emphasis on sensory experience, perception, and creative-functional capacities. Compared to Lowenfeld's system, Rubin's analysis tends to emphasize the process and the experiential component more than the final product. This makes sense, given that Rubin is an art therapist as opposed to a researcher or art educator. Her studies are based on insightful, anecdotal observation of children in art therapy sessions as well as similar observation in nonclinical settings.

Rubin's (2005) nine artistic developmental stages include *manipulating* (1–2 years), *forming* (2–3 years), *naming* (3–4 years), *representing* (4–6 years), *consolidating* (6–9 years), *naturalizing* (9–12 years), and *personalizing* (12–18 years). As with all developmental-stage theories, it is apparent that increased capacities, competencies, and complexities are built as the child evolves into an adolescent. In Rubin's stages, the emphasis is on a cumulative synthesis of sensory, emotional, mental, and physical expression that "are not so discreet in reality. Indeed they always overlap and in a very real sense, live on forever as possible modes of doing" (p. 35). Rubin's statement is relevant to all aspects of development. There is no purely linear progression, but rather there is an overall movement towards maturation and integration that continually evolves. This evolution involves some loss; for example, a child may lose the sheer joy of making a mess while singing in gibberish. However, as other capacities are gained, the appreciation of sensory stimulation is retained in experiences such as manipulating soft clay to produce a personally meaningful artwork. Growth is an integrative process as opposed to a series of stages that are successively replaced. Thus it is necessary for child art therapists to be familiar with all developmental stages: remnants of earlier stages can be seen in later stages. The degree to which these remnants may indicate health or difficulties is a complex question involving many variables, warranting careful consideration with each child.

Art Expression and Maturation

Inherent in any study of child development is the fact that children progress from having minimal fine motor control to having considerable fine motor control. They progress from experiencing simple concrete thoughts to the capacity for complex abstract thought. In general, as children's thinking and behavior become increasingly multifaceted, they become less innocent and less spontaneous. Their playfulness is replaced gradually by the ability to think deeply, to plan, and to analyze. Both Lowenfeld's (Lowenfeld & Brittain, 1987) and Rubin's (2005) classifications of artistic developmental stages encompass mental and emotional experience in a progression that culminates in the increased ability to express one's unique identity through artwork. It makes sense that art should ultimately reflect this. Identity formation, an active function during adolescent development, is the culmination of childhood (E. Erikson, 1968).

Figure 1.6, a portrait by a 16-year-old boy, illustrates the introspection and conceptual abilities as well as the fine motor control and sense of identity that epitomizes adolescent development. As evident in this sensitive portrait, adolescents demonstrate increased attention span, understanding of complexity, ability to plan, and the desire to be understood by others. Psychotherapy pioneers such as S. Freud (trans. 1938), A. Freud (1939), and E. Erikson (1968) shaped current concepts regarding child development. Art therapy assessment and practice continues to build on this foundation while reshaping its focus to emphasize the art-based language of children.

Figure 1.6 Portrait by 16-year-old boy

Psychological Theories of Child Development

Psychosexual Development

S. Freud (trans. 1938) was a pioneer in his attempts to systematize child development, and the first theorist to conceptualize child developmental stages. He characterized the first stage as the *oral* stage followed by the *anal, phallic, oedipal,* and *latency* stages. Physiological drives were a primary focus in these stages. His conceptualization of stages, however, provides a symbolic way to look at the experience of development. It starts with the early experience of pure physicality and the need for oral satiation followed by establishing self-regulatory abilities, gaining a sense of one's own power, developing relationally, and participating as a member of a community. The whole process leads to the gradual putting aside of the exclusive pursuit of need gratification and evolves into the capacity to experience adult sexuality and loving relationships.

S. Freud's (trans. 1938) studies were not based on systematic study of children but on clinical observation during the therapeutic process and this is a major reason Freudian terminology and concepts are no longer widely used in the field of contemporary child psychology. However, their influence fostered increased interest in research and theories about child development. Factors such as pleasure seeking and destructive propensities, which were salient in Freud's formulations, continue to be at the forefront of child therapy. A central focus of child psychotherapy and art therapy is the struggle to convert excessive desires for pleasure and aggression to meaningful higher-level expression (Kramer, 1977, 1993, 2000).

Psychosocial Development

The study of artistic development mirrors psychosocial developmental theories. Child art expression provides a visual narrative of psychosocial stages. Both Viktor Lowenfeld (Lowenfeld & Brittain, 1987), in his study of graphic art development, and Erik Erikson (1950), in his study of psychosocial development, provided well founded systems for understanding the stage-related emotional, cognitive, physical, perceptual, and interpersonal experiences of children. Together, these systems conceptualized the complex development of children and the multifaceted evolution of their artwork. Erik Erikson's recognition of the need to expand Sigmund Freud's (trans. 1938) study of psychosexual drives and developmental stages was the impetus for the theory of psychosocial development (Friedman, 1999).

Erik Erikson (1950, 1968, 1980) completed systematic studies of individuals as they progressed through the life cycle. He developed a framework that delineated the "eight ages of man." Prior to becoming a psychologist, Erikson was a practicing visual artist (Friedman, 1999). Perhaps it is because of this that his conceptualization of developmental stages lends itself well to understanding the role that creativity plays in maturational processes. Although Erikson's studies are scientifically based, his background as an artist may explain his ability to see and describe general truths about the human experience. All of the qualities inherent in stage-related conflicts that Erikson identifies, such as *basic trust versus basic mistrust* and *autonomy versus shame and doubt*, are observable features within creative art processes.

Erik Erikson (1980) strove to develop a theory that did not oversimplify the complicated nature of what it means to be human. Therefore, he studied fairly large samples of people over long periods of time. He included cross-cultural study in order to understand how the basic human experience differs for those who live in nonindustrialized settings (E. Erikson, 1968). He identified general themes that are characteristic of individuals as they develop. Each stage encapsulates a dynamic tension between opposing forces, emphasizing the role that reconciling conflicts plays in maturation. Each stage involves loss in addition to enrichment that is strong enough to offset that which is relinquished.

Maturation is a lifelong process that involves effective struggle at each developmental stage so that the strength necessary to become a well functioning human being can be built up cumulatively. If conditions are optimal, each stage builds on previous ones as the individual matures. However, deficits in an earlier stage may impede growth in a later stage. A common example of this is the child who does not learn to control impulses and continues beyond the preschool years to lash out when faced with disappointments. This tendency interferes with mastery and friendships in school, thus impeding resolution of the tasks associated with progression that involves striving for a sense of control. When the course of development is built on a faulty foundation, the child is at risk for repeated failures throughout life. Child art therapists assess children to determine the level of their maturation and use art therapy to facilitate corrective processes.

Experiences during later stages may afford opportunities for reworking earlier stages. For example, Vaillant (1993) describes the importance of the choice of spouse during adulthood regarding the possible affects on maturation. A spouse who expects and supports a healthy relationship provides the context for developing increased resilience during adulthood. In therapy with children, the idea is similar; the therapeutic process builds on the propensity to use current maturational strengths to work through areas of weakness. For example, a child who did not master potty training at the appropriate stage due to conflicts with parents may produce messes with art media during art therapy that he or she learns to control. This becomes a means to establish the necessary sense of control that allows for both regulated toilet habits and cooperative interpersonal relationships with perceived authority figures.

As stated above, the outcome of developmental struggles is growth, for which human beings naturally strive. The concept that all human beings instinctively strive for growth and maturation underlies developmental theories. This also provides a basis for understanding a central aspect of psychotherapeutic art interventions. The therapist builds on the human instinct to seek out opportunities for growth and development. Although this instinct may be more difficult to access in severely disturbed individuals, the therapist's role is to try to nurture this propensity that is inherent in all life.

Erik Erikson's (1980) theory is based on the belief that individuals and society mutually stimulate each other and enhance each other's survival. This begins in utero and proceeds within early familial relationships and culminates in participation in communities and societies. Therefore, clinical work is related to the health of the culture at large.

Childhood Defenses

Childhood defenses are evident in art therapy expression and in patterns of behavior and interaction. A conceptual understanding of defenses assists art therapists in evaluating strengths, difficulties, and goals for their clients. Anna Freud (1939) studied various aspects of child development that built upon her father's study of the ego and pioneered the concept of defensive structural development during childhood (Friedman, 1999). Anna Freud's research involved direct observation of children as a means of conceptualizing the developmental progression of defense mechanisms (among other psychological and behavioral aspects of childhood functioning). Her research included observation of normal children in Vienna and children who experienced traumatic disruptions during World War II in Britain (Edgcumbe, 2000), and the accumulated data served to form the basis of an innovative and complex developmental theory.

Subsequently, numerous theories have described and further systematized the concept of defense mechanisms. The current *Diagnostic and Statistical Manual of Mental Disorders* (DSM-IV-TR) (2000) states:

> Defense Mechanisms (or coping styles) are automatic psychological processes that protect the individual against anxiety from the awareness of internal or external dangers or stressors. Individuals are often unaware of these processes as they operate. Defense mechanisms mediate the individual's reaction to emotional conflicts and internal and external stressors.
>
> (p. 807)

Defenses as Maturational Process

The study of ego defenses provides a system for classifying maturational processes that affect behavior, emotion, cognition, and interpersonal relationships. Art therapists are familiar with this framework as it aids in providing diagnosis and assessment when integrated with children's overall functioning and art expression. Children's growth process is characterized by defensive maturation throughout development. Infants are primarily driven by instincts, seeking physical pleasure and comfort. During the toddler and preschool years, instinct-based states begin to be tamed, spurred by parents' encouraging and even insisting that children relinquish infantile states in concordance with their enhanced cognitive, physical, and emotional capabilities. Gradually, parents' understanding of reality is imparted to children, who little by little let go of their superstitions and magical beliefs and fears as well as their attempts at dictatorship (Fraiberg, 1955). By their sixth year, children have largely become functioning members of society, and as such, are capable of holding back impulses, engaging in school-based learning, and conforming to rules. Anna Freud (1939) used the term *latency* developed by her father to describe this period because reactivity and impulsivity are largely dormant until the onset of puberty. She observed that school-age children appear like little adults in their ability to engage in quality work and in both competitive and cooperative group activities. These observations are useful to art therapists when attempting to identify if children are functioning age-appropriately and to design treatment to fit the level of actual development if they are not. Development can involve areas of immaturity or it can involve pseudomaturity; in either case, the art therapist designs treatment to provide appropriate repair.

Defenses are tools employed by the self to protect and defend against actual or perceived danger (A. Freud, 1939). They are a necessary part of the structure of the self that allow for adaptation and coping with challenges. Vaillant (1993) likens defenses to an immune system that buffers individuals from the dangers of facing reality too directly. Defenses are not used consciously and are, therefore, "imperceptible to the user" (p. 19). They play an important "role in regulating aggression, grief, dependency, tenderness, and joy" (p. 13). As individuals advance through the life cycle, they tend to incorporate increasingly mature defenses. In healthy development, flexible use of a variety of age-appropriate defenses occurs.

Throughout the lifespan, well adjusted individuals shift from using lower-level defenses, such as projection and acting out, to increasingly higher-level defenses, such as altruism and suppression. Understanding which defenses individuals rely on is necessary for formulating treatment goals. In assessing children, it is important to understand the age-appropriateness of defenses so as to respect rather than attempt to rush or delay developmental processes. For instance, it is expected that young children use fantasy and projection and that they often egocentrically disregard consideration of others. Frequently, children with cognitive or psychological deficits incorporate less developmentally mature defenses than their peers. Therapeutic goals can be designed to help children use increasingly mature defensive processes For example, a child can incorporate *displacement* through the use of imaginative art processes as a gradual replacement for *acting out.* Contrary to the popular idea that it is bad to be "defensive," defenses, when employed in developmentally appropriate ways, are healthy and creative tools for coping (Vaillant, 1993).

Art Therapists' Studies of Defense Mechanisms

Artwork reveals much about the defenses an individual incorporates. Some of the pioneers in the field of art therapy were influenced by Anna Freud's (1946) study of ego psychology. They integrated this study with their observations that artistic endeavors are inherently strengthening for children and that artwork reflects and facilitates developmental processes. It stands to reason, then, that children's art can be used to assess defensive organization. Myra Levick (1983) was one art therapist who conducted systematic observation of child art and connected graphic indicators with specific defense mechanisms, whereas Edith Kramer (1977, 1993, 2000) observed defensive structures of children within art therapy treatment as related to the qualities of their artworks. Kramer's significant and innovative contributions are further described below.

Edith Kramer (1977, 1993, 2000) explored artistic growth and quality in art as indicators of the defensive structures of emotionally disturbed child artists, many of whom were severely aggressive and traumatized. As a result, *sublimation*—the process of redirecting undesirable urges—became the cornerstone of Kramer's approach. In studying the role of sublimation in art, Kramer observed that the quality of children's artwork revealed interpersonal and psychological functioning, particularly with reference to the capacity to handle aggression. Her formulations became a central aspect of art therapy because creative work can assist in transforming unmanageable feelings into socially productive, personally meaningful products, which can benefit both the self and the viewer. In the process "form and content become an inseparable whole" (Kramer, 2000, p. 44).

Kramer's case studies involved children who used art therapy to facilitate defensive maturation. She noted that significant raw emotion was channeled into intensely absorbing art expression. The artwork, which reflected the complexity of strong and sometimes contradictory emotions, indicated aesthetically charged personal struggles. It also served as a safe symbolic equivalent for life, restoring equilibrium to children for whom traumatic experiences had produced rampant feelings of being unsafe. Sublimation through art provides a means to higher-level organization of defensive structure.

Whereas artistic sublimation as described by Kramer (2000) may be an outcome of art therapy, other examples of defenses expressed in children's artwork appear spontaneously. These include reverting to scribbling, which reflects the use of *regression* (an immature defense), depicting a violent scene as a means of *displacement* of aggression (a defense of middle childhood as well as adulthood), and achieving a high level of aesthetically meaningful artwork demonstrating *sublimation* (a mature defense). Kramer maintained that the defensive maturation of a child is facilitated through the art therapy process and is observable in art therapy products. For example, sadistic qualities in art produce sensationalism, a low quality form of art. In contrast, if aggression is artistically redirected into sublimation, compassion may be conveyed.

Theoretical Underpinnings as Tools

The theorists that contribute to art therapists' understanding of art-based development span areas such as art therapy, psychology, and education. Their studies have evolved over numerous decades, providing a substantial foundation for assessment and treatment. Such exploration and research are important tools for child art therapists as they provide a framework for understanding both generalities and individual differences inherent in developmental processes. Although the theories are solid, they continue to be subject to minor revision as cultural shifts impact children's development and art imagery (Cox, 2005). For example, the constant bombardment of digital visual material and access to computer-generated imagery plays a role in shaping cognition, perception, and creative art expression in children (Golomb, 2011). Further, in western culture, relational and familial patterns have shifted from the relatively recent period when intact heterosexual marriages with one working parent were more common. Although it is important to continue to reevaluate the impact of cultural shifts for individuals and society, it is also necessary to keep in mind that many aspects of development and human experience are universal and timeless even though some are subject to generational, technological, and cultural shifts. Based on a large body of cross-cultural, art-based research, Silver (2002) speculates that similarities among individuals have a biological basis whereas differences result from cultural influences. Similarly, Bowlby's (1982) and E. Erikson's (1950) cross-cultural research findings suggest that there are universal features of emotional aspects of developmental experience—although further research continues to be warranted in order to tease out *which* features transcend cultures (van IJzendoorn, 1990). The combination of factors that involve both constancy and change make for a healthy spirit of inquiry that assists art therapists in their commitment to understanding the language of child art expression. This knowledge effectively supplements the art therapist's intuitive sensitivity and fluency in understanding the visual language of children.

2 Artwork Tells the Story of Child Development

This chapter serves as a continuation of the preceding chapter in that it takes a more in-depth look at material presented there. It explores the following developmental stages: infant, toddler, preschool, middle-childhood, and preteen levels of development. Within each stage, art expression is used to facilitate understanding of psychosocial functioning, defensive structure, and artistic development. Artwork provides a narration of the stages of child development.

Infancy: The Basis for a Sense of Hope

The basis for establishing trust occurs during the first year of life, at which time development is influenced by parental attunement in providing physical care. Erik Erikson (1980) noted that in the first stage of the infant's life, experience largely occurs via the mouth, the eyes, and the body. Babies who are maltreated, neglected, or physically ill are unlikely to develop the belief that their needs can be met. Due to the fact that infants lack a cognitive framework for understanding pain or hunger, entrenched and lasting feelings of anger, victimization, and despair may endure into later stages. On a basic level, traumatic early experiences may instill the belief that the world is an unsafe or cruel place (Stern, 1985).

Caregivers influence the infant's lifelong sense of mutuality and frustration tolerance, which contribute to belief in the dependability of self and others (E. Erikson, Erikson, & Kivnick, 1986). The outcome of this early struggle is not a conscious experience; but rather, it is expressed through interpersonal behavior, attitudes, and inner states. Effective struggle with the first stage of life results in a sense of hope that is strong enough to provide the basis for dealing with later interpersonal challenges. This lays the foundation upon which the development of mutual involvement with individuals, groups, and the community takes place.

Art Expression and Early Experience

Although infants do not paint, draw, or sculpt, art can express states that infants experience. Feelings of pleasure and comfort or discomfort and fear extend far beyond infancy. They can be observed in art expression and in human relationships throughout life. Needless to say, during art therapy sessions such themes are often expressed through subject matter, use of materials, and interactions with the therapist. A 12-year-old boy completed Figure 2.1 during a late stage of art therapy. At this point, he was able to focus on soothing

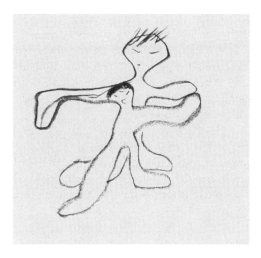

Figure 2.1 Relational figures by 12-year-old boy

and self-care whereas previously he focused on exploration of fears, abandonment, and trauma. In order to complete the drawing, he used me as a model and requested that I hold my arms out so that he could render the intended pose of the figures in the drawing. The artwork depicts two fluid and connected figures in a manner that expresses a state of comfort and support. While viewing the drawing, he said that he felt supported by me and that this had helped him to have more belief in himself. This drawing depicts the experience of dependency and safety, which is what an infant needs in order to develop a psychologically healthy foundation. As illustrated by this example, this is not just a feature of infant relationships, but of significant relational experiences throughout the lifespan. This interpersonal state is pivotal to developing a belief in the value of self and others.

Defenses Through Physicality

Early experience takes place most prominently on a physiological level. Kestenberg (as cited in Levick, 1983) has observed that infant inhibition of motor impulse and discharge is a precursor to the development of a personality structure. The primary means of coping takes place through physicality. For example, a baby who is anxious due to physical discomfort or separation may cope through attempts at physical self-soothing, diminished interaction, helpless motor activity, or screaming. In contrast, a mature person who must live with physical discomfort has access to more complex mechanisms such as suppression, intellectual understanding, and sublimation

The Terrible and Wonderful Twos

The second stage of psychosocial development, which covers the toddler years, involves a struggle between outer control (parents) and inner control (self). It is a time of both exuberance and conflicted dependency needs. A toddler has many new capabilities and must navigate the potential disappointments and constrictions imposed by potty training, fatigue, and unwanted naps. Figure 2.2 displays a painting by a toddler. It illustrates the physicality and newly developed energetic independence of this stage. The love of action that is apparent in this painting is characteristic of very young children who run instead of walk, experiment and explore with determination, and have limited speech and boundless curiosity. When these efforts are met with restrictions, such as limits from adults or an accidental tumble to the ground, the child—who has been temporarily crushed—may react with extreme distress.

If the toddler can struggle effectively, learn to tolerate disappointments, and still feel strong in the world, the result is a sense of will. Due to the toddler's lack of impulse control, instability, and potential emotional volatility, this can be a difficult phase for both parents and child. Even in healthy development, each stage brings daunting conflicts for which there are no simple solutions, but rather the child's innate demand to achieve more strength and complexity.

Toddlers: Art Expression

The Scribbling stage is the first of Lowenfeld's (Lowenfeld & Brittain, 1987) graphic developmental stages. This stage is characterized by pure action, randomness, and minimal awareness of cause and effect. Figure 2.3 is an example of a toddler's scribble. Note that physicality is primary. Toddlers do not attribute representational or symbolic qualities to their artworks. They experiment and manipulate in a process that is far more sensory than intellectual. As is evident in this drawing by a 3-year-old girl, interest in con-

Figure 2.2 Painting by toddler (2-year-old male)

Figure 2.3 Scribble by 3-year-old girl

trolling marks increases during the toddler and early preschool years. Lowenfeld noted the progression from random to controlled scribbles, which indicates a refinement in motor skills, cognitive development, and increased desire to gain control. Figure 2.3 includes some attempts at forming circular shapes as well as random scribbles.

Children at this stage take delight in pure action (Golomb, 2003) and have very short attention spans. Often they begin to attribute narrative or representational meaning to their artworks, but only when encouraged to do so by adults. Children increasingly realize that there is a connection between their actions and what appears on the paper. After about 6 months of scribbling, children's artworks become more elaborate with increased amounts of time invested in the activity. For a young child, scribbling is a meaningful and exciting experience that reflects a developing sense of self-activation, control, and autonomy that is inherent in this stage. (See Table 2.1, based on the ideas found in Lowenfeld and Brittain, 1987, and Rubin, 2005, for descriptions of early stages of graphic development.)

Toddlers: Defenses

The behavior and artwork of very young children certainly reflects the use of motor discharge (pure action) as a primary focus. The beginning of language heralds the use of defenses such as denial, fantasy, avoidance, and projection. These defenses are commonly used during the preschool years. *Acting out* is a defense described by Vaillant (1993) as "direct expression of an unconscious wish or impulse" (p. 53) with a focus on immediate gratification, and involves behaviors such as temper tantrums and even self-harm (such as screaming with a level of intensity that produces a sore throat). This resembles the acting out behavior of delinquent teenagers or adults with self-regulation difficulties; however, its connotation seems too negative to describe innocent infants

Table 2.1 Stages of Graphic Development

Stage	Graphic characteristics
Scribbling stage, 2–4 years:	
Early: Disordered scribbling	Gross motor actions, kinesthetic focus, action valued rather than product; may draw on top of previous marks; uses fist to hold tool; may ignore boundaries; no interest in representation.
Middle: Controlled scribbling	Increased fine motor action and smaller marks; increase concentration on certain areas of drawing. More deliberate action and defined, enclosed forms such as circles, swirls, loops; may have prefigural appearance.
Late: Named scribbling	Increased use of fingers to hold tool; increased verbal definition of shapes; more variety of forms; ever-changing descriptions of subject matter and movement of forms; longer attention span.
Preschematic stage, 4–7 years:	Unrelated shapes are scattered with subjective size relationships; rotation of images in various directions on the page; objects are distorted to fit on the page; human figures are subjective, initially evolving from scribbles; early figures often include only head and legs; gradually more details such as clothing, hair, decorations, and details of body parts are included; distortion and omission of body parts are normal; spontaneous, playful, imaginative, and shifting modes of representation that often include verbal dialogue with self are present.
Schematic stage, 7–9 years:	Systematic representation of forms based on greater knowledge of the environment; increased expressive and fine motor abilities; repeated schemas that rely heavily on geometric shapes and flat, bold representation; human figures rigidly proportioned; schemas are altered for unfamiliar subjects and those holding special meaning; limited cognitive understanding of spatial depiction of depth; minimal use of overlapping; objects are lined up on a baseline that is either drawn or implied; skylines are common; attempts to portray depth and movement or passage of time include x-ray drawings (e.g., drawing the interior of a house on the exterior wall), multiple baselines, distorted forms to convey an action or emphasis (such as elongated arms when depicting two people shaking hands); aerial views mixed with frontal views.
Gang Age, 9–12 years:	Greater emphasis on details evident in portrayal of the environment, clothing, hair, body parts, etc.; attempts to portray depth through overlapping, proportional size representation, depiction of a shallow plane and of relationship of objects; more modeled/realistic, individualized shapes to represent objects and figures; no understanding of shading; tendency to be self-critical in attempts to improve artistic skills.
Pseudonaturalistic stage, 12–14 years:	This stage is limited to children who have particular artistic interest/ability; increasingly personal meaning conveyed in artworks; portrayal of depth perspective, action, and details; increasingly accurate proportions; exaggeration of sexual characteristics and use of cartoon-like imagery may be present.

and toddlers. A marked inability to delay gratification of needs is characteristic of and developmentally normal for very young children. (See Table 2.2, based on work by the American Psychiatric Association, 2000; Davies, 2005; A. Freud, 1946; McWilliams, 1994; and Vaillant, 1993, for definitions of defenses.)

Table 2.2 Defenses: Developmental Sequence and Definitions

Defenses	Definitions
Early Childhood	
Projection	Falsely attributing one's own unacknowledged or undesirable feelings or impulses to others.
Denial	Inability to acknowledge or believe a painful or unwanted aspect of reality.
Fantasy	Substituting or superimposing made-up or imagined experience on reality.
Acting out	Acting without regard for negative consequences
Splitting	A perspective characterized by a view that is all good or all bad as opposed to integrating both negative and positive aspects into an overview. (Illustrated in chap. 12.)
Middle Childhood	
Displacement	Redirecting a feeling onto another less threatening subject.
Intellectualization	Engaging in focus on abstract and often detailed thought in order to take the focus away from something difficult.
Reaction formation	Substituting acceptable, often opposite feelings for those that are unacceptable.
Repression	Disconnection from feelings or memories in order to preserve one's sense of well being.
Sublimation	Expressing problematic impulses and feelings in socially useful, constructive, and creative ways.
Undoing	Engaging in activity designed to make amends for a regretted action, thought or feeling. (Not illustrated.)

The Play Age, Years 3–6

The "play age" marks the beginnings of the sense of responsibility, which is accompanied by the desire to prove oneself and to feel powerful. E. Erikson (1980) stated that each of his designated stages "is a potential crisis because of a radical change in perspective. There is, at the beginning of life, the most radical change of all: from intrauterine to extrauterine life" (p. 57). The stages mark shifts in functions relating to interdependency versus independence and activity versus passivity and involve the balancing of opposing forces. During the play age, which entails a struggle of initiative versus guilt, children do not eliminate feelings of guilt. Rather, they learn to cope with these feelings and to experience them in appropriate ways. The outcome generated is developing a realistic sense of conscience, self-control, and dependability. For a 5-year-old, breaking a sibling's toy may lead to the gradual capacity to feel remorse, but only after consequences such as punishment or disapproval have ensued. As children incorporate a conscience, initially provided by parents, they become increasingly constructive and accountable. This lays the groundwork for a sense of responsibility and purpose. The early stages constitute the basis for law and order.

The Play Age: Art Expression

Figure 2.4 is a drawing of a genie rising out of a bottle by a 5-year-old boy. It conveys much about the Eriksonian stage of *initiative versus guilt* (E. Erikson, 1980) in depiction of a powerful magical figure that is yet undeveloped, clumsy, and based in fantasy. A 5-year-old lacks impulse control and sound reality-based judgment. The drawing

Figure 2.4 Genie emerging from bottle by 5-year-old boy

portrays a fun-loving creature, similar to the preschool child in its apparent intense energy and purpose that remains unregulated. The composition is bold, dynamic, and centered. It lacks any ground line or reference points as these organizational features appear in artworks done during the first few years of elementary school.

The Preschematic graphic developmental stage (Lowenfeld & Brittain, 1987) of preschool and early school-aged children heralds the beginning of the shift from the sensory and tactile to representational artwork. During this playful stage, floating objects, hybrid creatures, subjective depiction of proportions and colors, distortions and omissions of body parts are often portrayed. In general, there is a greater emphasis on communication with the self than on producing recognizable or realistic imagery. Figure 2.5 is a map for pirates, which shows a landmass and the location of buried treasure. The 4-year-old boy who drew it worked both impulsively and purposefully. His drawing had more meaning for him than for others, characteristic of age-appropriate egocentricity. As evidenced by the features of this artwork, preschool children are egocentric, highly imaginative, and driven.

Figure 2.6, by a 5-year-old boy, depicts a quickly executed (which is typical for this age group) humanized cat that appears at center stage. Preschool children often mix human and animal figures. Their compositions and use of color are random with no logical organization, often resulting in artwork work that is aesthetically interesting and harmonious and that conveys physical energy. For example, in Figure 2.7 (by a 5-year-old girl) note how the lack of arms and the bent leg create a geometrically interesting and balanced figure. The simplicity of the tadpole, with circular and other simple forms, provides an armature to which greater development of details and forms is added as the child matures (Golomb, 2011). Once again, the child's creativity, egocentricity, and

Figure 2.5 Pirate map by 4-year-old boy

Figure 2.6 Humanized cat by 5-year old boy

sense of purpose are apparent. The above art examples communicate the physicality and individualized fluid impressions of reality that characterize this developmental stage.

The Play Age: Defenses

The composite animal depicted in Figure 2.8 is an example of the use of fantasy and projection, defenses that preschool children frequently use. The 5-year-old boy artist

Figure 2.7 Person by 5-year-old girl

depicted an animal that is based only loosely in reality. The drawing contains the child's projection of human and highly imaginative qualities that reflect early childhood fantasies and personal feelings. Defenses used by preschool children include projection, fantasy, denial, and regression. Children of the play age are free to embellish reality. They dwell within the realm of imaginative states, becoming fairies and pirates as well as teachers and parents. Reality is often distorted at this age whether in imaginative play, fearful states, or distortion of imposed restrictions.

Figure 2.8 Fantasy animal by 5-year-old boy

The defenses that are incorporated quite actively during the preschool years can be observed in artworks, behaviors, play activity, and verbalizations. For example, the chalk castle depicted in Figure 2.9 is from an experience that took place in my neighborhood, and demonstrates the child's use of denial and fantasy. When I asked one of the children (a 4-year-old) who drew the chalk castle on the sidewalk about it, he told me that it was the kingdom that was owned by his family. His same-aged peers chimed in, competing for my attention in discussing their own family kingdoms. A parent of one of the children then questioned the reality of their statements, and they acknowledged begrudgingly that this was make-believe. But they were visibly irritated at the adult's imposition of reality as it interfered with the fulfilling absorption in fantasy.

When a small child engages in the use of denial and fantasy, it is often seen as quite charming. When adults do this, they are not viewed as sane or trustworthy, and they likely have interpersonal or functional difficulties. For example, adults frequently deny substance abuse problems, even to themselves. Actively psychotic adult patients have difficulties differentiating reality from fantasy. For the preschool child, fantasy and denial are normal. The inhibition or lack of these defenses in early childhood sometimes indicates psychological difficulties such as anxiety, depressive, or autistic spectrum disorders.

Preschool children also use projection, a defense involved in attributing one's own qualities to those of others, real or imaginary. The friendly yet aggressive dinosaur depicted in Figure 1.1 serves as an example of the latter. Projection through art expression is constructive and useful. It allows for examination of one's own states but with a safe degree of distance. Projection can also involve blame. A small child may do this by saying, "Bad Mommy!" when he is reprimanded for a transgression. Adults who rely heavily on

Figure 2.9 Chalk castle drawn on sidewalk

the defense of projection tend to have relational difficulties. In order to function well, older children and adults develop more reality-based and responsible ways of coping.

Middle Childhood, Years 7–9

The elementary school years involve balancing a sense of industry with opposing feelings of inferiority (E. Erikson, 1980). While feelings of inferiority can be debilitating, they are also an important and necessary measure of reality. Children develop the ability to tolerate and use feelings of inferiority as an impetus for growth. Erikson stated that the resulting virtue in the struggle between industry and inferiority is a lifelong, deeply felt sense of competence. The artworks of children during middle childhood portray a new level of self-criticism and rigor. Attempts to convey images or ideas in a particular way may be demonstrated through increased level of detail, more frequent erasures, and preference for controllable media, particularly pencils. At this stage many children decide that they are not good at art and may cease to develop artistically, choosing to focus on other interests where they experience feelings of success and mastery.

During middle childhood, children compare and evaluate themselves in relation to others. In order to preserve self-esteem, they may choose not to engage in activities at which they believe they are unsuccessful. Children who learn to struggle with mastering some activities, whether it is academics, sports, art, and so on, are engaging in important experiences that promote self-esteem, thereby creating a foundation for healthy functioning in adulthood. Art therapists observe children's capacity for struggling with feelings of inferiority by noting degree of effort invested in art making, whether the child attempts to repair perceived mistakes, and how much control is exercised in art production.

Middle Childhood: Art Expression

Lowenfeld and Brittain (1987) described the stage typical of 7- to 9-year-old children as the Schematic stage. This phase involves an increase in order, exemplified by depictions such as a skyline and baseline and repeated schemas to symbolically represent familiar objects and figures. There is usually a geometric and conformist quality inherent in this stage that represents a notable shift from the artwork of younger children.

Often, the shift from one developmental stage to another is gradual, involving transitional periods in which features of both earlier and later stages are quite observable. Figure 2.10 displays artwork by a 6-year-old girl with one foot in the Preschematic stage and the other in the Schematic stage. She used realistic color to depict two figures standing on the ground in an orderly fashion. This replaces random organization of the previous stage with a more realistic and formulaic depiction. The figures convey an interesting combination of early (impulsive rendering, large heads) and middle childhood features (realistic color and early schematic representations). The picture reflects awareness of two figures in relationship to each other and to the environment. Lowenfeld and Brittain (1987) observed that children in the Schematic stage do not yet have the cognitive ability to show depth perspective. Spatial depth may be represented through seemingly arbitrary short cuts, such as aerial views (e.g., Figure 2.11, picture of a baseball field by a 9-year-old boy) and x-ray views (e.g., Figure 2.12, picture of a house with see-through walls by an 8-year-old boy). Schematic artworks most frequently line up objects on a

Figure 2.10 Two girls by 5-year-old girl

Figure 2.11 Aerial view of baseball field by 9-year-old boy

Figure 2.12 X-ray view of house and tree by 8-year-old boy

baseline at the bottom of the page, or the bottom of the page itself provides an "implied baseline" (see Figure 1.3).

Middle Childhood: Defenses

As children make the transition into school, defensive structure shifts. The result is orderly behavior, restraint, and grounding in reality. Figure 2.10 (mentioned above) is indicative of the transition from the play age to middle childhood. The drawing includes both impulsive and idiosyncratic elements of early childhood and orderly formulaic elements that are more characteristic of middle childhood. The two figures seem to be based on the same recipe, while the background is scribbled and somewhat random. The figures are ordered and realistic regarding color and composition. This is evidence of the desire to follow rules, embrace reality, and incorporate restraint and discipline.

Anna Freud (1946) described *repression* as a major defense that is very necessary in normal development as the child begins school and participates in activities that demand socialization, competition, and task mastery. She observed that instinctive behavior goes underground, allowing for productive learning, which essentially constitutes the basis of what will later become adult productivity. Children who do not develop increasingly mature defenses (which facilitate the taming of intense feelings and impulses) often prove to be sore losers, have "behavior problems," be poor students, and so on. Control and self-discipline are evident in children's artwork during middle childhood. They line figures up on baselines; they use realistic color, although somewhat rigidly; they develop formulas for how to draw particular objects. These features encompass the Schematic stage of graphic development (Lowenfeld & Brittain, 1987).

The capacity to repress impulses and strong emotions permits a sense of order and conformity. Objects and figures are often carefully organized in artworks. Note how the members of the family are presented in terms of relative size in Figure 1.3. It is as though children at this age take a reactionary position to their previous impulsivity. *Reaction formation*, a defense that characterizes this tendency, involves responding in a manner that is the opposite of an undesirable feeling and serves as a condemnation of that feeling (Vaillant, 1993). Children adaptively use reaction formation when they are faced with difficult circumstances as a means of protecting self and others from negative emotions. A 12-year-old girl who was rejected by her father frequently hogged my most expensive supplies as a way to fill this void. She shifted to making gifts for others during her art therapy sessions, which indicated increased maturation although difficulties were still present. Her focus on giving eased the burden of longing and need. Reaction formation is difficult to identify in artworks. It may be represented by a contradiction of subject matter and emotional tone in an attempt to reverse a painful state. As with any assessment, in order to recognize the manifestation of reaction formation in children's artworks, it is necessary to be familiar with the child's circumstances.

Artistic Development and Defenses of the Preteen Child, Years 9–12

The Dawning Realism or Gang Age stage (Lowenfeld & Brittain, 1987), evident in artworks produced by older (preadolescent) school-aged children, reflects a shift to increased self-consciousness and awareness of the environment. This stage is characterized by emphasis on details, gender differences, and flexible schemas, unlike the formulaic approach of the Schematic stage. Cognitive developmental abilities enable children to conceptualize depth representation and spatial distance through overlapping and relative size of objects. Although the figures tend to appear stiff, they are no longer made up of geometric shapes and may include much detail. During later childhood as adolescence approaches, graphic stages progress to include expression that is increasingly complex, realistic, self-aware, and self-critical. As mentioned previously, it is clear that the evolving development of the self is depicted in art and that individuals become increasingly complex as they develop throughout childhood.

Figure 2.13, completed by a 10-year-old boy, is a portrait of Theodore Roosevelt. The use of more mature childhood defenses is evident in this drawing, which characterizes the Dawning Realism or Gang Age stage (Lowenfeld & Brittain, 1987). An increasingly reality-based focus in the subject matter and use of detail is evident. The use of erasure is part of the increased attention to detail and apparent need for control. The defense of *intellectualization* is apparent. This is an age-appropriate defense that involves separating thought from emotion in order to be productive. Often children between the ages of 9 and 12 complete detailed depictions that involve well thought-out, intellectually based pencil drawing. Vaillant (1993) points out that when this defense goes overboard, the result is an obsessive-compulsive style of coping. Indeed, during middle childhood, obsessive traits such as erasing, redoing tasks, or memorization of numerous facts is common, and they are an important developmental function that promotes developing the necessary sense of mastery, control, and competence.

Sublimation, a high-level defense employed during middle childhood, may be apparent in the Teddy Roosevelt drawing. Sublimation involves a conversion of instinct into constructive activity (A. Freud, 1946) and, in this case, an artistic product. Artistic sublimation, a concept coined by Kramer (1977), involves an interplay of defenses, such as displacement, reaction formation, and intellectualization. The act of artistic sublimation

Figure 2.13 Theodore Roosevelt by 10-year-old boy

involves communicating and expressing experience that results in artwork that brings meaning to complex and contradictory emotions and perceptions. Both the artist and the audience are enriched by the new understanding generated by the artwork. Portraits serve "to preserve the essence of another human being," (p. 17), which demonstrates the synthesis and aesthetic sensibility relating to positive areas such as empathy, admiration, and interpersonal relatedness, as well as negative feelings such as envy or revulsion. Art expression can transform these complex emotions into meaningful statements, allowing for a high level of shared gratification.

In general, the 10-year-old has experienced a massive shift from the 5-year-old in the capacity to repress potentially overwhelming emotions and socially unacceptable behaviors. The use of age-appropriate defenses enables individuals to be appreciated by others, to fit in, and to contribute meaningfully to their communities. Defenses employed by school-aged children allow them to be successful in school, at play, and in a variety of increasingly complex interpersonal relationships. This is especially important as the anxieties and hormonal and physical body changes relating to puberty begin to mount. Defenses help to neutralize pressures of physical, social, and academic demands.

Concerns about sexuality are often conveyed in artworks by older school-aged children through inclusion of exaggerated detail in depicting gender-related characteristics. The process of creating an artwork provides the opportunity for feelings relating to impending adulthood to be safely displaced onto the art process and product. *Displacement* involves redirecting a feeling about something threatening to a less threatening object. This is evident in Figure 2.14, a highly detailed pencil and watercolor rendering titled "My Dad" by an 11-year-old boy. The gender-specific details, such as facial hair nubs and male hairstyle, are executed using an almost painful level of detail. In doing so, the child is able to neutralize possible worries about impending puberty-related body changes. The background includes an organized repetitive pattern that indicates a level of intellectualization resulting from more developed maturational processes. As previously mentioned, organization and self-structure are important functions of later childhood.

Figure 2.14 "My Dad" by 11-year-old boy

In a similar way, Figure 2.15 by an 11-year-old girl incorporates thoughtful, intellectually based detail in depicting a female hairdo. Once again, because sexual characteristics in drawings during this stage are often exaggerated, intellectualization and displacement are apparent in the attention to detail in the figure and attire. Through displacement, the anticipation and anxiety concerning impending sexual maturity are dealt with. The use of defenses makes it possible to examine and cope with stressful subjects. In the therapeutic process with school-aged children, age-appropriate defenses such as intellectualization and displacement are encouraged because they facilitate safe ways to look at threatening material. For example, a child dealing with parental conflict portrayed a story about the marriage and resulting children of a cat and dog. The offspring of this couple were mutations that suffered as a result of the parents' mismatch. The drawing and story allowed this boy to engage in the use of displacement and attention to detail through artistic and verbal narratives as a means of neutralizing overwhelming feelings.

Defenses as a Means of Adaptation

As mentioned above, defenses provide immunity, a form of protection. Defenses, such as denial, characteristically used by preschool children, are used adaptively by older individuals who face stress. For example, "Leo," an 8-year-old boy who described his father as kind, loving, and fun, completed Figure 2.16. In reality, his father, who was allowed

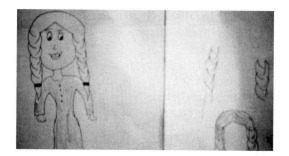

Figure 2.15 Female figure by 11-year-old girl

Figure 2.16 Father and son interaction by Leo

only brief parental visitations, experienced severe mental illness that caused him to have poor judgment and inappropriate behaviors. Rather than accept the reality of having a parent who was severely compromised, Leo believed that his father protected him. This drawing of time spent with his father depicts an experience of being treated roughly and appearing helpless. When asked if the drawing expressed danger or discomfort, Leo confidently described it as "My dad cracking my back; its just plain-old-fun father and son rough-housing." Although the drawing revealed a frightened state, direct acknowledgment of this feeling would have been too destabilizing to bear. Leo found a useful means of protection by focusing only on the positive feelings he had for his father. This buffer contributed to his ability to function well in many areas of his life.

Although the use of defenses is individualized and subject to ongoing shifts in response to stressors and developmental shifts, major defenses of middle childhood include repression, intellectualization, reaction formation, sublimation, and displacement. This is a stage of control, achievement, heightened competition, and self-consciousness that provide the basis for increasingly complex identity formation.

Conclusion

Theories provide a framework for understanding generalities. Child development and its relationship to art expression is a very complex topic that cannot be simplified. In understanding each child's developmental progression, it is important to take into account that development is a complicated process that always includes some regression and areas of immaturity. Because each person demonstrates a unique artistic and developmental style, it is helpful to look for general qualities of developmental stages when evaluating children.

This chapter has explored child development and art expression. As children progress developmentally, they develop judgment skills and original modes of expression. If development proceeds without major disruption, children acquire the capacity to become increasingly constructive human beings, thus inspiring hope about the future world. This is a world they will create when they leave behind the crayons and modeling clay that enlightened adults provided to help foster industry and imagination.

In providing art therapy, the hope is to help children to become well functioning adults who can contribute positively to the world. This type of long-term view is a necessary element of the work that child art therapists undertake. E. Erikson (1980) recognized S. Freud's simple and clear observation that what a normal adult should be able to do is "Lieben und Arbeiten" (to love and to work) (p.102). Erikson observed that by *love* Freud meant not only sexual love but also love for children along with expansive and genuine forms of generosity. And by *work*, he had in mind productiveness, but not to the exclusion of the ability to be a loving and interpersonally connected being. In providing child art therapy and in studying child art expression and child development, it is not only helpful but also potentially very gratifying to keep in mind the vision of the well functioning adult of the future who can love and work in a meaningful and generous way. The experiences, relationships, and struggles of childhood are preparation for these abilities.

Part II

Interpersonal Developmental States

An Art-Based View

3   The Pictorial Language of Early Developmental States

Early relational experience is an important area of study for clinical practice. The origins of interpersonal and emotional functioning can be observed in infants' relationships with parents. Art expression by children gives voice to these developmental states, which are fundamental for human beings in general. It is useful for clinicians to label and identify the characteristics of such states in conceptualizing the needs, struggles, and eventual fulfillment that exist within a developmental progression. Although child art therapists may sometimes work with infants (a practice that inevitably includes parents and their methods of care), understanding infantile states goes a long way in working with people of all ages.

In other words, theories of early interpersonal development are useful tools for art therapists in addition to other aspects of development already discussed. Object relations, attachment, and neurobiological theories, as well as research regarding brain development, provide a framework for understanding the importance of symbolic expression and the emerging relational self. These are crucial elements of the child art therapist's theoretical knowledge as they provide the basis for helping children utilize creative art expression as a means of integrating affect, perception, and cognition. The roots of these functions are established during the first 3 years of life. In addition, early relational models apply throughout the lifespan and support key components of psychotherapy. As already noted, the primary aim of art therapy with children (and frequently with adults) is to repair developmental disruptions. The disruptions that child clients experience often begin early in life and serve to impede interpersonal development.

Observational research of infants, neurobiological research, and studies of treatment indicate that relationships with caregivers, along with opportunities for independent self-activated expression, help to facilitate the emergence of a healthy self. Art-based therapeutic work provides the opportunity for children to access nonverbal material while incorporating age-appropriate cognition. The child's act of creating artwork allows for spontaneous affective expression. Art therapists assist children in using expression as a vehicle for depicting and subsequently organizing overwhelming feelings that could not previously be managed. Therapeutic goals often encompass helping children to gain a sense of mastery over chaotic feelings. This parallels the role parents serve with infants in making possible the means to cope with potentially overwhelming states.

During the first few years of life, children literally learn to stand on their own two feet. Autonomous functioning is an important and complex accomplishment. A child art therapist deals with children who experience problems that interfere with the capacity to effectively face the demands of standing up to increasing responsibilities and of trusting self and others. In optimal circumstances, genetic potential is strengthened and more fully realized. When the situation is less optimal, inadequate care produces deficits in the development of psychological strengths. Research indicates that these deficits can persist throughout the lifespan and that the first years of life are most crucial to whether they occur (Siegel, 1999).

The Developing Brain

Recent advances in infant brain research scientifically validate attachment and object relations theories that have been established through observational research (Bowlby, 1988; Mahler, Pine, & Bergman, 1975). Schore's (1994) research supports the existence of a symbiosis between the primary caregiver and the infant. It also supports the hypothesis that during the period Mahler described as *practicing* (10–18 months), unparalleled brain development takes place. (Mahler's stages are discussed more thoroughly below.) The caregiver's gaze and attunement influence the infant's developing brain. Over time, the infant's affect-regulating capacities advance, largely as a result of the caregiver's modeling. Increasingly sophisticated cognitive functions (cortical control) arise and are integrated with earlier, more primitive (subcortical) functions. This critical period of brain development constitutes the basis for emotional regulation, impulse inhibition, self-cohesion, and interpersonal reciprocity including empathy (Schore, 1994).

In sum, the reciprocal engagement between mother and infant stimulates growth in important areas of the infant's brain (Schore, 2003). The mother's caregiving—feeding, handling, playing, soothing and comforting, and responding to the infant's cues (largely physical, at first, but followed increasingly by emotional and then cognitive cues)—serves instinctive purposes. It involves many levels of sensory engagement including sight, sound, touch, feel, and taste. Infants' brains cannot develop normally without such caregiving, which provides the foundation for successful survival.

The mother's modeling of emotional states gives the infant the information for building self-protective abilities. Laboratory research demonstrates that an infant approaching an unknown and potentially dangerous situation will look at the mother's face and retreat if her face shows fear (Stern, 1985). Mothers also tend to empathically mirror infant's emotions with their own facial expressions. This behavior, referred to as *marked mirroring*, lowers the intensity of the emotion. Marked mirroring is a form of emotional regulation that helps the infant develop the ability to handle affective states (Fonagy et al., 2004). Schore (2003) describes this reciprocal process as incorporating right brain to right brain communication between mother and infant that serves to stimulate brain growth in its emotion-regulating regions. This early relational position has similarities with the art therapy relationship, which facilitates the processing and managing of nonverbal experience.

Repairing Disruptions Through Art Therapy

Schore (2003) and Siegel (1999) have established that the mother's playful interactions bring about the release of serotonin, fostering the infant's capacity to experience joy and leading to massive right brain development. This is followed by development of cortical functions that are associated with cognition, providing the basis for making sense of feelings. Visual, affective, and sensory components of art therapy practice involve subcortical functions and thus may offer the possibility for reparative work for children who have sustained difficulties in early life. Art-based therapeutic interventions provide a framework for cognitive organization of affective material, a process that simulates early relational experiences.

Stages of Early Relational Development

The exploration of early development that follows is twofold. It examines both the experience of infancy and the significance of interpersonal states as evolving conditions of the human experience throughout life. Mahler et al. (1975) developed a conceptual model for understanding the psychological experiences of infants and toddlers, a model that describes stages towards gradual separation from caregivers during the early years. These descriptions illuminate universal human themes, focusing on relational states that are first evident in infancy but which persist throughout life. Although Mahler's research has been criticized for failing to screen participants in order to distinguish between disturbed and well adjusted individuals, this does not detract from its relevance for clinical work; the emotional, interpersonal struggles of love, loss, and abandonment are universal (Masterson, 2000).

Psychological Birth

Mahler et al. (1975) conducted research involving extensive observation of infants (0–31 months) and their mothers and coined the term "psychological birth" of the infant. This refers to a gradual process of separation and individuation from the mother's physical and empathic care. Like Winnicott (1971a), Mahler emphasized that the mother need not be perfect but rather "good enough" and that the infant internalizes the mother's reflection and care. This internalization provides a secure foundation for the developing self. Discrete interpersonal developmental stages constitute the psychological birth of the human being. Whereas biological birth is a dramatic one-time event, psychological birth is a gradual process that takes place during the first 3 years.

Relevance of Early Relational Stages for Clinical Work

Interpersonal states are experienced in the therapeutic relationship as well as in infant–parent relationships. These states are inherently difficult to describe, as they involve nonverbal and instinct-based experience. My hope is to use Mahler's terms to provide a vocabulary for conceptualizing aspects of expression relevant to child art therapy. In work with severely traumatized children, it is especially difficult and important to find a language to describe interpersonal and self-regulatory states because nonverbal experiences are inherently difficult to put into words.

The following vignettes emphasize art therapy as a tool for addressing interpersonal states. Mahler's terms are used because they are especially suitable for describing both early relational experience and states that occur in clinical work. The child art therapy examples that follow illustrate parallels of clinical practice and early relational states. The language of art becomes a relationally based means of therapeutic communication within which interpersonal functioning can be not only expressed but also strengthened.

Early Relational Stages and Child Art Therapy

Normal Autistic Stage (0–2 Months)

The autistic stage constitutes the transition from existence within the womb to external life. Infants exist in an unformed and insulated state. Although infants respond to physical stimuli, relationships are largely one-sided; the caregiver holds the responsibility for maintaining the relationship. Mahler et al. (1975) believed that the infant is aware of stimuli but does not perceive people or stimuli as separate entities. Experience for the newborn infant involves primarily half-wake, half-sleep states. Objections have been raised regarding the accuracy of these observations of the normal autistic stage. Contrary to Mahler's observations, laboratory research has demonstrated that even in early infancy, some cognitive functions occur and that the infant's state is not exclusively quasivegetative, as Mahler's description implied (Stern, 1985). For example, infants turn and show increased responsiveness to familiar smells. Mahler's research did not involve experimentation, but rather observation of infants and mothers so these nuances were not detected. She observed the cocoon-like state of infants and their minimal responsiveness to stimuli. She also concluded that the mother's role is instinct driven, exclusively focusing on the infant's survival.

Clinical Implications for Art Therapy

In clinical practice with children, a most obvious parallel to the normal autistic phase is work with children who have autistic spectrum disorders. In general, these children have not acquired relational abilities or well developed language. Although previously attributed to poor maternal care, this condition is currently considered a neurological disorder characterized by diminished capacity for interpersonal engagement. Intellectual abilities are often impaired in more severe cases of autism, but mildly impaired individuals on the autistic spectrum may have superior or normal cognitive functioning. Similarly, children with autism have impaired language development whereas children with milder autistic spectrum disorders usually have impaired abilities to relate but may not experience language deficits.

CASE EXAMPLE 1

"Teddy" was a 7-year-old boy who was diagnosed with mild autism. His symptoms included delays in language development and an isolative interpersonal style. He was easily threatened by peers and would lash out at them. He focused repetitively on his interest in trains and cartoon animals. He did not make eye contact (a feature shared by children with autistic spectrum disorders). Teddy was very happy to engage in art therapy although he did not actively relate to me and seemed minimally aware of my presence. At the same time, it was clear that he was dependent on me to provide structure, engagement, and supplies. Without these provisions, he would have occupied himself in his own world. Like the mother of a very young infant, my role was to offer nurturance with the goal of fostering interpersonal development. His art expression portrayed fairly well executed repetitive images of his limited range of interests. Figure 3.1 depicts cartoon characters based on one of his favorite television shows and exemplifies a preference that is typical of autistic children who may feel more comfortable with cartoons than with peers. Teddy did not voluntarily depict people. When asked to draw people, he drew them very quickly and, as shown in a drawing of his family (see Figure 3.2), did not illustrate or discuss any of their personal characteristics. This drawing was completed quickly, lacking both investment and artistic development.

Teddy was not able to tune into the nuances of relationships. He experienced a sense of investment when depicting inanimate objects, and he preferred copying to spontaneous expression. His experience of the world was an insulated one, similar to the infant's normal autistic phase. My methods involved offering structure and

Figure 3.1 Cartoon characters by Teddy

Figure 3.2 Family drawing by Teddy

responsiveness. I encouraged Teddy to draw the cartoon characters he liked and to make up stories about the characters so that he could further develop both his thoughts and his drawings through color and detail and communicate his unique perceptions. I also encouraged him to interact with me and with his artwork. I gave him a variety of pictures of animals to copy so that his limited repertoire of themes could be broadened.

Figure 3.3 depicts a variety of animals, based on Silver's (2007) "Drawing from Imagination" stimulus images. Using stimulus images and receiving close support allowed Teddy to pick up new ideas, which he was unable to do on his own. I encouraged Teddy to describe through art expression the nuances of his experiences such as what it is like to see something scary. He drew a picture of a vampire based on what he described as a frightening episode of a television show (see Figure 3.4). He verbalized that he felt frightened by the vampire's fast movements and multiple sets of eyes and faces. In response to my supplying a square within which to draw something funny, Teddy drew what he described as an airplane disguised as a lion (see Figure 3.5). As is evident from these drawings, increased interpersonal connection and a higher level of graphic expression occurred with the provision of structure.

Like the mother of a baby in the normal autistic phase, I was required to provide considerable structure and engagement, similar to nourishing an infant in order to facilitate growth. The amount of structure that I offered was extreme. I sat fairly close and maintained as much eye contact as possible. I talked to Teddy while he worked so that he would not retreat into an isolative state. I "fed" him pictures to copy. To offer this degree of structure and interference to a child more capable interpersonally and cognitively would thwart creativity and therapeutic progress. The therapeutic goals focused on increasing Teddy's impaired capacity to formulate ideas, engage in making choices, and participate in meaningful communication.

Figure 3.3 Animals by Teddy

Figure 3.4 Vampire by Teddy

Figure 3.5 Airplane disguised as a lion by Teddy

CASE EXAMPLE 2

"Keith" was a 12-year-old with a diagnosis of Asperger's syndrome. Like Teddy, he did not initiate interpersonal contact and did not make much eye contact. As is characteristic of Asperger's syndrome, Keith's intellectual development was not impaired. Although he was socially isolated, his handsome appearance and artistic talent were admired by his peers. As was true of Teddy, Keith shied away from depicting humans in his artwork. He preferred to portray robotic super heroes and villains. When I asked him to draw real people, he often portrayed them with a robotic appearance, in disguise, or with their backs facing the viewer. For example, in Figure 3.6, Keith chose to portray himself in a concealing Halloween costume when completing a self-portrait, indicating his need to maintain some distance from others. Figure 3.7 illustrates him at home playing video games, with emphasis on the details of the surroundings and of the screen as opposed to his personal characteristics. In depicting himself at school, Keith created a stiff, isolated image (Figure 3.8), effectively capturing his negative feelings about school. These images reflect attention to detail and strength as a visual artist. This strength enabled Keith to portray his interpersonal style, which was characterized by a state of self-protective and self-soothing isolation and a tendency to be absorbed in a fantasy world involving action-figures. This interpersonal style is exemplified in Figure 3.9, a portrait of a somewhat grotesque superhero—his favorite genre. I encouraged Keith to depict characters that interested him, to develop them, and to talk to me about his artistic struggles as well as the qualities of the characters' personalities. Eventually, he worked on technically challenging clay statues of futuristic science fiction characters. Figure 3.10 displays a well developed clay sculpture approximately 10 inches in height that demonstrates Keith's strength as an artist. We spoke of his artistic goals, which were to portray surreal and grotesque cartoon-like figures that included accurate human anatomical structure. I felt privileged to be included in Keith's discussions about his artistic struggles and vision because I knew that he had difficulty sharing his thoughts with others.

Figure 3.6 Self-portrait by Keith

Figure 3.7 Keith playing a video game

Figure 3.8 Keith at school

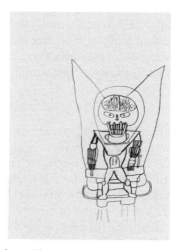

Figure 3.9 Robotic superhero by Keith

Figure 3.10 Sculpture by Keith

My approach fostered Keith's development, accessed his strengths, facilitating artistic and verbal description while encouraging sharing of his unique perceptions. He was able to bring form and substance to his ideas and to do this in a relational context. Because extreme insular functioning can lead to feelings of isolation, a reluctance to seek help when needed, and diminish ability to clarify one's own priorities, the treatment goals focused on building increased interpersonal reciprocity. The artwork and conversations facilitated significant communication, reducing the degree of insularity. This encouraged Keith to communicate his well developed inner world, a process that could be generalized to relationships with other adults and with peers. Due to the nature of his diagnosis, Keith would most likely continue to be restricted in his capacity for interpersonal connection. Thus treatment focused on improved coping rather than cure of autistic spectrum symptoms, which is not possible.

The use of a progressive model of interpersonal development supports realistic treatment. I viewed Keith's progress as evidence of interpersonal experience on a developmental continuum. He was minimally aware of me but began to make eye contact sporadically. I remained active in eliciting expression. Art expression was a suitable way to accomplish this because it allowed for long periods of solitary self-absorption that did not disturb Keith's developmental and comfort levels. I sat fairly close to him in a perpendicular location at a table to facilitate more frequent eye contact. An important aspect of this process was my active use of eye contact and verbalizing in attempts to gain a sense of mutuality in understanding Keith's inner world.

ADDITIONAL COMMENTS

The role of the art therapist with children who experience autistic symptoms parallels the relationship between infant and parent. The degree of engagement, structure, and interpersonal effort on the part of the therapist is intensive. The aims of treatment respect not only the child's need for insularity and predictable routines but also encourage communication at the highest level the child can tolerate. The therapist has a significant responsibility to maintain interpersonal interaction in the therapeutic relationship just as parents are responsible for sustaining the interpersonal bond to facilitate the child's survival. In the case of the infant, the difference is that the parent's role is both physical and interpersonal whereas the art therapist's role is exclusively interpersonal. Further, in the parent–child relationship, the normal infant develops interpersonally, which assists in sustaining the relationship. In therapeutic work with an autistic spectrum child, the therapist keeps the relationship alive with little help from the client. Only gradually will the impaired child assume increased interpersonal abilities such as eye contact, sharing perceptions and thoughts, and asking for help.

Symbiosis Phase (2–4 Months)

When the infant begins to emerge from the autistic stage, *symbiosis* with the mother becomes a striking phenomenon. During the course of the symbiotic stage, the infant's stimulus barrier shifts from an extremely protective position to one that allows for greater awareness of the mother. Freud likened the bright-eyed little face peeping out at others during this stage to a baby bird beginning to crack through the eggshell (Mahler et al., 1975). At first, the infant does not take in stimuli that exist beyond the symbiotic union. Physicality and the visual image of the caregiver's face are significant organizers of the infant's experience. Gradually, an ability for self-soothing develops (e.g., intentional thumb sucking), but during symbiosis, the infant relies primarily on the caregiver for soothing. This is the earliest period of transition to a more active relational position and the beginnings of reciprocity, characterized by a high level of vulnerabilty and virtually no ability to function independently. The parent unconditionally anticipates and meets physical needs so as to provide comfort and safety.

Clinical Implications for Art Therapy

The art therapist may assume a symbiotic role in certain situations. These instances often involve children who lack the capacity for independent self-activation. This may be due to mental retardation, brain injury, severe depression, or extreme anxiety. In such cases, it may be necessary to collaborate on the same artwork in order for the child to engage at all. The goal is to bring the child to a higher level of self-activation through providing support.

CASE EXAMPLE

"Charlie," a very depressed 6-year-old boy, was withdrawn and appeared to have caved in on himself. The only way I was able to engage him was to work on the same page. Even with this support, he rejected opportunities to do any creative work and agreed only to play tic-tac-toe. Gradually, I began to introduce the idea of drawing animals instead of Xs and Os in tic-tac-toe games. Due to the close support he felt, he was able to engage in creative activity, drawing small images of animals on the tiny tic-tac-toe board he had drawn (see Figure 3.11). This enabled him to feel protected enough to risk more personal expression than would have been possible without interpersonal support. In

Figure 3.11 Tic-tac-toe board containing animals by Charlie

later art therapy treatment, he was able to produce some bigger drawings, but it was still necessary for me to provide some contributions on the same page.

In Charlie's case, the goal was to promote self-expression to help him emerge from his crumpled, withdrawn position. To achieve this, it was necessary to supply a level of safety akin to the infant–mother symbiotic experience. I recognized the tic-tac-toe game as a tenuous expression of Charlie's need for connection that required careful support for him to develop further. Winnicott (1971a) explained that healthy developmental processes in young infants are facilitated by the mother's recognition and response to the infant's cues. Healthy development is impeded if the mother substitutes her own needs and attempts to force these on the infant. Reading and responding to nonverbal cues is also an important function of child art therapists.

Differentiation: First Subphase, Hatching (6–10 Months)

At about 4 to 5 months of age, the infant begins to differentiate individuals and to show some growth beyond the former state of fusion. The first phase of differentiation, *hatching*, is characterized by increased alertness, goal-directedness, and persistence (Mahler et al., 1975). The baby strains to look at faces or plays peek-a-boo games and pulls at hair, clothing, and so on. These explorative patterns are a result of simultaneous relational, cognitive, and physical development. The baby experiences persistent devotion to manual, tactile, and visual exploration even before there is a capacity for independent locomotion. The differentiation phase heralds the beginnings of manipulation of materials, which in later childhood, is used as a way to enact a sense of purpose, to facilitate self-soothing, and to connect with self and others. It provides the basis for confirmation of one's ability to produce cause and effect (Sroufe, Egeland, Carlson, & Collins, 2005).

During this subphase, babies engage in studying and comparing different people, reacting cautiously to strangers. This is the first stage in which interpersonal anxiety is apparent. The hatching baby who inspects the faces of strangers seems to be saying, "Is this world a safe enough place for me?" Clearly, sometimes the answer is "no" as babies may collapse into a state of worried desperation when encountering an unfamiliar person. They turn their heads away and sometimes cry in apparent anguish, indicating that the sight of a stranger is unbearable. The scrutiny and evaluation of others to assess for safety has its roots in this stage—although the level of vulnerability and dependency decreases over time as independent functioning increases.

Clinical Implications for Art Therapy

For some children, anxiety towards unfamiliar people and situations retains the quality of infant stranger anxiety. For example, school-age children who experience school phobia and separation anxiety manifest similarities to differentiation-phase infants. Sometimes anxious children perceive the therapist in a manner that resembles babies' perceptions of strangers. Such may be the case with the child who cautiously peers at the art therapist, covering his or her artwork with his or her hand, both suspicious and curious about whether there is any hope for a positive relationship.

In working with an anxious child, an art therapist can foster the soothing use of art materials, providing support and assistance in order to reduce anxiety. Without reduction of anxiety, the child may remain frozen and unable to engage in constructive therapeutic work. The same is true for a differentiation-phase infant. Without a reassuring caregiver, anxiety interferes with the baby's capacity to develop the ability to feel independent, strong, and safe in the world. Art therapy methods can provide a structure that helps children to experience a sense of organization and security. With insecure children, the goal is to gradually develop the ability to self-soothe and to rely on their own strengths.

CASE EXAMPLE

During art therapy treatment of an anxious 7-year-old girl, I provided supportive structure in order to reduce anxiety. "Natalie" had been afraid to attend school, clinging to her parents. She appeared to experience a sense of overwhelming dread, believing that the world outside of her family was inexplicably dangerous. Her family members were high achievers, and she put a lot of pressure on herself to perform well. Although generally an ethical person, she cheated in school due to her fear of failure.

In art therapy sessions, my focus was to help Natalie to gain a sense of organization because she tended to work in a state of anxious impulsivity. She worked quickly and frantically with minimal attention to detail. This caused her to ruin her artwork and then to become discouraged, at which time she would request that I complete her work for her—which I gently declined. Provision of emotional support and structure helped to reduce her anxiety and impulsivity. Initially, I suggested mainly neutral themes and provided small boxes and canvases for her to paint on as this helped to soothe her and facilitate belief in her ability to perform successfully. Rather than giving in to suggestions that I draw for her, I attempted to offer manageable experiences. In one session when she spoke of her fear of going to school and leaving her mother, I drew an outline of a person and asked her to complete the image to show what her body felt like during these difficult times (see Figure 3.12). This image depicts a desperate, crying girl, described as feeling sad. Artwork

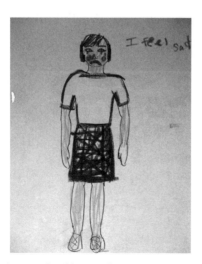

Figure 3.12 The feeling of going to school by Natalie

such as this allowed Natalie to portray and externalize her anxiety. Within this therapeutic framework, she became more able to manage overwhelming feelings. She subsequently had more success in separating from her parents and gained confidence in her ability to represent and make sense of her experience, which ceased to be so unmanageable.

Natalie also gained confidence in her ability to perform, in part, as a result of my expectation that anxiety can be managed. The use of small canvases and boxes for painting served to provide security for her, allowing her to navigate through art processes more safely. Frequently, her artwork depicted scenes conveying danger and discomfort and provided an outlet for her fears. For example, Figure 3.13, painted on a small board, shows a colonial girl (a safe subject choice) who is literally lost at sea. It conveys the feelings of abandonment and fear that Natalie was familiar with on a daily basis as she faced separation from her family. We talked about the anxiety and terror that a colonial girl might experience. This served to comfort Natalie and helped her to feel less alone as a result of reflecting on the universality of experiencing fear when confronting danger.

Art therapy methods increasingly fostered Natalie's sense that she was capable of soothing herself, organizing her chaotic and fearful emotions, and experiencing enjoyment in activities and decision-making. This gradually helped to decrease her anxiety regarding school performance and separation from parents. The challenge of regulating separation anxieties is first experienced in infancy and may recur in later stages. Just as the role of the infant's parent is to facilitate sturdiness and soothing, the therapeutic process with anxious children promotes gradual development of strength in regulating overwhelming emotion.

Differentiation: Second Subphase, Practicing (10–18 Months)

During the *practicing* subphase, the baby becomes enamored with creeping, crawling, and finally walking. This provides an exhilarating sense of freedom, which indicates an early capacity for substantial self-activation. The child craves and thrives on the emotional support and admiration from parents; the practicing subphase is considered a stage of exuberant narcissism. The toddler appears to experience a sense of omnipotence

Figure 3.13 Colonial girl by Natalie

in the drive to keep moving regardless of bumps and falls. Although for most parents this is a joyous and exhausting time, some have difficulty tolerating the toddler's independence and may become anxious and critical. Parental anxiety can deprive the child of the admiration that helps to promote self-confidence. Literally, the first steps are taken away from the parent. Parents' continued support, encouragement, and protectiveness facilitate healthy development for the bumbling little creature who has very little use of language or self-protective functions.

Clinical Implications for Art Therapy

In child art therapy, the therapist may become the audience from whom the child receives admiration and applause for nonverbal activity (Kramer, 2000). Parental admiration nourishes a child's sense of having intrinsic value. Whether or not their work has artistic merit, children who have not developed a sense of being valued can benefit from opportunities to be admired for their courage in experimenting with art materials. Messy and ugly expressions as well as the creation of beauty can be appreciated in art therapy. Children who have experienced toilet training difficulties often exemplify this issue by struggling to maintain control.

CASE EXAMPLE

This was the situation with a bright 7-year-old girl, "Brenda," who had not experienced successful potty training and who engaged in ongoing control struggles with her parents. Although Brenda could perform well, she was in apparent rebellion against performing for others. Consequently, she stubbornly held in her bowels, which led to stomach pain and sometimes "accidents."

In art therapy sessions, Brenda was initially controlled and rigid. She created tiny, meticulously detailed clay pieces and cleaned up excessively, demonstrating her need for control. I provided both controllable and expressive art materials as well as emotional support and appreciation for all of her efforts, thereby validating both the need for control and her forbidden but increasingly gleeful fascination with chaotic expression. Gradually, her clay pieces became bigger and involved ever more messy materials, signifying a loosening of control. I supported this trend in an unobtrusive way so that independent efforts were confirmed. To release the bind with control struggles, it was crucial that I maintain a position of acceptance of all expression. My ability to be comfortable with excessive and seemingly unproductive rigidity along with messy, unformed expression was especially important. I had to put aside any expectations that Brenda create beautiful art and strive to see the beauty in her exploratory victories. Interestingly, the toileting difficulties resolved during this time period. This was likely due to Brenda's acceptance of her messy creations while getting support for doing so. Art therapy can offer a means of repair that even loving and conscientious parents cannot facilitate.

The above case illustrates an example of a child in need of the opportunity to rework developmental functions. My approach emphasized using the child's existing strengths to encourage loosening and reestablishing control. It was important that the child, as opposed to an outsider, generate this control. Using a medium such as wet clay was especially suitable because it allowed for both messy and controlled expression. This media choice would be unsuitable for a child who was disorganized or explosive as this could be frightening and cause uncontrolled aggression and overwhelming confusion. In addition, I did not push any materials on Brenda. I admired her creations whether they were rigid and obsessive or messy.

Art therapy is well suited for supporting the development of healthy narcissism in children. Kramer (2000, p. 93) described the art therapist's role as simulating the "gleam in the mother's eye," referring to Kohut's description of the therapist as a benign and accepting presence who is akin to an admiring parent. The therapist's admiration of creativity and genuine self-expression supports children basking in their own glory. Brenda established a more healthy level of narcissism, one that was related to her own expression rather than generated by her perception of what others would admire. Her previous simultaneous wish to please and resulting anger about this expectation had resulted in control struggles, a battle in which both parents and child experienced defeat.

Differentiation: Third Subphase: Rapprochement (15–24 Months)

During the *rapprochement* subphase, the toddler experiences a clash between autonomy and dependency. This is characterized by increased vulnerability and volatility, impotent rage, projection, and splitting. The child lacks the ability to neutralize emotions or to be able to experience simultaneous emotions (e.g., love and anger). Projection and splitting are used as a way to tolerate painful affect. For example, a 3-year-old client refused to end the session, stating that he liked working with clay and that he needed to make three more snowmen. After I gently insisted that we had to end our time for today, he told me that he hated this place and that he would never return. The only way he could tolerate leaving the enjoyable experience was to denounce it wholeheartedly, which allowed him to feel more in control of the separation. The fragile state of the toddler involves a sense of omnipotence that meets with the inevitable fate of facing dependency needs and relinquishing control. Although increased language and motor skills facilitate greater independence, the irrational wish for complete control leads to rage and deflation. In what is often a no-win situation, toddlers wish to be understood and magically gratified while demanding control; this leads to an overwhelming sense of fragility and insatiability, the essence of what Mahler et al. (1975) described as the *rapprochement crisis*. During this stage, parental ability to provide reality testing, support, and boundaries are instrumental in facilitating the child's capacity for frustration tolerance and affect regulation.

Some of the manipulative and self-regulatory difficulties of individuals with personality disorders are similar to the interpersonal patterns of the rapprochement phase (Masterson, 2000). However, in-depth emotional and interpersonal experience also begins at this stage. In reference to observation of toddlers, Mahler et. al. (1975) stated, "One could see with a special clarity during this period the roots of many uniquely human problems and dilemmas—problems that are sometimes never completely resolved during the entire life cycle" (p. 100).

Clinical Implications for Art Therapy

In child art therapy treatment, interpersonal and art-related experiences reminiscent of the rapprochement crisis are common. Many children receive treatment because they have difficulties accepting controls, which inevitably results in conflicts with authority and related problems at home, at school, and in the community. In art therapy sessions, these difficulties may take a wide variety of forms including destruction of artwork, anger at supplies provided, and rejection of suggestions by the therapist. However, very often during sessions, the problematic behaviors are not directly evident (at least initially) because it is easy for children to express strong feelings through art as opposed to relying on the usual destructive patterns.

CASE EXAMPLE

A second grade boy, "Rich," received weekly art therapy for about 9 months. The reason for referral was that he experienced frequent temper tantrums that were triggered by minor disappointments. During these tantrums, he would scream, kick, and punch others in apparent rage analogous to the behavior of a 2-year-old. His family had been chaotic for most of his life. Tantrums were a way to express his rage and overwhelming and uncontrollable feelings. Although his emotional development was similar to that of a 2-year-old, his cognitive and physical developmental levels were appropriate for his 7 years. In art therapy sessions, Rich demonstrated a tendency to be impulsive by working quickly and messily on his art. Nonetheless, his creativity and emotional intensity enabled him to artistically express and verbalize personally meaningful themes.

My role was to provide manageable tasks so that Rich could put coherent form to strong feelings while remaining in control. I asked him to do a picture of a scene reflecting something that interested him, providing a small piece of paper so that the possibility of becoming emotionally overwhelmed would be lessened (see Figure 3.14). He used a combination of paint and pastels to create a picture of a train running into a mountain. I responded to the artwork by saying that I thought this did not look very safe; he replied by enthusiastically saying, "Yes! And I'm driving the train." The fact that Rich could *safely* share the very familiar and terrifying feeling of losing control was a new experience for him. During our sessions, there was a sense of mutual understanding and safety. Although previous experiences of expressing emotion had repeatedly caused antago-

Figure 3.14 Train driving into mountain by Rich

nism, isolation, and abandonment, the therapeutic use of art facilitated a meaningful interpersonal connection. Art expression became the basis for portraying and regulating strong feelings in the context of a supportive relationship.

The value of transforming expression into nonverbal and verbal understanding cannot be underestimated as it lays the groundwork for developing the behavioral controls that are necessary to function adequately in the world. For a 2-year-old or a chaotic 7-year-old, it is necessary to learn that frustration can be managed. The parent of a 2-year-old and the therapist of an aggressive 7-year-old are charged with a similar task of providing safety and containment so that the child can entertain the possibility of surviving disappointment. In an observation applicable to both parents and therapists, Sroufe et al. (2005) state that the exuberance and strengths of a toddler's desires are important human characteristics. "With caregiving assistance, they can become the cornerstones for later creativity and agency" (pp. 106–107).

Approaching the Preschool Age: Object Constancy (24–36 Months and Beyond)

Three-year-old children tolerate temporary separation from parents due to the cognitive and emotional ability to understand that parents still exist even though they have left the room. By the third year, children have usually developed a realistic and consistent image of the parent that can be called on when needed. This ability is known as *object constancy* and engenders the capacity for more sophisticated levels of self-soothing, cognitive skills, and affect regulation. A sustainable self-image and gender identity also begin to emerge. Children can engage in symbolic play activities and art expression. These activities further promote growth and are spurred by tremendous physical, cognitive, and emotional development. In healthy development, an early form of identity has now been established.

An Ongoing Exploration: Early Development and Art Therapy Theory and Research

Research and laboratory studies (Fonagy et al., 2004; Schore, 2003; Sroufe, et al., 2005; Stern, 1985) confirm Bowlby's (1988) and Mahler's (Mahler et al., 1975) hypotheses that successful early development is dependent on responsive care. Mahler's framework regarding interpersonal stages of development was built upon observational research that involved mothers and babies for several years in a home-like setting. These findings have uniquely illuminated much about the progression of development in addition to providing an understanding of interpersonal–psychological states that have origins in both normal and pathological development. Within these states lie the potential for the creative and therapeutic focus that fuels the visual modes of perception inherent in art therapy process. The early dyadic relationship can serve, to some degree, as a model for the therapeutic relationship. Both address developmental areas such as reality perception, interpersonal interaction, trust, self-regulation, self-soothing, and self-activation. Art therapy process focuses on facilitating such functions in the service of strengthening the child while repairing stage disruptions. Emotional and relational states are expressed within artwork and the art therapy relationship. The integration of theories of interpersonal development with an understanding of the pictorial language of early states is a valuable tool for promoting healthy growth in child art therapy clients.

4 The Pictorial Language of Early Relational Trauma

Infants are amazing beings that evoke much fascination and curiosity. Although it is not possible to remember what it was like to be an infant, it is well worth the effort to try to understand as much as possible. Studies involving infant observation help to illuminate some aspects of this subject. Additionally, exploring the effects of infant maltreatment provides valuable information about an infant's experience of vulnerability. Undoubtedly, infancy is characterized by a state of fragility and total dependency, qualities that are present in later years but to a lesser degree. Individuals who experienced maltreatment during infancy sustain damage that is evident as they proceed through later development (Schore, 1994; Sroufe et al., 2005). Sameroff and Emde (1989) explain:

> When things go well, there is a tangible sense of thriving and accomplishment for caregiver and baby, and this is shared with others who see it. When things go awry, the opposite happens. Distress and frustration, although normal and necessary in the short run, can be unmanageable in the long run.
>
> (p. 3)

Although infants do not create artwork, older children may incorporate what appear to be infantile images in their art. This imagery can serve to delineate important information about early experience. The sensory and nonverbal qualities of art expression provide a fitting means for portraying aspects of infant experience.

The Importance of Early Experience

Practitioners of child art therapy must be versed in theories of early relational development for the following reasons:

1. The early years constitute the initial formative period, which influences basic personality structure and the internal working models for subsequent experiences.
2. Children of all ages may still have some areas in which they function at a more infantile level due to a variety of familial, cultural, and biological causes.
3. Individuals' earliest development and history provide clues to the kind of supplementation that needs to be offered in treatment.

4. Art therapy, in particular, provides a tool for addressing deficits relating to early experience because of its nonverbal and sensory therapeutic components.

The Early Self: A Relational Being

Winnicott (1965) stated, "There is no such thing as a baby" (p. 35). What he meant by this is that a baby does not exist without its mother (or caregiver). Human beings are highly relational creatures as evidenced by the fact that they form families, civilizations, and societies. An infant's extreme dependency on parental care is the foundation from which socially constructive, related beings emerge. Erik Erikson (1950) emphasized that even in utero, the infant and its environment mutually stimulate each other, and that this mutual stimulation between the individual and the environment continues throughout the life cycle. The question of the degree to which parents shape their children has been disputed (nature versus nurture). Conclusive answers are difficult to pin down considering the multitude of biological and environmental variables that shape all aspects of a developing person.

During infancy parents must meet the physical needs of the infant. The degree to which this is compromised produces related problems. In the beginning, an infant exists at a primarily physical level. Physical sensations and the parents' response to these provide the basis for later emotional mastery and the capacity to trust others. As mentioned previously, E. Erikson (1950) described the psychosocial struggle that infants engage in as trust versus mistrust. Infants experience a range of potential discomforts and gratifications. Parents strive to soothe and care for their children to ensure healthy adjustment and survival.

The strident and upsetting sounds of an infant's cries are generally enough to activate parents to soothe their babies. Parents do not analyze the matter because their actions are based on instinct. Although they do not think about trust versus mistrust, it is the parents' instinctive provision of care that helps to facilitate a sense of hope for the baby. The fact that parents try hard but are not perfect teaches children to struggle with small increments of unmet need and to cope with difficulties in later stages of life. Through trial and error, infants teach their parents to correct mistakes in the care they provide. Research suggests that is it is more important that parents facilitate opportunities for infants to experience repair in relation to unpleasant experiences than that they shelter their young from all discomfort (Sroufe et al., 2005). For infants, this facilitates a belief in others as well as a capacity to struggle, both independently and interdependently, with challenges. Repair and struggle are also salient processes throughout the course of life and are highly significant within child art therapy treatment. The belief that repair is possible is an important component of healthy relationships, developmental processes, and optimal functioning. Art therapy can offer children who were deprived of adequate interpersonal care during infancy opportunities to engage in repair on interpersonal, physical, and symbolic levels.

The struggle of infancy facilitates the capacity to feel trust as well as mistrust in a healthy and realistic way. Both lack of trust and blind trust are undesirable outcomes in the developing human being. Fortunately, the majority of infants master the struggle between trust versus mistrust and thus develop what E. Erikson (1950) described as basic trust that results in a sense of hope. Basic trust provides belief in oneself and others at a fundamental level.

Disrupted Early Attachment and Treatment

The art-based study of infant and toddler attachment that follows focuses on the relevance of the earliest developmental stages in working with children. Although early intervention is preferable, many children are not referred for treatment until they begin to experience difficulties in school (Sroufe et al., 2005). Treatment of infants and toddlers most frequently includes parents or guardians. This approach involves helping parents to understand and meet their babies' needs. It involves supporting parents to forge attachments with their infants. Cycles of disrupted attachment can be intergenerational, and therapeutic work with parents strives to shift the tide of destructive long-term relational patterns.

Implications for Treatment

Many children who receive art therapy have experienced early maltreatment. The effects of infant physical abuse or neglect are difficult to repair. Among children maltreated as infants, there is a higher incidence of school failure and social problems as well as increased risk of adult psychiatric conditions and criminal behaviors. This places a burden both on the victims of maltreatment and on the community (Schore, 2003). Ill-treated children, even though later adopted into supportive and loving families, often experience severe disturbances throughout childhood, adolescence, and adulthood. These individuals never mastered the earliest struggles due to anxiety about whether they could depend on receiving basic care. Consequently, the internal working models they developed have caused them to see all adults as cruel or depriving (Stern, 1985). It is difficult to reverse early templates and very often a total cure is not possible. However, even in cases where damage is severe, treatment can reduce destructive behavioral and interpersonal patterns.

Art Therapy Intervention

Art therapy expression illuminates the struggle between trust versus mistrust with children who experienced attachment disruptions. Children who have experienced maltreatment during infancy often express strong emotions in their artwork. For these children, emotions are not understandable or manageable, illustrating the fact that development of the capacity to regulate emotions is dependent on the provision of adequate early care. The feelings expressed in artwork of children who were maltreated as infants often include a sense of helplessness, rage, and despair. Such feelings are the only imaginable responses for a totally dependent being in the face of severe attachment disruptions. This artwork is often reminiscent of an infant's psychomotor agitation and cries of distress.

Case Example 1: Unmanageable Need

"Nina" was a 12-year-old girl who had experienced severe early neglect. She was adopted at age 2 and, at that time, had physical signs of maltreatment including scars and malnourishment. Although the physical symptoms healed, it became increasingly apparent that Nina could not be satisfied or comforted. She was increasingly envious and needy. Although envy is a normal emotion, Nina's experience of this emotion was tied into a desperate and overwhelming need that related to experiences during which her very survival had been threatened. As a school-age child, she hoarded food and stole from her family and friends. By the time she was 12, her parents were totally frustrated. No matter how much they gave her, the effects of early unmet needs were not diminished. One can only imagine an infant's response to being left hungry and cold for extended periods and of having no reliable person to turn to when in distress. It seemed Nina was unable to believe that her needs could ever be satisfied and she was unable to trust adults. She explained that she perceived their expressions of good wishes as lies. Her perception was that she had to be sneaky to be taken care of; she lied, stole, and cheated.

In art therapy sessions, Nina had difficulty organizing her thoughts and feelings. She was avoidant and detached, which made it difficult to facilitate a connection with her. Her frequent response to questions was, "I don't care." She was intelligent and attractive. However, she lacked friends, and she did poorly in school. Although Nina was creative and clever, her motivation to invest in artworks was not well developed, similar to her approach to schoolwork. Even though her ideas sparkled, her ability to follow through was weak. When confronted about stealing and lying, she focused on her dislike of others and her feeling that she never received her fair share of material items, privileges, and recognition (regardless of whether she had earned good grades or other rewards). Her goal was to be pop star, which would afford her the fame, wealth, and glamour she felt entitled to.

Figure 4.1, a painting of a person in the rain, was done during one of Nina's early art therapy sessions. It portrays an ungrounded and vacant figure surrounded by clouds and rain. Nina appeared to find doing this image soothing, and she noted that the figure appeared to be part of the storm. The image conveys a sense of despair reminiscent of infant neglect and characterized by emptiness and lack of containment. Being held, responded to, and cared for provide physical boundaries and a confirmation of one's own existence during infancy. In contrast, Nina's painting portrays an unsafe, passive, and unformed experience of emotional and physical distress. During infancy, physical sensation and emotional experience are intertwined whereas cognitive understanding is absent. Emotional mastery during infancy is critically tied to the physical and relational experience of care (Schore, 2003). An important aspect of early development is the gradual capacity to make sense of and find comfort in emotions and physical sensations. The functions initially performed by parents are gradually integrated as attributes of the self, resulting in the ability to self-soothe. Although Nina did not relate the image to herself, it appears to serve as a kind of autobiographical representation of abandonment. Nina said that the person in the image appeared sad. And because she did not associate the image with herself, she could safely share that emotional material with me.

Later in art therapy treatment, Nina was able to organize strong feelings into more developed statements—both visually and verbally. Figure 4.2 portrays a small, enraged child in a supermarket, described as engaged in a temper tantrum that resulted from "wanting more than she is allowed to have." When questioned, Nina said that she could relate to the feeling of rage and that she often felt extremely disappointed. This artwork is more clearly developed than Figure 4.1 because it was done after more organizational ability and cognitive understanding had been established. Still, strong emotions relating to the profound experience of unmet need (of feeling like a bottomless pit) continued to reign.

Figure 4.1 Person in the rain by Nina

Figure 4.2 Temper tantrum by Nina

An important goal in treatment with Nina was to help her to develop the capacity to control rage and to find ways to get her needs met through communication rather than through stealing and blaming others. The early stages of treatment focused on developing a sensory, visual, and verbal vocabulary to express need, and later therapy focused on reflecting upon experiences, behaviors, and choices. At age 12, she continued to angrily blame her parents and others when she faced seemingly minor disappointments. The overall focus in treatment, then, was to simulate parents' tasks when fostering infant development: modeling organization, providing soothing, mitigating frustration, containing rage, and supplying a language to describe experiences and express needs. Art therapy expression promoted important aspects of these tasks by bringing forth preverbal material for examination in a context removed from the early battleground. In addition, it was important for Nina's adoptive parents to be partners in treatment; they worked on establishing behavioral containment as well as empathy. Needless to say, they required considerable support in their efforts.

Regarding relevant defenses, Fraiberg (1987) has stated that infants who are mal-treated are vulnerable to developing pathological defenses. These infants tend to negate "every expectation for normal social interaction" (p. 187). They do not seek out the mother but instead avoid contact with her. Rather than attributing benevolence to the mother, they perceive her as a threat and assume a position of relational freezing, which involves disorganization and disconnection characterized by a state of immobility and dissociation. The disconnected and vacant state apparent in Nina's painting of a person in the rain (Figure 4.1) resembles Fraiberg's description of *infantile avoidance*.

In later infancy, *fighting* (Fraiburg, 1987) is a pathological defense that is induced by perceived danger. Fighting involves a state of acute anxiety that is motivated by terror and results in tantrums in an attempt to ward off feelings of helplessness. Individuals experiencing extreme danger have been described as resorting to "flight or fight" responses. Whereas avoidance is akin to the flight response, protesting through aggressive behavior or crying is akin to the fight response. Figure 4.1 resembles an avoidance or flight response, and Figure 4.2 portrays a fight response. It was a major accomplishment for Nina to express this latter inherently aggressive and chaotic state in a controlled, expressive work.

Case Example 2: Confusion about Love and Safety

"Chris," a 10-year-old boy who was severely neglected during infancy, completed Figure 4.3, a person-in-the-rain painting. After years of neglect and repeated temporary removal from his drug-addicted mother's care, Chris was now in a loving foster home; however, he had difficulty believing that all would be well.

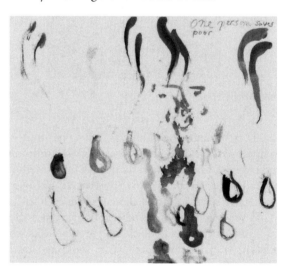

Figure 4.3 Person in the rain by Chris

Chris's painting features a small incomplete human figure (bottom center) described as next to a fire and surrounded by streaks of fire and smoke in addition to huge drops and streaks of rain. He wrote the vague sentence "One person saves poor" at the top of the page and explained that, amid storm and fire, another person rescued a poor person. The unformed and fragmented image suggests disorganization and appears to symbolically reflect this child's wish to be cared for as well as his difficult struggle to integrate his new placement with his former experience. In his new placement, Chris misinterpreted loving gestures as harmful, which caused him to respond in a combative manner. Similarly, the painting belies its description; the tiny figure, barely visible and cut off at the bottom of the page, appears threatened and alone.

This artwork exemplifies what Fraiberg (1987) describes as another pathological defense of infancy, *transformation of affect*, which involves replacing a painful feeling with a pleasant response. For instance, Fraiberg described a maltreated infant who, while sucking contentedly, had a bottle removed suddenly from his mouth. The infant responded by smiling and laughing whereas a normally attached infant would have displayed disturbance. This behavior signifies a profound disruption in the ability to read cues and to make sense of physical and emotional experience. It suggests an inability to distinguish care and safety from neglect and danger, a failure commonly demonstrated by children with histories of early relational trauma. The early experience of lack of attunement by the caregiver that takes place on a physical level (and may initially involve hunger or physical pain and discomfort) produces a sustained tendency to misread the intentions of others. This can result in repeated experiences that expect and invite interpersonal dysfunction such as abusive or provocative relationships and perceiving violent or high-risk behaviors as pleasurable.

Attachment Research

Children who are maltreated during infancy do not develop the ability to recognize, organize, and regulate their feelings and bodily sensations because these functions can only be established in the context of adequate early care. The bottle or the mother's breast provides nutrition for the growing infant, and emotionally and physically responsive care provides nourishment for psychological functioning such as self-regulation, trust, frustration tolerance, interdependence, and empathy. For both humans and animals, healthy development is contingent on the experience of secure early attachment. This is the context in which a person learns how to love and be loved (Ainsworth, 1969).

Bowlby (1982, 1988) studied the impact of attachment on children as well as the instinctive and formative nature of early relational experience, establishing that prior to formation of the self, the parent–child relationship provides the basis for survival and self-protection. Subsequent formation of a self that is secure is thus contingent on early attachment relationships. More recently, Schore (2003) has linked deficits such as lack of empathy, violent behavior, and poor impulse control to failures in brain development in poorly attached youngsters. This has been confirmed by brain research studies, and it is now widely accepted that inadequate care during infancy negatively impacts brain development. In addition, Schore provides evidence to support the conjecture that relational experience within the context of emotionally attuned psychotherapy can facilitate neurological repair relating to interpersonal functions and affect regulation.

As illustrated by the above cases, severe infantile anxiety constitutes a faulty foundation for the developing self and is a very serious risk factor. Pathological defenses of infancy can interfere with the experience of pleasure and security that are necessary to a solid neurobiological foundation. The importance of the infant's experience of comfort and trust cannot be underestimated (Hughs, 1997; Klorer, 2008; Siegel, 1999). When this is compromised, later development inevitably suffers in a manner that is similar to building a house on a damaged foundation.

The artwork completed by Nina and Chris, both of whom experienced very early trauma, have an emotional intensity that helps to provide understanding of the importance of early care. Stern (1985) described how the baby is apt to see the parent as cruel when faced with unmet needs. In severe circumstances, children transfer such perceptions onto others and perceive the world as cruel, producing feelings of global abandonment. The experience of insurmountable need becomes a deeply entrenched belief. This perception results in symptomatic behaviors such as stealing, lying, tantrums, and interpersonal manipulation designed to defend against extreme helplessness. Frequently, these children attempt to hide their neediness, adopting a superficially engaging and appreciative facade (Hughs, 1997). Such was the case with Nina and Chris, both of whom were ingratiating and charming. Their engaging personal style served as a survival mechanism and as a means of hiding the substantial shame that is inherent in overwhelming neediness.

A Conceptual Framework

Parents provide a form of scaffolding for the formation of a healthy self. The scaffolding is very gradually removed as the child's self becomes more solid (Davies, 2005). Early attachment experiences greatly influence child development. As with other types of problems, art expression can reveal considerable information about the ways that children have been affected. Nonverbal modes of expression, such as art, provide a language for expression and repair of the damage that results from disrupted attachment. Attachment disordered children are severely at risk, and treatment can provide, if not a total cure, a protective influence. The prognosis depends on many factors including inborn personality strengths, the level of damage that has been sustained, and ongoing support systems.

Although infants are not consumers of art therapy, knowledge of normal and pathological infant development is an important tool for child art therapists. In addition, sensitivity to the pictorial language of infant relational trauma assists in maintaining a grounding and compassionate approach to working with children who have experienced severe disturbance. A solid conceptual framework is especially important when working with severely at risk children as this helps to provide a grounding influence in the context of chaotic expression. Tolerating and understanding chaotic expression is an inherently difficult clinical responsibility. Children who do not feel safe tend to provoke strong emotional responses in those who work with them. When working with internally chaotic children, theoretical support as well as supervision and self-care serve as important anchors for therapists.

Part III

The Pictorial Language of Resilience and Vulnerability

5 Resilience
The Capacity to Struggle with Challenges

Resilience is a form of immunity that is associated with capacity to cope with stress, to recover from difficulties, and to use challenges in the service of personal growth (Davies, 2005). Resilient children believe that they can master difficulties as opposed to feeling at the mercy of external events. This quality is known as internal locus of control (Werner & Smith, 2001). Flexible use of age-appropriate defenses is also an indication of resiliency (Vaillant, 1993). A variety of age-appropriate and effective means of coping contribute to a child's level of sturdiness, an important factor in insuring a steady course of maturation. Although negative experiences impact resilience levels, some children who experience tremendous adversity manage to triumph impressively whereas others who live within supportive environments do not develop significant strengths. Research shows that children who consistently triumph over adversity possess internal strengths as well as a repertoire of experiences in which they previously handled challenges successfully. Most importantly, research findings by Sroufe et al. (2005) and Werner and Smith (2001) indicate that secure early attachment is the strongest predictor of resilience in children. Research findings also indicate that resilient individuals had at least one significant highly supportive early relationship. Sroufe and Siegel (2011) maintain that children's brains are remodeled in a template that is based on early relational experience, thus reproducing enactment of the successes and failures that parallel those that occurred during infancy and early childhood.

Protective and Risk Factors

Analysis of risk and protective factors is useful in determining resilience levels (Davies, 2005). Risk factors cause vulnerability within children whereas protective factors help to foster resiliency. These factors can be external or internal. External risk factors include socioeconomic hardship such as poverty or minority ethnicity and related discrimination; parental dysfunction; parental level of education; exposure to violence, sexual, physical, or emotional abuse; divorce or death of a parent; harsh discipline practices; and multiple moves or placements. Parents with disrupted attachment histories place their own children at greater risk. Internal risk factors are qualities of the child; they include intellectual and physical impairments and difficult temperament. Cumulative effects of risk factors, as opposed to specific hardships, contribute to the possibility of negative outcomes (Canino & Spurlock, 1994).

External protective factors include areas such as environmental, economic, and parental support and stability; high quality schools and childcare; family support systems; and enriched cultural and recreational opportunities. Internal protective factors include attributes such as physical health, positive temperament, and intellectual aptitude and talents.

Individual art therapy treatment can address risk factors that relate to children's ability to cope with stress, whereas case management, community services, parental support, and family therapy can address environmental and external risk factors. Treatment aimed at building protective factors often enhances resilience. As adults, those who have experienced lower levels of internal resilience in childhood are at greater risk for developing psychiatric disorders, addictions, economic difficulties, criminality, and relationship difficulties (Werner & Smith, 2001).

Background information about children that includes relational, physical, familial, school, and behavioral functioning provides a broad view of resilience levels. This information can be gathered from those who have regular contact with the child and provides a starting point for art therapy assessment. Art therapy evaluations can shed light on children's levels of resilience as well as risk and protective factors, offering a lens for understanding children's perceptions and states. In general, art therapy evaluation does not uncover surprising findings, but rather serves to confirm existing information about a child's strengths and problems. Nonetheless, art therapy expression may reveal thoughts, feelings, and perceptions that were hidden from view. Most significant is the potential of art expression to specify the unique experience of each child and to pinpoint creative strengths that may not be as apparent in other activities. These strengths can be mobilized in treatment to build higher resilience levels.

As mentioned in previous chapters, achievement of age-appropriate developmental functioning is dependent on many factors. All people experience some fluctuation in the capacity to function optimally. Fluctuations may be caused by discomfort, disappointments, and a variety of stressors. Major disruptions (domestic violence, divorce, abuse, death of a loved one, critical physical illness, and so on) often present severe challenges to development, resulting in symptoms. One way to view this is that the psychological energy needed for maturation must be used to survive the disruption. For example, in the case of parental conflict, many children devote their energy to trying to help their parents to get along better and then blame themselves for failure to succeed in this effort. This consumes an enormous amount of energy that would normally be used in peer relationships or in activities that could produce an experience of age-appropriate success. Repeated successes foster higher resilience levels, but failure to wholeheartedly invest in activities thwarts healthy development. The bulk of what follows in this chapter focuses on protective factors, and the next chapter (chapter 6) takes risk factors as its main topic.

Building Resilience

Case Example 1: Art Therapy as Resilience Booster

Soon after her parents divorced, "Greta," a 6-year-old, manifested symptoms such as interrupting and the inability to sit still that exasperated her first grade teacher. Anxiety and distress had taken the form of physical agitation, interfering with school performance. During her first art therapy session at a community mental health agency, Greta completed Figure 5.1 in response to my request that she draw her family. The

Figure 5.1 Family drawing by Greta

cheerfully colored scene includes a house and shows her standing between both parents. She stated, "I'm trying to clap my Mom and Dad together." Greta further revealed her unwillingness to accept her state of powerlessness because she labeled each window with the initials of Mom, Dad, and her own name. "We can each have our own window," she insisted. When I said, "You really love *both* of your parents," she emphatically wrote "I love you" on the drawing, explaining that these words were intended for me as well as her parents. I assume she expressed love for me, in part due to the insecurity she was feeling and in part because she was appreciative of my validation of her feelings. She was also an effusive and kind child.

The portrayal of Greta's wish to reunite the family provided an outlet for her intense anguish related to her parents' divorce—anguish that was apparently causing the behavioral symptoms at school. The drawing, though, also shows Greta's strengths; it is well organized, age-appropriate, and directly conveys her thoughts and feelings. During 4 months of weekly art therapy, this bright, active child was encouraged to discharge and make sense of her disappointment. She came to understand that although she could not repair her broken family, she could express her views to regain a sense of control that helped to resolve her agitation. Greta learned that she could handle even a very severe disappointment, cope with anxiety, and reestablish the ability to be successful in school. Internal locus of control, a feature of resilience, was reinforced. During the first session, Greta revealed not only that she was struggling, but also that she had many internal protective factors including intelligence, a very likeable personality, a positive attitude, and the ability to face difficulties head-on. Resilient individuals tend to acknowledge disappointments and are able to use them in the service of growth (Werner & Smith, 2001).

Greta's external protective factors included supportive and cooperative parents and a very loving grandmother who had provided childcare since infancy. Greta's parents were blue-collar workers who struggled financially and were not well educated. Although they occupied a relatively low socioeconomic stratum, they maintained steady employment and income, a protective factor that fostered a sense of stability. Internal and external protective factors helped to support Greta's progress in therapy and adjustment to the divorce.

Form, Content, and Expression of the Problem

The child art therapist strives to understand fluctuations as well as more entrenched areas of difficulty. Impulsive responses to all activities during sessions indicate something very different from an impulsive response to one theme or type of art process. Some children become very disorganized or excessively rambunctious when using potentially messy art materials whereas other children demonstrate high levels of creativity and organization in such activities. These responses reveal important information about coping styles and appropriate therapeutic interventions. Children's developmental level of graphic expression and behavior is often influenced by the subject matter being portrayed. For example, a child may produce a careless artwork when depicting potentially difficult or unpleasant subject matter.

In Greta's case, her initial drawing of house, parents, and self (Figure 5.1), which was organized and direct, demonstrated strength and courage in facing difficult material. During the following session, Greta drew "a house on fire" (Figure 5.2) in response to my request that she draw a house. This drawing indicates less control and more acceptance of the fact that her family structure had been destroyed by the divorce. I encouraged Greta to talk about what it would be like to see your house burn down, and she described how angry and sad a person would feel. Then I suggested that divorce feels a lot like that and she agreed.

As noted above, Greta gained some control over the physical agitation and grief that she experienced through art therapy expression. This helped to facilitate resolution of behavioral problems, providing a constructive and alternative outlet for discharge and reformulation of despair and agitation. This second drawing certainly communicates disruption, doom, and disorganization. It also shows Greta's ability to express distress and to loosen control without escalating to a state of chaos. The structure of the

Figure 5.2 House on fire by Greta

house remains intact although it was described as surrounded by smoke and "burning up inside" (an apparent metaphor for herself). Greta remained very cooperative and engaged throughout this process. She was careful not to mess up the art supplies or the work area, indicating the ability to be present with her own feelings while remaining considerate of others. Once again, Greta showed features of resilience in her ability to engage in a useful learning experience in which she readily made use of art expression and the therapeutic relationship. Children who possess features of resilience tend to make highly effective use of therapy, but in contrast, children who are more vulnerable often have difficulty making use of such opportunities for growth.

Media and Theme

In my initial evaluation of Greta, I was aware that she was willing and able to face difficulties. I observed that she was relieved when given the opportunity to share her pain. My approach to themes for art and discussion emphasized directness as this elicited Greta's cognitive strengths. I knew that she tended to become physically excited and thus did not encourage the use of messy materials. When eliciting personally evocative material, it can be especially helpful to offer more controllable media such as pencil, markers, or collage. This provides a balance so that a child is not placed under the double stress of using a hard-to-control medium—inducing the possibility of literally creating a mess—while portraying potentially upsetting content. Media selection can make the difference between successful experiences and a disturbing loss of control. This method can be viewed as promoting features of resilience in the here and now by supporting an internal locus of control. The therapeutic and assessment process can strengthen the qualities associated with self-sturdiness. In Greta's case, the ability to express, explore, and contain difficulties with a trusted adult was reinforced.

Behavioral Fluctuations

An art therapy assessment session is a novel situation during which both characteristic and unusual reactions may be demonstrated. Often, children behave as they normally do during sessions; however, there are numerous examples where neither presenting problems nor strengths are revealed through behavior. For instance, a timid child may become more outgoing when receiving an invitation to be creative in an intimate setting; a disruptive child may behave compliantly due to the level of nurturance offered during the session; and a child who is defiant at home may be ingratiating to the art therapist. Behavioral observation during the session does not provide a comprehensive overview of a child's functioning. It must be integrated with a holistic view that includes art expression, behavior, verbalization, and background information. If a child behaves differently during a session than was described by parents, teachers, and others who see the child regularly, it is likely due to the novel experience of the art therapy session. If there have been behavioral problems, it is helpful for the child to be told, in a sympathetic way, that the art therapist is aware of the reasons for referral. This can alleviate a child's inclination to hide uncomfortable facts.

In treating Greta, I immediately informed her that I was aware that she was seeing me because she had been having trouble with interrupting and being able to sit still at school since her parent's divorce. She appeared relieved that I was direct in acknowledging that this was the case. She was very active and talkative, which was consistent with the descriptions of her overall functioning. In addition, her cooperative and earnest participation indicated considerable developmental strengths. These factors contributed to a straightforward therapeutic focus.

Direct and Metaphorical Themes

A child's descriptions of artwork are very important indicators of personal information and coping skills. Children frequently describe their artworks very accurately. Conversely, descriptions may involve disguise (Rubin, 2005) or contradictions. Symbolic expression and failure to recognize visual communication can veil material that is too frightening, embarrassing, or difficult to face. Children may use metaphor or direct expression. Both modes of expression are age-appropriate. Imaginative, symbolic art expression permits a means of displacement. The previously discussed drawings by Greta, whom I saw several times following her parents divorce, exemplify art expression involving direct communication.

When her grandmother became terminally ill later that same year, Greta returned to art therapy. I had met the grandmother who had sometimes transported Greta to her appointments, and it was apparent that Greta was very close to this kind and doting woman. During the period of her grandmother's illness, Greta initiated imaginative themes, including a collage-drawing, described as "a ghost and its friend falling into a hole in the ground" (see Figure 5.3). Greta did not make any connection to the painful reality of the

Figure 5.3 "Ghost and friend falling into hole" by Greta

impending loss of an important relationship, but rather, safely expressed morbid and potentially overwhelming feelings using the buffer of imaginative themes. The media that I offered for this activity allowed for a combination of control (through cutting and gluing the figures) and gentle expression (through using oil pastels that can produce emotionally based coloring). Greta's ability to use displacement and symbolic expression in order to express grief was a developmentally appropriate defense. This strength helped her begin to face the impending loss, which she was later able to speak about. Greta's parents were concerned that the grandmother's imminent death would cause agitation, as had been the case with their divorce. The image of the ghost and its friend expresses the emotional experience of irrevocable loss and the horror of death. Such expression helped Greta to discharge and neutralize anxiety and may explain why only minor behavior problems ensued. Following her grandmother's death, there were incidences of clowning behavior at school. However, she responded well to support and admitted that she was acting silly because she "didn't like feeling sad about Grandma's death."

Greta experienced internal and external protective factors that contributed to her ability to struggle effectively with loss, producing a successful outcome in relatively short-term therapy. Greta's strength was apparent in her art expression that demonstrated intelligence, flexibility, a willingness to engage in problem solving, and the ability to use imagination in a playful and constructive way.

Case Example 2: A More Vulnerable Child Builds Resilience

"Daphne," a 7-year-old girl, received art therapy when experiencing parental divorce and longstanding difficulties at school. Unlike Greta, who was seen as good-natured, Daphne's parents described her as having been fussy and difficult to manage since birth. She had witnessed her parents fighting for much of her life, a severe environmental stressor that had disrupted her internal sense of security. High levels of parental conflict present significant risks for children (Garrity & Barris, 1997).

At school, Daphne was seen as bossy and an instigator of conflict. Her schoolwork was disorganized and included problems with reading, writing, and following directions. She also had strengths not always apparent at school that comprised innovativeness, independence, creativity, and intelligence. In addition, she was fond of animals, which she demonstrated by passionately discussing cats, dogs, hamsters, and rabbits with me. External protective factors included familial financial security, a supportive extended family, advanced parental educational levels, a high-quality school, and familial willingness to access resources.

Avoidance of Stress-Related Themes

During an initial art therapy session, Daphne quickly drew a picture of her house, which she said was haunted by ghosts (see Figure 5.4). As I inquired about the impulsive but well executed, monochromatic drawing, Daphne suspected I did not believe her and defended her position. I asked how she knew it was haunted, and she said that she heard the ghosts banging around in the attic and that she was the only one who knew about this. She admitted that she was a little scared but that she was used to ghosts because they had been there since she was a baby. Perhaps Daphne related this theme to her parents'

Figure 5.4 Ghosts in the attic by Daphne

fights as a result of the pressure to deal with the ensuing stress alone. When parents fight, "The children who live in fear of being ejected from the home have no power, no bargaining chips, no champions. Instead they are swept into a conspiracy of silence" (Wallerstien, Lewis, & Blakeslee, 2000, p. 103).

It is especially hard for toddlers and preschool-age children to make sense of parental conflict because their sense of reality and security is inherently fragile. Daphne's confusion of fantasy and reality was an understandable means of coping with stress (Garrity and Barris, 1997). She had substituted a frightening but less painful fantasy for the more painful reality of parental conflict. The use of fantasy is characteristic of preschool children, but Daphne, as late as age 7, still found comfort in this means of coping that gave her a sense of control, enabling her to handle realities too difficult to bear.

Daphne's organized drawings and her ability to function very well in many areas, such as sports and independent activities, indicated significant strengths. She was organized and self-assured in pursuits that involved creative self-expression and problem solving. My treatment focus included building on Daphne's sense of self-assuredness so that she could be more successful in relationships and school performance. In Daphne's case, finalization of the divorce provided a sense of relief even though adjusting to visitation schedules and residing in two homes was an added challenge.

Building Resilience Through Media and Interpersonal Support

Daphne would not discuss or depict her family or school life. When I asked her about these subjects, she became withdrawn and uncomfortable. The difficulties she experienced were too painful to face and had prevented her from developing the ability to organize emotional experience. Although it was not possible for her to focus on the reality of her life circumstances, her love of artwork and creativity provided a vehicle for focusing on here-and-now reality. She was playful, tough, and experimental in a manner reminiscent of a kitten, stalking media and themes as though they were prey. She applied paint as though she was performing wizardry, scolding it for defying her control. I was her accomplice, agreeing with her anger regarding the paint's audacity for misbehaving.

As I cheered her on, I thought of her former state of utter helplessness in hearing her parents' constant fighting.

Figure 5.5 is an example of a painting in which the layers of paint obliterated the form. This initial loss of control, for which the paint was harshly admonished, was followed by imposing structure on top of the mess through the overlay of a defined circular geometric pattern. Daphne demonstrated her anger and rebellion in relation to the medium. Art therapy processes and the therapeutic relationship provided ways to explore both repulsion and tolerance of structure. In the harmless realm of painting, she waged a war that she could win and experienced being the boss of a menacing mess. Somewhat paradoxically, her level of strength allowed her to use fluid media as a means of gaining control.

Daphne had previously discharged chaotic feelings by making up stories and insulting other children. She had trouble following rules. Her rejection of rules and behavior codes at school had raised alarm and caused further isolation. During sessions, Daphne's ability to be creative and find comfort in experimentation was apparent as was her defiance and desire to impose control. In the "virtual reality" of art expression, she felt that I was rooting for her in her attempts to master her emotions and behaviors. This helped her to see attempts at control and organization as worthy and constructive. Her peer relationships and school performance and behavior improved. Daphne's strengths assumed a more prominent position in her daily life. Among these strengths was a heartfelt appreciation for things that were strange and beautiful, exemplified in Figure 5.6, a

Figure 5.5 Painting by Daphne

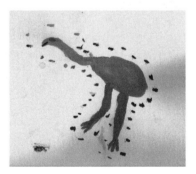

Figure 5.6 Flamingo by Daphne

decorative painting of a flamingo. During the final period of treatment, Daphne strove to build sturdy clay structures that were balanced and solid. She was confident and self-directed in completing the sculptural vessel shown in Figure 5.7, which she described as modeled after ancient ruins and a safe place to store important items. When I asked her if she would keep it at her mother or father's house, she explained a plan to have one at each location.

Daphne received art therapy for over 3 years, which included several extended breaks during seasonal sports activities. By the end of her treatment, she had adjusted to the divorce, demonstrated good school performance, and was enjoying peer relationships. During this time she had also received academic assessment and tutoring. Her home-life had stabilized. A year after the divorce, I asked Daphne about the possibility of ghosts in her house. She accused me of having invented this ridiculous idea, indicating that she no longer had such fears. At this point, she acknowledged that the transition between two homes was "a pain," but she relished the fact that she had "two Christmases, two birthday celebrations, and two Easter baskets filled with candy."

Although parental volatility remained and caused notable stress, several external protective factors had significantly improved including a more peaceful home life and increased academic support. Throughout the course of treatment, I maintained contact with the parents and the school counselor. Child art therapy does not exist in a vacuum. It is most effective when supported by external factors. In Daphne's case, age-appropriate strengths were built through art therapy and were used to improve external factors that facilitated a constructive engagement in tasks and relationships. This is not to say that there were no longer concerns that would likely crop up at later stages of development. Daphne was unable to discuss the impact of parental conflict and needed to keep a stiff upper lip in order to withstand this stressor. Her level of self-disclosure about family matters was extremely low, which served as a means of protection and assisted her in functioning successfully.

Figure 5.7 Sculptural form by Daphne

Summing Up

Assessment of resilience helps in formulation of treatment goals for initial and ongoing art therapy treatment. The case examples just discussed illustrate the integration of these goals within a relational approach that uses art media and themes to foster internal protective factors. Although the features that make up resilience can be generalized, the therapeutic process is always unique and based on the personality and preferences of each individual. Ironically, more resilient children are apt to make better use of the therapeutic process because their growth is boosted by internal and external protective factors. Successful art therapy treatment in the preceding cases was accelerated by the presence of supports that were available to the children within their lives. The next chapter explores necessary adjustments to approach, expectations, and methods with highly vulnerable children who lack significant internal and external protective factors.

6 Vulnerability and Fluctuating Developmental States

Shifting Developmental States

A 97-year-old psychiatrist, with whom I consulted, remarked that he did not feel old. When I asked him how old he felt he said, "Oh, 3 or 30 or 50 years old." (He was not senile, quite the contrary.) His statement referred to the idea that maturation involves not so much replacing as gaining access to multiple developmental states. Joan Erikson (1988) depicted the completed life cycle as a weaving involving intermingling and blending threads to represent all the stages. Individuals are a tapestry consisting of all the ages that they have been and currently are. Although maturation may have a linear progression, earlier stages never truly go away. Well integrated individuals have access to and awareness of multiple self-states. These remain to be drawn upon in current experience and thereby provide a structure for how to live. Thus, development can be viewed as both linear and multidimensional and comprises both the past and present self.

It is reasonable to expect, then, that within the progression of child art development, remnants of earlier stages are present. Sometimes this is pervasive and due to a serious developmental delay or regression whereas in other cases it is transient, comforting, or used to enhance artistic form. In the execution of art, access to the use of imagery associated with early development, such as scribbling or primitive forms, can be used to enhance artwork and is a sign of growth. But earlier styles of art can also appear as distorted, disorganized form or content that is a sign of cognitive or emotional disturbance.

Series of art pieces by the same child can show variations in levels of development. Indeed, the artistic level of development may decrease when children incorporate subjects that they do not know how to draw, that they are disinterested in, or that provoke stressful reactions. Fatigue, illness, or distress can cause artistic regression. Very frequently, less controllable media induce lower levels of graphic development. The capacity to engage in age-appropriate levels of graphic development, however, is viewed in the context of responses persisting over time rather than theme- or media-related responses. Conversely, it should be noted that children with severe disturbances often have areas of age-appropriate strength as well as areas of immaturity; their fluctuating developmental states are often apparent in their artwork.

At risk children reveal manifestations of vulnerability in their artwork that are highly individualized. Observation of such art expression allows the viewer to empathize with the child's experience, providing the basis for effective treatment. It is unusual to encounter a child who does not reveal strengths via art expression. Sometimes children's strengths are more prominent in creative artwork than in other areas of functioning, which helps to facilitate the therapeutic process because these strengths may be further developed in art therapy and later transferred to other areas.

Degree of Disturbance, Different Settings, and Associated Interventions

Children in residential settings require significant levels of intervention and structure in order to supplement their impaired functioning due to a poor sense of reality, suicidal inclinations, high levels of impulsivity or aggression, and inability to control emotions and behaviors. In contrast, children in outpatient and school settings tend to be more stable than those in residential settings as their difficulties are manageable within a less restricted environment. Although at times they may be severely at risk, they are less likely to pose active threats to self or others.

The following case examples describe the treatment of three girls who received art therapy in different settings. The first, which took place in an outpatient clinic, provides an example of a child who was able to function within the community but who suffered from anxiety along with interpersonal, academic, and behavioral difficulties. The second deals with a child in a residential school who exhibited acute anxiety, poor reality testing, and highly impulsive behaviors. The final example concerns a girl who attended a day-treatment school program and who manifested poor reality testing and severe cognitive and psychosocial deficits. Nonetheless, she was stabilized and able to live safely within the community.

The examples presented help to delineate varying degrees of high-risk behavior, the most severe of which necessitated that the child receive residential treatment. Furthermore, as discussed above, fluctuations in graphic development were present within the different examples as well as between them. These fluctuations were primarily related to themes depicted in the artwork.

Case Example 1: Outpatient Setting—Pseudomaturity, Trauma, and Need

Many children take evident pleasure in producing autobiographical imagery, but for others, it is confusing and overwhelming to depict self-portraits and personal memories. Drawing oneself in the future can be an evocative task that is comforting and exciting for some but stressful for others. Eleven-year-old "Dina" gained satisfaction from depicting a series of drawings about distant and recent past and future. Fluctuations in artistic developmental levels were apparent in her artwork and were consistent with her overall functioning.

Dina was described as "age 11 going on 30," by her father. She had been physically abused by her stepfather while living with her mother but was now in her father's custody. She had experienced many moves. In addition to having been physically abused by her stepfather during the previous 2 years, she had experienced familial instability and periods of neglect and had witnessed significant parental conflict throughout her life. Not surprisingly, these experiences had taken a toll on Dina's development. Her father initiated treatment because he was concerned that Dina was trying to be too grownup, that she pried into his affairs and bossed him around but lacked interest in age-appropriate pursuits such as peer relationships, youth activities, or schoolwork. For example, he complained that she insisted on joining him in adult recreation such as card games with his friends when she should be playing with girls her age.

Dina appeared mature and composed. With a neutral facial expression she told me about her sadistic stepfather and said, "That is why I am here." In a manner that seemed beyond her years, she emphasized feelings of victimization and seemed to relish the attention I provided. I had the sense that she was afraid of losing me even before I had a chance to get to know her. Although she remained calm, her eyes appeared very sad while she poured her heart out. She told me that she would like to draw about her life.

I asked Dina if she would like to draw a memory of something that happened when she was a little girl, which she was eager to do (see Figure 6.1). She began by drawing a wavy fence and then painting the figure representing herself with a small brush. She told me about the picture as she worked, stating that her earliest memory was of falling off of a fence that she had attempted to climb at age 3. She worked quickly and blotted the paint with a tissue, almost obliterating the figure. I said that I wondered why she had chosen paint for the self-image, and she replied that paint would be good for showing tears. She said that the picture illustrated her crying out for her mother, who was far away, and explained that she was alone, undiscovered for a long time. After this description, she took a brown marker and added more lines to the drawing of the fence.

Although the image was sad, Dina's facial expression remained pleasant. She completed the remainder of the drawing with markers and stated that she did not think her drawing was very good. She had attempted to show multiple views of the fence, a gate, and a football field, but her artistic skill faltered in undertaking this technically demanding task. In addition, her art expression and organization were understandably compromised by difficult emotional material relating to early feelings of abandonment. Dina had recalled a traumatic experience that affected her ability to develop and organize the artwork because trauma can impair cognitive and organizational skills (van der Kolk, 2003).

Dina then stated that she wanted to draw a memory from the past year and immediately set out to portray herself being beaten by her stepfather (see Figure 6.2). Once again, her facial expression remained neutral as she drew and described her stepfather beating her

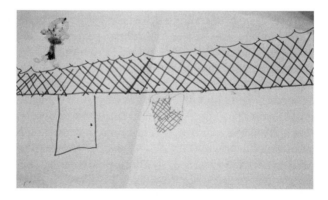

Figure 6.1 Early memory of fall from fence by Dina

Figure 6.2 Memory of being beaten by stepfather by Dina

with a club. She said that he was both mean and ugly, with a potbelly and a horrible laugh. When I asked why he beat her, she explained that he accused her of wrongdoing (such as not drying the dishes); however, she never knew exactly what she had done wrong, which made her feel that she was "just plain bad." She was composed and able to verbalize clearly. Her drawing was not well developed, in keeping with the starkness of the theme.

Figure 6.3 is Dina's response to being asked to draw herself 10 years from now. Dina stated that at age 21 she would be a fashionably dressed beautician and that she would be thinking about having babies. She worked more slowly on this drawing and smiled as she envisioned herself working in a beauty shop and thinking of having babies. When I asked her if there were any other wishes or hopes she had about being an adult, she said she could not think of anything else. She appeared quite happy about this image in contrast to the previous two drawings. She said that she thought it was a pretty good drawing and that she loved babies.

Dina intently engaged in art therapy treatment with me. Although there were variations in the level of care and organization in completing the three-drawing series, Dina remained composed and able to verbalize clearly. Her pseudomaturity contrasted with her naive eagerness to trust me with very personal material. The interpersonal themes in the artwork included abandonment, victimization, and unmet need.

Figure 6.3 Future projection by Dina

Dina demonstrated the most age-appropriate level of graphic development in her third drawing where she portrayed more positive subject matter. This drawing illustrates an organized, detailed, and well proportioned figure with attention to the gender-identifying features typical of Lowenfeld's (Lowenfeld & Brittain, 1987) Gang Age.

The first drawing, which reveals a state of vulnerability and abandonment, includes features of an earlier level of graphic development. The disorganized composition and scattered figure–ground relationships have similarities to artwork by preschool children and evoke the precariousness of tottering and being about to fall. In contrast to an attempt at order suggested by the repetitive pattern of the fence, formal elements also convey messiness through the blurred rendering of the self-figure and the wavy lines of the fence. These features indicate losing control (messiness) and attempts to regain control (repetitive patterns). Certainly, the ability to regain control is a strength, but nearly obliterating the self-figure conveys distress.

The second drawing, a stark depiction of an overwhelming recent memory, was completed quickly and displayed dramatic yet relatively undeveloped imagery and an impoverished style. Faced with a harsh reality, Dina's omission of color, detail, and effort created a measure of emotional distance. She used the "shorthand" of stick figures to depict an experience of victimization, precluding more developed expression. Using impoverished imagery provided a form of self-protection through decreased engagement, that was consistent with Dina's lack of engagement in suitable activities for her age group.

Dina did not use much color—probably because color tends to increase emotional expression (Kramer, 2000). Her first drawing is the most expressive whereas the following two drawings were neater and better organized, expressing emotional distance. Dina remained detached during their execution, perhaps in a state of trauma-induced numbness. She strove to be controlled and organized, age-appropriate abilities that promote a sense of self-efficacy. Her facility for facing very distressing material and showing no emotion was consistent with posttraumatic symptoms, which include feelings of detachment and restricted range of affect (American Psychiatric Association, 2000).

Controllable media helped Dina to portray emotionally charged themes and, at the same time, supported the protective degree of numbness and restriction that helped her to function effectively in many areas. Children are not well served by the experience of becoming overwhelmed during initial art therapy sessions. Conversely, they should be encouraged to take modest risks so that they can have the experience of self-regulation to whatever degree they are capable. I provided only a few ounces of water and small paint brushes, which Dina used carefully. I did not offer media that could become excessively messy, such as wet clay or substantial amounts of paint, because the themes that I offered were evocative. It is helpful to offer controllable media when providing potentially difficult themes. Both evocative themes and less controllable media have a tendency to induce some regression, which can provide decreased feelings of safety, particularly with traumatized or disorganized children.

Graphic Development

Dina's drawings illustrate the manner in which emotionally difficult themes may bring about lower than age-appropriate levels of graphic development. Her pictures of personal memories were less organized and included less detail than projection about the future. This fluctuation in drawing development parallels the psychological and behavioral processes of Dina's coping patterns in response to familial turmoil, neglect, and abuse. Pseudomature and overly controlling behaviors—such as bossing her father around and neglecting the age-appropriate tasks of schoolwork and peer relationships—were present in her life. Her artwork contained undeveloped imagery, negative themes, attempts at control, and idealization of adulthood.

Defensive Structure

As described in earlier chapters, children at age 11 tend to displace strong emotions through physical activities such as sports, competition, teamwork, and creative endeavors. They also focus on intellectual mastery and control through learning facts and emphasizing details. Their artwork reflects this through detailed work that is frequently completed in pencil. Art themes of 11-year-olds often include both serious and humorous, sometimes cartoon-like subjects. Dina was able to engage in detailed and controlled art expression, indicating a capacity for age-appropriate expression. It was also apparent that there were areas of extreme vulnerability and helplessness. As revealed in her art, Dina tried to feel and act grownup. But her facade of composure and bossiness was no replacement for genuine sturdiness; she was a vulnerable child. Although her high level of trust was a strength that could be worked with in therapy, it also placed her at risk. She indiscriminately coveted attention from adults and was detached from peer relationships and childhood pursuits. She was comforted by the thought of having babies, perhaps as a means of soothing her feelings of failure and abandonment.

Dina's ability to maintain control was a strength, particularly given the difficulties she had experienced. She incorporated age-appropriate defenses such as intellectualization and repression. Her ability to emotionally distance herself was overdeveloped. Although this had allowed her to survive, it had left her compromised in her ability to invest in developmental tasks.

Case Example 2: Residential Setting—A Fragile Sense of Reality

The following case illustrates a more severe level of disturbance, which is to be expected in a residential setting. The client's art expression and behavior exemplified fewer age-appropriate features and considerably impaired functioning.

"Jenny," another 11-year-old girl, had a history of being immature, impulsive, and demanding and of clinging to her mother. Following a horror movie that she had attended with peers on her eleventh birthday, she was convinced that an alien was following her. She impulsively talked about killing herself by threatening to jump out of windows and running into traffic. Her single mother reported that Jenny had always had behavioral difficulties and that she used physical discipline. Her agitation, hyperactivity, and refusal to be separated from her mother had been ongoing. Jenny's mother experienced depression and had a possible bipolar disorder. Jenny slept in the same bed with her mother. She was thought to be at risk for self-harm and residential placement had been determined as the only safe option; she was extremely angry about this.

Upon admission, Jenny screamed and cried when her mother left. She was restless and noisy, apparently plagued by tremendous fear and agitation. She eventually became clingy with staff, angrily blaming them for her residential placement and insisting that she was well enough to go home. As she denied suicidal ideation, some of the staff believed her and proposed that she be discharged. It was not clear what her diagnoses were. It was speculated that she was experiencing either the effects of trauma, bipolar disorder, or childhood schizophrenia and that she had some features of borderline personality disorder. Regardless of diagnosis, it became increasingly clear during initial art therapy sessions that Jenny was in great distress.

During these individual sessions, Jenny was angry and clingy. She made loud gulping noises, becoming especially angry at the end of the sessions as though the pain of transition and separation was too much to bear. While in her presence, I remained very calm, which was not easy in the face of her agitation. The only art materials offered were small pieces of paper and pencils with erasers, necessitated by how fragile and disorganized she was. I came to understand that this was due to the fact that her thoughts were tormenting her.

Jenny also attended art therapy groups shortly after her admission. In these sessions her behavior was quiet and subdued. Her drawings were undeveloped copies of artwork by older girls, consisting of hearts and flowers (see Figure 6.4). She hid in the shadows of these girls in much the same way that she had clung to her mother prior to her placement.

Figure 6.5 shows a drawing that Jenny completed during her first individual art therapy session in response to the request that she imagine what she would be like as a grownup. She impulsively dashed off the drawing. When I asked her to tell me about

Figure 6.4 Drawing done in group session by Jenny

Figure 6.5 Future projection by Jenny

the picture, she said in a rushed manner, "It shows me at age 25. I am going with my mom to the polls and voting for Obama." Jenny did not see the lack of logic inherent in confusing current events with her future. She appeared extremely agitated and began making gulping noises. I suggested that perhaps she would like to make a pattern design, in response to which she quickly drew a series consisting of heart, star, and cloud shapes (Figure 6.6). She calmed down for a few minutes and then started pacing around the room and making guttural sounds.

In response to the request that she draw a person during a session that took place on the following day, Jenny quickly drew a small floating figure (Figure 6.7), which she quickly described, mostly in response to my questions. She stated that it is "a little girl" and that it is "an alien." When I asked about the age of the figure, she spoke angrily and rapidly, "She's as old as the hills." Jenny elaborated about the drawing, confusing fantasy and reality and producing a flood of thoughts about the alien being kept at this residential school against her will. She said, "I hate it here. This place scares me." When I asked,

Figure 6.6 Design drawing by Jenny

Figure 6.7 Little girl alien by Jenny

"Can you tell me what you are afraid of?" she angrily grabbed the pen from my hand and quickly drew the picture in Figure 6.8, saying, "Evil alien." Throwing the drawing at me, she said, "This is what I am afraid of, an evil space alien, and it is following me." Jenny began making clucking noises, which went on for several minutes. She was very upset, perhaps experiencing a hallucination or a dissociative episode.

Even though it was suspected that Jenny had experienced abuse, I never found out what had triggered her decompensation. Whether due to trauma or a biologically based disorder, Jenny was terrified, necessitating a focus on reducing anxiety and emphasizing stabilization and safety. I told Jenny that although I appreciated knowing what was frightening her, I thought that drawing her fears was too hard for her. I told her that we should think of something that was not quite so distressing, which helped to calm her. She then lay down on a couch with her eyes closed. I talked to her about the fact that I now knew how scared she was and that we needed to help her feel better. Although Jenny's expression of extreme distress was difficult to tolerate, my knowledge about her thoughts was very useful in helping the treatment team understand how to provide appropriate support within the context of her treatment.

Graphic Development

During the next session, Jenny continued to be angry and restless. She immediately did an impulsive pencil drawing of a figure and wrote "You" on top (see Figure 6.9). She stated that it was a picture of me and that she drew me because I made her angry. She said, "You are smiling and you got me locked in here." She wrote the word "angry" on the top of the page. Although it was not the case that I was responsible for her placement, I did not argue with her. I carefully looked at the drawing and told Jenny that I was impressed with the quick picture she had done of me as it captured a very good likeness. This intervention helped her to focus on present reality as well as her strengths, which was calming for her. I then asked Jenny if she could do a picture of something from her own life, something that had really happened. After quietly thinking for a few minutes, Jenny drew a pony ride that she explained was a memory from a few years

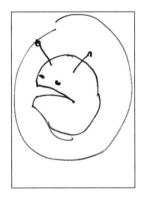

Figure 6.8 Scary alien by Jenny

Figure 6.9 Portrait of therapist by Jenny

ago. In this drawing (see Figure 6.10), Jenny was more organized and demonstrated an increasingly age-appropriate level of graphic development. As Jenny responded to my questions about what she remembered from that day, it became clear that the drawing was not based on a memory but rather on a photograph of the event that was on display in her home. When questioned, she said that she did not remember the event, but that she liked the photograph and had tried to duplicate it from memory. We discussed that this was her best drawing yet and she appeared pleased. Whereas Dina was disconnected and frozen when depicting the harsh reality of her life, Jenny was comforted by reality-based themes and had fond associations when thinking about her home.

Jenny was more organized when reproducing a preexisting image. Her behavior, demeanor, and abilities were age-appropriate as she engaged in the production of and discussion about the pony-ride drawing. She was overwhelmed by intrusive thoughts

Figure 6.10 Pony ride by Jenny

on an ongoing basis. When she engaged in artistic expression that was reality-based and limited her associations, her agitation subsided.

Jenny's art expression revealed her difficulties as well as her strengths. When left to develop her associations, she became frightened by her fear of aliens and her agitation, impulsivity, and hostility mounted. I could see how difficult it would be for her to engage in normal tasks such as attending school or even watching television. However, when Jenny focused on an organizing and reality-based theme, she was more successful and well regulated.

Jenny's highest level of graphic development emerged when she portrayed a picture based on memory of a soothing photographic image. This is because free association was too stimulating for her. Her ability to remain grounded in reality was fragile. Unlike most 11-year-old children, Jenny lacked the internal structure that would allow her to screen out upsetting thoughts. Often children who are placed in residential settings have very severe difficulties in managing their thoughts, emotions, and behaviors. Jenny was a very vulnerable child who experienced serious risk factors, including parental psychiatric illness, a possible biologically based thought disorder, a history of corporal punishment, and poor academic success. Her treatment would focus on stabilization and developing increased safety and connection to reality.

The information that Jenny shared with me was useful to all the staff who worked with her. She had not previously admitted that she believed she was under siege by aliens and that this was driving her panic and suicidality. Art therapy helped her to disclose this material. It is important to know the truth in order to help. Jenny was prescribed antipsychotic medication, which lessened but did not eliminate her disordered thoughts and anxious, volatile state.

Defensive Structure

Jenny's defensive structure was fragile and underdeveloped for her age. She was afraid of aliens and had limited means of calming herself. Her inability to ground herself in reality left her frightened, agitated, dependent, and more like a preschool-age child in terms of her ability to self-sooth and to differentiate fantasy from reality. She was unable to function well in her life because at age 11 children are expected to work industriously and to differentiate reality from fantasy. Preschool children are protected and comforted in relation to their fears. They eventually develop cognitive and emotional regulatory skills that allow them to engage diligently in sports, schoolwork, and creative activities without becoming disorganized. Jenny lacked such age-appropriate defenses due to a variety of risk factors because of the following possiilities: effects of traumatic experience, neurochemical imbalance, and familial stress.

Case Example 3: Therapeutic-Day-School Setting—A Stabilized but Vulnerable Child

Mary, also an 11-year-old, attended a day school for low-income children with psychiatric disorders. She was developmentally delayed and functioned both cognitively and academically at a third-grade level. In addition, even with the use of antipsychotic medication, Mary experienced psychotic thoughts and believed that she had personal relationships with famous pop-stars. Although her fascination with popular musicians was age-appropriate, she could not get a handle on what was real or imagined. Although Mary was quite pleasant to be around, she was ridiculed by her peers who perceived her tangential speech, thick glasses, and somewhat lopsided gait as odd. She got along well with a younger girl who was also considered a misfit by her classmates. Early in life, Mary had been removed from her drug-addicted mentally ill mother's custody and resided with her maternal grandmother.

When asked to complete a picture of a person, Mary drew a portrait of me (see Figure 6.11). She captured a good likeness and worked industriously with colored markers. In drawing and in viewing the picture, Mary remained focused and engaged. I was aware of feeling more connected to her than when she became lost in her delusional fantasies. She was quite proud of the drawing, which she gave to me as a gift. This served as a concrete boost to her sense of value, as she did not generally feel that she was capable of giving due to both economic poverty and interpersonal deficits.

Comparing Example 3 With Example 2

Like Jenny, Mary was focused when copying something from real life. The flat, simplistic image reflects Mary's cognitive delays. Without structure, Mary talked incessantly about her fantasies and was unable to complete coherent imagery. Her usual drawings were disorganized doodles that included the names of popular music bands. The drawing of a real person demonstrates concrete organization as a means of blocking psychotic thoughts, as well as skill and mastery that was difficult for her to accomplish in many areas of her life. In ongoing art therapy sessions, Mary worked on sewing pillows with animal faces and a doll, soothing activities that helped her to organize and focus on tasks.

Although Mary was a very vulnerable child, she was stabilized and lived successfully within the community within the framework of protective services that included medication, a secure foster home, and a therapeutic school. Her fantasies about popular musicians were comforting but threatened to subsume her ability to maintain relationships

Figure 6.11 Portrait of therapist by Mary

to reality and other people. Mary's ability to trust is evident in her portrait of me (Figure 6.11), which portrays a kind and solid stance. This contrasts with Jenny's depiction (Figure 6.9) in which the figure is fragmented, weak and undeveloped. A significant difference between these two girls involves Mary's capacity to trust versus Jenny's perception of constant danger. Not only did this necessitate residential placement for Jenny, it made it very distressing to work with her. In general, it is far more difficult to work with children who lack basic trust. Although the treatment goals for Jenny and Mary emphasized maintaining a reality focus, Mary was capable of soothing herself whereas Jenny required that the therapist provide the soothing function of which she was incapable.

Risk Factors, Art Therapy, and Treatment Goals

The art therapy examples by three vulnerable 11-year-old girls illustrate shifting perceptions and developmental states. Because 11-year-olds have progressed through several stages of childhood, their artwork is likely to reveal both age-appropriate development and regressions or delays. Indeed, the girls' artwork did reveal both disturbance and strengths in relation to their shifting developmental states.

Children who experience significant risk factors often require long-term therapy and support. The art therapist may feel like a blip on the screen, given the intense level of need and the chaos that often characterize these children's lives, but this does not negate the value of working with them. It is important, however, to maintain a realistic understanding when working with very vulnerable children who lack significant internal and external protective factors. The goals must focus on cultivating existing functional strengths and emphasizing safety, connection, and stabilization rather than cure. This often involves offering less fluid art media to facilitate building a sense of control. Ideally, the type of media used is part of a bigger picture in which long-term support is present that reinforces external protective factors. Some children with severe disturbances and environmental risk factors may never achieve the ability to function independently. However, therapy can greatly assist them in developing their strengths, thereby boosting their capacities for constructive participation in the world around them.

Part IV

Tuning In to Children and Parents

7 Planning, Practical Matters, and Safety

Healthy development is facilitated by permission to engage in creative exploration, experimentation, and risk taking. From the first days of life, sequences of holding, handling, and support provide conditions that spur growth and maturation (Winnicott, 1990). Similarly, the art therapy environment offers holding and handling through both physical use of materials and relational means (Robbins, 2000a). The art therapy office, art materials, and art therapist maintain focus on self-generated expression, which is ultimately used in the service of understanding children and helping to build sturdiness in them.

Therapist and Client Anxiety

Therapist Preparations

It is stressful to face the unexpected. Although it is natural to want a plan before meeting with a child for the initial and subsequent sessions, exercising clinical judgment in the here-and-now is the primary tool for treatment. Techniques and art directives are simply aids whereas the therapist's flexibility and clinical sense truly foster the therapeutic process. I always feel nervous and excited before I meet with a new child client. Although I have spoken with the parent(s) or another party such as a case manager, I do not yet know how the child will react to the unusual experience of an art therapy session. Prior to sessions, I often think about what I will ask the child to do. But more than a plan, what is needed is the readiness to tune in to each child. Every clinical situation demands a unique response, and even though it is necessary to provide structure, I agree with Yalom (2000) that it is ideal to "create a new therapy for each patient" (p. 32). The approach that I recommend for conducting initial art therapy sessions involves incorporating a structure that is flexible. The art therapist's knowledge of development along with art as a communication tool is the foundation for this endeavor.

The first session establishes an understanding of the importance and value of art therapy. The art therapist accomplishes this through conduct that helps the child feel at ease while gradually introducing challenges. The aim is to set a tone that invites creativity and also elicits expression of the child's problems and strengths. It is crucial that clients feel recognized and understood for their unique qualities. In addition, it is important that efforts by parents and treatment facilities to help clients are supported. Meeting these demands puts a certain amount of pressure on the therapist, so some anxiety is to be expected. On the other hand, awareness of such issues assists the therapist in maintaining a calm demeanor, which is especially important given that child clients often anticipate the initial meeting with anxiety. Indeed, according to Yalom (2000), Sullivan described a psychotherapy session as a discussion between two people in which one of them is more anxious than the other. The fact that the therapist is vulnerable has the potential to enhance the value of the encounter. Sensitivity and self-awareness can be used to understand and address the needs of a new client and to present a calm invitation to participate in therapy. Self-awareness on the part of the therapist is a vital tool that helps to modulate the anxiety of both parties.

Preparing the Child

Prior to initial sessions, it is helpful if children can receive a simple explanation of what to expect. In a school or residential setting, the art therapist can handle this responsibility. The explanation to the child might be something like this: "We will meet for about 45 minutes and you will get to do some artwork and to talk with me." In outpatient settings, the parents or guardians can perform this function. Whether in a tone of anger or support, parents often explain to children that the session will address specific problems that they have already discussed with the child. Many parents appreciate being coached about how to prepare children for the first session. Sometimes a parent will attend the session with the child due to the child's severe anxiety, very young age, or the need to assess the parent–child relationship. Often, the expectation is that the child attend some initial sessions unaccompanied, which permits opportunity for assessment of the child's independent functioning.

Upon entering the session, it is productive for the therapist to ask what the child has been told and to elicit expectations of therapy. This can help put children at ease and engage them right away in the process of self-reflection. If comfortable doing so, the child may then initiate discussions about problems. If the child expresses confusion about the reason for attending therapy, an opportunity is provided to explain and reassure. Explanations might include, "This is a time to do artwork and to tell me all about what is going on in your life." Or, "Your parents wanted you to come here because you are having a hard time getting along with other kids, and they want you do some artwork with me so that I can get to know you." But different situations may demand different responses. The explanation should be very simple, developmentally appropriate, and individualized to the child's ability to face difficulties directly. It is important to assess the impact the explanation has on the child. Most children respond best to minimal explanation; this gives them the message that they are responsible for communication as opposed to expecting that the therapist monopolize the session.

Safety

Worries about doing the right thing on the part of the therapist can be put to good use. It can remind therapists to provide a sense of safety and to be cautious when implementing activities. Any therapy session has the potential to be uncomfortable and overwhelming. An art therapist can enhance a child's self-regulation through offering opportunities for successful art expression and meaningful self-disclosure. When experiences result in loss of control that is triggered by unmanageable art media or overwhelming personal exploration, it can be difficult to repair the ensuing shame and disorganization. Ideally, the child art therapist's approach is analogous to driving slowly on a hazardous road. Just as reading road signs assists the driver, reading client cues through keen observational skills is helpful in maintaining client safety.

Maintaining Safety Through Flexibility: An Example

"Rita," a 10-year-old girl, was referred by her single mother due to angry outbursts that included scratching other children. I asked Rita why her mother had initiated therapy for her, and she stared at me with a frozen facial expression. I then inquired about how things were going in her life and if there were difficulties, to which she replied that there were no problems at all. Although my desire to please the mother had initially led me to consider asking Rita to draw pictures of what makes her angry, I quickly reevaluated this. Rita appeared terrified not only of me but also of the very idea of spending an hour sharing about herself. After gently inquiring about what she was willing to do, it became clear that drawing and painting outdoor scenes and flowers put her at ease. Rita's anxiety seemed to diminish as she worked silently. Her intense feelings were expressed in her artwork, which portrayed scenes containing explosive flowers described by Rita as showing "Happy Days" (see Figure 7.1 for an example). Although Rita was not aware of this, the intensity of her artwork matched the explosive anger that her mother reported. Through the artwork, I could begin to understand the feelings she was unable to verbalize. The drawing in Figure 7.1 appears unsafe due to the large waves that threaten to attack a flower that seems to be flying apart. Similar to Rita's notion of a happy day, her personal appearance was beautiful and placid rather than that of an aggressive child whose outbursts she denied.

During this initial session, I learned that asking Rita to depict problems or feelings would have shamed and frightened her. Nonetheless, she revealed strengths via sensory expression as opposed to direct exploration of problems. I did not know if Rita's limited verbal disclosure was due to the stress of the initial session or if it was pervasive. I later learned that she was unable to verbalize her feelings most of the time and that she

Figure 7.1 "Happy Days" by Rita

experienced feelings of deeply rooted abandonment and shame. These feelings were related to her father abandoning the family when she was a toddler. The art process provided an avenue for safe expression of her strong feelings. In ongoing therapy, artwork gradually led to Rita's increased ability to face disappointment directly. My observation that she liked soothing art activities but felt on the hot seat when talking about her feelings influenced my decision to proceed initially with soothing media and themes. This led to including her mother in sessions to provide support for facing disturbing behaviors and feelings. Together we helped Rita to find ways to express and make sense of her concerns and feelings.

Ensuring Confidentiality

Respecting a client's privacy goes beyond the legal aspects of confidentiality; there are therapeutic ramifications as well. All evidence of other clients' work should be removed from the therapy office even if consent to display has been given. This reduces distraction as well as meeting ethical requirements. It minimizes the possibility of overt feelings of rivalry towards other children and promotes feelings of being in a safe environment.

Confidentiality Versus Bolstering Self-Esteem: An Example

An 8-year-old boy with very low self-esteem asked that I permanently display his painting for other children to see. When I explored with him why he would like this artwork to be displayed, he explained that it was his best painting and that he was proud of it. He added that it would help other children to feel encouraged to see that good work was possible. I tried to think quickly of a response that would not burst the bubble of his newly found sense of accomplishment. I agreed that this work was worthy of display, further explaining that unlike school, all children's conversations and artworks are private in this setting. Although he was disappointed, I provided empathy and support along with the assurance that he could depend on having privacy and my undivided attention. His chaotic and impoverished daily life did not afford the opportunity for having his own space or for receiving individualized attention from adults. This interaction served, in part, to help him believe that he was worthy of having adult attention and protection.

Providing Structure

The factors that constitute the structure of child art therapy sessions are logistical, physical, and interpersonal. They also involve time frame, materials, setting, and approach. The best setting is free from interruption and is well organized so as not to be overwhelming. The physical layout, the media presented, and the therapist should convey a calm and inviting atmosphere.

Art Materials

Although each setting is different, it is important to make sure that organization and support are facilitated by the physical environment and choice of media to the extent possible. When it comes to the media, it is advisable to display a limited range of materials. These may include several sizes of drawing paper, markers, colored and graphite drawing pencils, crayons, oil pastels, small paint sets, erasers, scissors, and glue sticks. Clay, fabric, ribbons, liquid paints, and various other supplies can be kept available but out of view. Specialized equipment such as a glue gun, blow dryer, and wood-carving tools should be stowed away. Sharp tools and potentially toxic materials are used infrequently. These materials should not be offered during initial sessions. In ongoing therapy, they are only used with children who can handle them safely and only during individual sessions where close supervision is possible. Although it is tempting to grant children's requests for complicated, expensive, or potentially dangerous materials, the anxiety evoked in the therapist and the potential for harm are not worth the risk. Providing safety with the expectation that valuable work can be done with available resources is a significant therapeutic intervention that trumps granting wishes.

Although my preference is to limit the amount of supplies that are displayed, I like to provide enough to offer some variety. The least messy and easily controlled materials are within reach, and messier or more complicated materials are available if therapeutically appropriate. However, when working with children who are easily overwhelmed (e.g., those who are severely traumatized, disorganized, or hyperactive), it is especially helpful to limit materials, perhaps offering only one or two options. And for preschool children or toddlers, displaying just a few art supplies that emphasize gross rather than fine motor control enhances therapeutic work. These latter supplies could usefully include dough-type modeling medium, squeeze paints, crayons, thick markers, and large paper. Further, since young children tend to be very curious, it is especially important to hide toxic media and sharp implements. Having to restrict children from exploring enticing materials can undermine the support needed to provide a therapeutic holding environment.

It seems clear that children who do not have the regulatory capacity to restrict or select appropriate materials have more successful experiences when suitable structure is provided. In addition, younger or hyperactive children may overuse or misuse materials, which can be costly and very messy. Prior to meeting with such art therapy clients, it is necessary to remove not only expensive, potentially dangerous, or toxic materials but also those that require skill levels that are not appropriate for the child.

Optimum Setting

My current office has an art table and storage space, but there is no sink in the room so I must go to the restroom to refill water containers. I have containers of premoistened wipes so that children can clean their hands without having to leave the room. In the past I had to improvise even more, sometimes by using drawing boards as a substitute for a table or by wheeling materials on a rolling cart into a room that was also used as a dining room. I have done in-home art therapy, setting out my supplies on the family dining room table (always insisting that the television be turned off). Art therapists tend to be very flexible, creative people who can make inhospitable environments safe and containing. Although this requires forethought and is often not easy, it well worth the effort because the structure of a quiet, safe environment allows the therapeutic process to develop. There is bound to be chaos at times, and a certain amount is even therapeutic; nonetheless, it is the therapist's job to eliminate intrusions and obstacles. Indeed,

Rubin (2005) aptly described the ideal approach to structuring child art therapy sessions as provision of a "framework for freedom" (p. 19), emphasizing that a balance of chaos and order is usually necessary for the unfolding of meaningful creative expression.

The inviting and orderly nature of the physical environment and the art therapist's acceptance of all types of expression counterbalance the disorderly aspects of the creative process. Silver (2002) posits that structure enhances rather than restricts creative expression. Still, art therapists seek to individualize the level of structure so as to elicit the most therapeutically useful expression from each child.

Finding a Balance

The question of how much structure to provide is ever-present in child art therapy. This pertains to directives, media, degree of inquiry regarding presenting problems and artwork, as well as when to intervene in the face of potentially disruptive behaviors. Art expression and creative processes allow children to find answers from within. The danger of the therapist exerting too much control concerns the potential restriction of self-generated insight, mastery, and problem solving. A unique and valuable aspect of art therapy is its propensity to facilitate the development of self-trust. Art expression that emerges spontaneously often holds the seeds of personal strengths that were previously unknown even to the artist.

Art therapists constantly face the challenge of providing just enough structure—but not more. One way to do this involves giving assistance with art technique, that is, giving feedback or instruction to whatever degree brings the child to the highest level of creative and therapeutic work. Kramer (2000) described this function as using the *third hand*, "a hand that helps the creative process along without being intrusive, without distorting meaning or imposing pictorial preferences alien to the client" (p. 48).

The most important goal of the initial session is to provide a positive introduction to art therapy. Because all children are different, there is no formula for how to do this. The art therapist's clinical sense, empathy, and creativity must be the guide for how to proceed. Some children need discipline and firmness from the therapist to have a positive experience whereas others need leniency and flexibility. Both physical and psychological safety must be priorities. As previously mentioned, sharp tools and toxic art media should not be offered. Although equally important, psychological safety often has less obvious components than physical safety. Particularly when conducting initial sessions, art therapists should not underestimate the potential of evocative themes or fluid media to be overwhelming. Because messy materials can stimulate feelings of agitation, it is sometimes better to offer only pencil or precut collage images to the child who is impulsive or aggressive or has poor reality testing. It is also important to improvise and restrict an activity when it escalates beyond a therapeutically indicated level of comfort.

Time Frame and Predictability

The length of individual and group child art therapy sessions generally ranges from 45 to 90 minutes depending on the setting, scheduling concerns, and the age of the child. Most often younger children have less developed attention spans necessitating shorter sessions. It is important that children be informed of the length of the session and that this time frame is kept consistent. The value of predictability cannot be over-estimated. This applies to arrangement of the room, therapeutic approach, and time of day. Predictability offers a structure that greatly enhances a child's sense of safety. This is especially important for the large percentage of art therapy clients who have experienced chaos.

It is beneficial to provide notice about how much time remains, particularly towards the end of the session. This helps children to develop self-regulatory skills that can be generalized to other transitions in their lives. Although children may ask for extra time, it is better to empathize with this wish than to gratify it. A response to this request can include reassurance about continuation of work at the next session such as, "It sure is hard to end when you are involved in an activity; but unfortunately, we have only 5 more minutes. I will keep your project safe so we can get back to it next week." Children who have difficulty ending can be reminded of this at the beginning of subsequent sessions to help them build the sturdiness needed to tolerate separation more smoothly.

Creating Directives

Art therapy directives are closely linked with the process of structure. Offering guidance to the client regarding what to create and how to proceed has a number of intertwined aspects.

Where to Focus

Information about the reason for referral, the child's age, history, interests, possible diagnoses, and cognitive abilities and difficulties shape the structure of an initial session. As already noted, preschool-age children respond well to art media such as easily manipulated modeling materials, squeeze paints, large paper, and chunky markers. These are materials that accommodate gross motor functions. In addition, younger children often respond best to simple themes that are reality-based or imaginary (e.g., self-portraits, favorite animals, or an animal family). These media and themes can be used to tailor art tasks that focus on the child's presenting problems in an individualized manner. The tasks can be designed to be both engaging and clinically informative. Ideally, art therapists possess the creativity and clinical insight needed to effectively personalize directives. In many cases, presenting problems can become the basis for a structured drawing task. For example, when assessing the impact of divorce on a child, it can be fruitful to ask the child to create a picture that tells about the divorce. Likewise, when evaluating children who present with explosive anger or restricted expression, requesting a drawing of "What makes me angry" can reveal important information. Note that in directing a child to depict autobiographical material, it is advisable to keep the instructions concrete, as opposed to requesting abstract expression (e.g., "What does anger look like?"). An abstract depiction of emotions is more overwhelming and less in keeping with the cognitive developmental level of young children. In addition, some children freely engage in narrative descriptions whereas others need to communicate nonverbally via artwork.

The Value of Negative Expression

A major benefit of art therapy is that art expression can facilitate transformation of fear and anger. During initial sessions, a child's propensity for this use of the creative process can be assessed. For example, when working with children who have experienced trauma, it can be revealing to request a drawing of something scary. This offers the child a choice regarding whether to complete an imaginary or realistic image of something frightening. Many children are relieved to be asked to depict something scary as it provides reassurance that the art therapist can handle frightening subjects. In depicting such subject matter, children can begin to master fears because they are in control of the process. However, if a child appears frightened and uncomfortable or refuses to complete a scary picture, it usually indicates an attempt at self-protection. Under these circumstances, self-protection is a strength that can inform the structure provided by the therapist. By following his or her lead, the therapist maximizes the child's ability to experience a safe level of control and self-regulation. The therapist then paces the therapeutic process so that difficulties are addressed when anxiety has been sufficiently reduced.

Structured Versus Free-Choice Directives

Both structured and free-choice art therapy directives have the potential to elicit creativity and to reveal important information about children. The level of structure is determined by the needs of the child and the related goals of the therapy. Factors such as short-term treatment and severe behavioral or cognitive impairment often demand a higher level of structure than long-term therapy or treatment of less impaired children.

It is helpful to consider the rationale for incorporating structured versus free-choice directives because this can provide a framework regarding which approach to use with each child. Understandably, children who easily lose control are likely to benefit from limiting the use of fluid, sticky, runny, and messy media. They will probably benefit from more structured activities as well. For instance, some children who have cognitive deficits or are easily overwhelmed may be unable to engage in spontaneous creative activity. It seems cruel to ask such a child to complete a free painting or drawing when filling in a drawn outline or responding to a stimulus image would be more manageable. On the other hand, some children cannot be creative when a specific directive is imposed. Regardless of the child's abilities, time-limited treatment or evaluation (e.g., a court-ordered custody evaluation) can necessitate a highly focused approach (Levick, Safran, & Levine, 1990).

Rejection of Directives

Children may reject directives supplied by the therapist and convey strong needs to assume control of art themes. In some cases, it is helpful to offer structured art directives as a starting point while permitting rejection of this directive. For example, "Jenna," a 12-year-old girl who had experienced a recent trauma, used permission to reject my suggestion as a means of regaining control of her ability to trust herself. She had been referred following disclosure of sexual abuse perpetrated by her grandfather. She said that she would not be able to do a drawing of "Something that is important to me" as I requested. Instead, she asked for a mirror and completed a realistic, sensitive self-portrait that conveyed a somber mood. Because her familial situation and internal state was turbulent following the disclosure of abuse, Jenna sought to do artwork that was controlled, comfortable, and familiar. She had been doing self-portraits at school that contributed to her ability to complete a well developed drawing. These portraits also served as confirmation of her identity, which had been disrupted by the sexual abuse. Her sincere and meaningful self-portrait indicated that I had made the right choice by supporting her rejection of my directive. In actuality, Jenna did complete my directive, a picture of something important to her: namely, confirmation of her sense of intactness as a person. I did not point out that she had rejected my idea but had done it anyway because the fact that Jenna needed to own this process was a strength. For children who have been sexually abused, art therapy is uniquely suited to assist in regaining the sense of basic control that has been damaged by violation of the body and the self. My initial assessment supported Jenna's attempts at self-protection and her capacity for making her own decisions. If the child who rejects a directive goes on to produce meaningful work, this is often an indication that the rejection was in the service of therapeutic growth.

In contrast to the above example, when some children refuse to complete directives, it is helpful to insist that they try their best. For example, "Kenny" was an anxious 5-year-old who intensely feared failure and gave up easily. During his initial sessions, I insisted that he try to complete artwork that was hard for him. His parents had informed me that he gave up too easily due to anxiety, so I repeatedly told him, "Try it and then tell me if it was awful." I provided very structured directives with themes that were not too over-whelming such as images of trees and fish, subjects that interested him. He was enticed by using colorful paint on large paper as the soothing media eased his anxiety. Figure 7.2 is Kenny's delightful painting of fish. With encouragement, proper support, and structure, Kenny demonstrated that he was more capable than he thought. In this way, he confirmed that my insistence that he complete directives was a helpful intervention.

Some children refuse all directives offered by the therapist. It is important to understand why this is the case while keeping in mind that there are often good reasons for refusal. Whether or not children provide explanations, background information offers possibilities that relate to relational, cognitive, cultural, emotional, or previous art experience factors. It is generally fruitful to inquire about dislike of the ideas being offered.

Figure 7.2 Painting of fish by Kenny

Although some will stare blankly or express annoyance, most children will answer such questions. I am frequently amazed at how the unacceptable becomes acceptable after children have been validated by the opportunity to express criticism.

Asking Questions

There are two main ways to obtain information regarding the meaning of client art expression. First, a thorough knowledge of the child's history contributes to a holistic understanding. If a child has been diagnosed with a mental health disorder, it is helpful to take the vulnerabilities inherent in the condition into account. For instance, keeping in mind that a child has an anxiety disorder provides information regarding excessively timid interpersonal behavior and hesitant artwork. It also informs the therapist concerning the degree of safety needed to put the child at ease. Likewise, in the case of a child who is known to be defiant and aggressive, it makes sense to offer boundaries and art directives that help to channel these behaviors while limiting themes and materials that could overstimulate.

Second, to learn as much as possible about the child, it is customary to inquire about the artwork. These questions are often based on observations of subject matter, media usage, and the child's apparent level of satisfaction with the product. Questions about either form or content can elicit significant associations. For example, "Fiona," a 6-year-old girl who had witnessed domestic violence and who was often derided by her father, experienced low self-esteem and had trouble coming up with original ideas. During initial sessions, she conveyed a preference for decorative pictures of hearts and flowers that were devoid of themes. I watched as she drew Figure 7.3, a flower comprised of purple and blue hearts. She struggled to fit the desired amount of hearts in the bottom section and added a stray orange heart under the flower. It looked to me as though the stray heart was trying to get into the circle. I asked Fiona to tell me if her picture reminded

Figure 7.3 Left-out heart by Fiona

her of anything, and she said that it looked like a circle of baby elephants. When I asked about the stray one on the bottom, she replied, "It's on the outside. It's trying to get inside, but they won't let it in. It's telling them to let him in." When I asked if they would listen, Fiona sadly shook her head from side to side. I responded, "Which one would you be?" and she pointed to the excluded heart. In this manner, I came to understand how alone she felt. My questions mainly related to the formal aspects of the drawing and fostered a loosening of Fiona's restricted imagination. In contrast to her previous artwork, she had revealed some of her struggles. This helped me in formulating a plan for Fiona's ensuing therapy that, through symbolic expression, would gently help her explore and cope with feeling marginalized in her family.

As a general rule, open-ended questions are to be preferred. "I am very interested to find out about this picture. Can you tell me something about it?" "How did you feel about working with this type of clay?" are examples. Most children appreciate the art therapist's genuine curiosity and interest in their ideas, associations, and creations. Occasionally, a withdrawn or very guarded child experiences discomfort when faced with such inquiry, and the use of questioning must be reevaluated and perhaps suspended, at least temporarily. Patience and support may result in finding ways to put such children at ease. Children who have been maltreated often wish to be understood, but they are unable to see even kind adults as benign because they have come to expect abuse and betrayal. It is important to remember that such children are difficult to engage for good reason, and it is best to accommodate their level of interpersonal functioning, whether through validating anger, tolerating silence, or both.

The Art Therapist's Attitude

On occasion, I have been asked if children are put off by being asked to complete structured directives. This question surprises me because I find that children are generally quite eager to engage in these processes. In most cases, the invitation to be creative and to share this experience with an encouraging, understanding, and interested adult is viewed as fun and meaningful. Many children have no greater wish than to be understood by a caring adult, and art expression affords this opportunity on a deeply felt level. Certainly, there are children who are resentful, frightened, embarrassed, or angry during art therapy sessions, and in these cases, the art therapist must try to understand why this is so, adjusting interventions accordingly to facilitate active engagement in treatment to whatever degree is possible.

It is the job of an art therapist to believe wholeheartedly in the benefits of engaging children in art. Therapists' anxieties about asking children to complete art tasks should be examined. The roots of such fears may lie in professional insecurity, a lack of comfort with art techniques, or anxiety about what children may reveal. It is helpful to determine if reluctance to offer a particular structure is based on an individual child's need for delicate treatment or on the therapist's anxiety. Doubts are part of the territory for child art therapists. Both clinical work and professional identity can be strengthened and enriched when pertinent questions are explored with the art therapist's supervisor or personal therapist. The child art therapist's doubts can be taken in stride if they are buffered by faith in the art therapy process.

Conclusion

According to Winnicott (1990), the facilitating environment fosters maturation. During initial and ongoing sessions, it is helpful to keep this vision in mind. Although there are no hard and fast guidelines for how to provide safety, structure, and a climate that supports therapeutic creativity for each child, the aim is to supply the optimal amount of each, a process that involves constant adaptation to the child's need.

Knowledge of early relational experience and developmental stages (as described in previous chapters), along with a deep understanding of art processes, helps to establish flexibility on the part of the therapist. Because maturation is an interpersonally fueled process, attunement to the child fosters emotional and cognitive growth. This maximizes safety and engagement but is more difficult to achieve with children who are not able to share their preferences and problems openly. Such children may express their needs almost exclusively by nonverbal means. In any case, familiarity with the child's history can help decode the meaning of nonverbal expression and increases the possibility of putting the pieces of the puzzle together.

The first meeting sets the therapeutic climate by establishing a tone of support, inquiry, and understanding. It also begins the assessment process (an important topic that is covered in the following chapter). During assessment, the child's problems, strengths and unique style of expression, as well as suitability for art therapy treatment, are evaluated.

8   Engaging, Assessing, and Learning From Children

I generally learn far more from initial art therapy sessions than I can grasp. In encountering new clients, I enter a world with its own culture and language, replete with belief systems, customs, and rules. The approach, as a guest in this unfamiliar territory, is one of interest and desire to learn. It is important to enter this territory with a map, which consists of as much background information as possible about each child. Knowledge of art processes, child development, and childhood disorders is another navigation tool. Such knowledge provides the context for a safe and focused approach that facilitates engaging with and learning from children.

Ways to Learn From Children

Although there are many surprises, it is helpful to know what to look for in embarking upon this learning process. Some areas of focus include formal elements, style, media usage, level of control, graphic development, verbalization, facial expression, and quality of interaction. The level of congruency of facial expression and subject matter in art and verbal content reveals information about how a child processes or tolerates thoughts and feelings. Shifts in content, style, mood, and verbalization are also important aspects to be aware of as these may indicate discomfort, distress, or loss of interest. Awareness of these factors provides not only understanding but also cues about how to put children at ease and keep them engaged. Style, mood, organization, size, and relationship of images may change within a series of art pieces. Some children vacillate between rigid control and disorganization whereas others freely use a variety of media without regression. Within these sequences, children present meaningful displays of coping styles and creative adaptation. Thus begins each child's story of perceptions and relationships to others and to the environment. The artwork completed during initial sessions can provide deep communication between therapist and child. For both parties, this is usually a sensory and mentally engaging experience.

The manner in which children relate to the art therapist is also informative. It may reveal typical or unusual responses for the child, which as mentioned earlier, can only be determined through comparisons with background information about how the child relates to both adults and peers. Kramer (2000) explored children's varying perceptions of the art therapist as teacher, supplier of goods, and audience. Ideally, these perceptions facilitate positive experiences during which children feel valued and supported and creative expression is encouraged. Rubin (2005) emphasized that children tend to project and transfer upon the art therapist "feelings and expectations relating to significant others" (p. 124). Therefore, the fact that the art therapist supplies materials and closely attends may evoke a host of possible reactions—some positive, some negative—including comfort, safety, nurturance, suspiciousness, greed, or shame. These reactions are likely to have strong associations with past and current relational experiences.

Reluctance to participate in art therapy invites exploration as well. It can indicate many possibilities including dislike of art, feelings of inadequacy, perceiving a stigma in regard to therapy, distrust of "the system," investment in maintaining a family secret (such as domestic violence or abuse), or depressive symptoms. To intervene effectively, it is necessary to find ways to understand the reasons for these reactions through paying attention to what the child says and does. Tolerating the unknown is often necessary.

The Need to Focus

It is often the case that children receive very short-term therapy, sometimes consisting of fewer than six sessions. This necessitates a focused approach so that individual creativity and strengths can be maximized and problems can be explored. Establishing a focus on problems while encouraging creativity involves a delicate balance. In short-term therapy, assessment and treatment take place simultaneously, a process that is justified by the fact that creative expression tends to harness individual strengths. In longer-term therapy, assessment also takes place both initially and continuously; however, the treatment develops increased levels of depth as the child becomes more able to engage reciprocally.

Artwork Series During Initial Sessions

In the best-case scenario, activities used in a session are designed based on what is most needed for the purposes of assessment and therapy. Moreover, it is worth mentioning again that it is preferable to rely on common sense and general guidelines regarding media and theme rather than formulaic approaches. The preceding chapter discussed structured and unstructured activities; the following explication further elaborates on both kinds of activities.

Free Choice

The initial invitation to complete artwork can begin by asking what art themes a child likes or what he or she would like to draw. Permission to choose freely affects each child differently. It may elicit anxiety, relief, or a host of other possibilities. It is the job of the art therapist to observe these reactions because they reveal important information about individual coping styles and ways to proceed during the session. If a child is uncomfortable with free choice and if after provision of validation and encouragement (e.g, "It's hard to think of an idea, but there's really no right or wrong way to do this") the child still refuses, then it may be a good idea to suggest a theme and offer validation (e.g., "I can see that free-choice was not quite right for you"). Accurate reflection helps to build trust and conveys the therapist's belief in a child's reactions. Ideally, the therapist validates and supports expression repeatedly, which contributes

to positive and self-generated experiences in spite of the fact that children are generally expected to work hard and face challenges in therapy.

Enlisting free-choice artworks several times throughout initial sessions serves to gauge
varying responses, both before and after the ice has been broken. Often the free-choice artworks, completed when the child is used to the setting, are more personal and creative. In
some cases, however, later free-choice drawings are increasingly constricted or less developed, which may be due to stress caused by the session, guardedness, fatigue, and so on.

Case Example: Free Choice, Anxiety, and Enthusiasm

"Josh" was an 8-year-old boy who faced many challenges. He had witnessed violent
attacks on his mother by his physically abusive stepfather—a man who reportedly derided
and demeaned him. Although Josh was intelligent and capable, he was self-deprecating,
demanding, and jealous of his younger brother, towards whom he often directed the brunt
of his anger. He had few friendships, and like many children, he was sometimes bullied. His
mother worked full-time; there were financial worries and he faced the current stress of his
mother separating from his stepfather. Josh's biological father had died of a drug overdose
when he was a baby. During the first session, he told me that this was why he did not feel like
a strong person. For most of his life, he had carried the weight of this overwhelming loss.

Josh was enthusiastic about the free choice drawing task. He told me that he planned
to be employed as a computer-game designer someday and that he was going to do a
drawing relating to a game he planned to invent. Enthusiastically, he proceeded to draw
Figure 8.1, which depicts what Josh described as the two forms of an alien named "Bob."
Bob is perched on a planet that is made of cheese, and Josh explained that Bob can take
the form of a strange three- legged creature or of a piece of cheese, changing forms in
response to the level of danger present. He stated that Bob is a serious name and so it is
a funny name for such a strange alien. Josh invented and narrated the scene, speaking in
computer game jargon. He added that Bob "loses lives," that is, can die numerous times
and then "win lives." Josh happily continued speaking rapidly, explaining that *both* the
alien and the planet are made of cheese.

As I listened intently, the story continued: "Anyone who tries to eat the cheese will spit it
out" as the cheese "turns rotten and smelly" when endangered. I commented that the planet

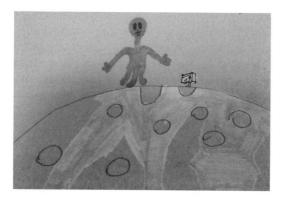

Figure 8.1 "Bob, the Alien" by Josh

and alien have found good ways to protect themselves from destruction, but that it must be hard to have to turn into rotten cheese. My statement recognized that finding effective ways to cope with threats is important, but that there is often an unpleasant cost involved. Josh agreed that it was hard for Bob, explaining that he often felt lonely and worried.

While coloring the planet with yellow maker Josh said, "I'm different from other kids because my father died when I was a baby." He also expressed turmoil about the upcoming separation of his mother and stepfather. With a serious expression on his face, he told me his stepfather had "anger management problems." Josh then verbalized resentment, stating that his parents favored his younger brother (the stepfather's biological child). He talked so much that he was unable to complete his artwork during the session. He appeared distressed that the session was ending and asked if anyone else was coming to see me as he wished to stay longer. I assured Josh that although I could not extend the session, I could understand why he wished for more time because it is terribly hard to end when you are in the middle of something. I told him I would save his work for next time when he could draw and talk some more. The drawing remained unfinished because by the next session, Josh's interest in this story had waned.

Josh had difficulty completing homework and chores. He was usually worried and agitated, a condition that was mirrored in his art expression and behavior. I was aware of the degree to which worry and loss had eclipsed Josh's ability to live as a carefree child. The initial session facilitated both assessment and therapy in affording Josh an opportunity to feel understood by examining difficulties both verbally and through symbolic art expression.

As is often the case, I was amazed at how much I was able to learn from the first session. The fact that Josh was bright, verbal, and trusting contributed to his ability to share openly. His mother was a concerned and loving parent who had helped to shape her son's belief that self-expression is affirming. It was also clear that he was anxious, needy, and distractible. His artwork was creative, providing opportunities for representation of thoughts and feelings. The alien art theme referred to unpleasant means of protection in response to mortal threat. The vulnerability expressed was not surprising given Josh's experience of death of a parent and exposure to domestic violence. Due to his quick, imaginative mind and the challenging circumstances of his life experience, he seemed to be working at rapid speed to keep up with a flood of thoughts and ideas. Imagination, verbal abilities, and desire to engage were strengths. Josh was able to displace his fears through art expression, an age-appropriate function that could help him work through his intense anxiety. Displacement of fears through art expression provides a means of neutralizing anxiety that is particularly useful for school-age children (Levick, 1983) and a helpful facilitator of art therapy treatment. Josh responded very well to a free choice drawing that afforded him the experience of control and safe expression of difficult material. Controllable drawing materials enhanced this experience.

Structured Directives

Case Example Continued: Structured Directives

Although free choice may allow for a glimpse of self-structuring abilities and shed light on thoughts, behaviors, and feelings, structured directives also reveal information that can be very helpful for purposes of assessment and treatment. For many children, structure fosters increased creativity and helps to provide a climate of safety. Themes can be tailored to contain distress for anxious or suspicious children, or they can provide a challenge, encouraging a greater degree of self-disclosure through technically difficult tasks.

DRAW A STORY

Silver's (2007) Draw a Story task is highly structured in its provision of stimulus images and specific directions. It has the potential to elicit imaginative and cognitively based creative expression. When Josh was asked to complete this activity, he immediately expressed a preference for using his own ideas, not someone else's. I explained that he could make all decisions but simply use two of the drawings as inspiration. He then enthusiastically began working on another complicated story, this time in comic-strip format. He selected Silver's mouse and cowboy images as the basis for his story titled "Cucumber Dude" (see Figure 8.2). The story involved a mouse who was offered one wish by a green ball. Contrary to his wish to be a cool cowboy, the mouse became a fat, old-fashioned cowboy. In a subsequent attempt to reverse this, however, he was turned into a cucumber. Searching for help, the cucumber entered a witch's house only to be put into a soup. Cucumber Dude found enough strength to escape from the soup but had to learn to live as a cucumber, a great disappointment.

Once again, Josh was unable to complete the story by the end of the session. He stood in the doorway, describing numerous difficulties that Cucumber Dude continued to face. I assured Josh that although it is hard to leave, we would get back to his important ideas next week. As during the initial session, I was faced with the task of validating and reassuring Josh to help him tolerate loss. Obviously, loss was a central theme in his life. I was aware of his desperate desire to keep my attention and his need for a sense of closure and containment in his life. The story of Cucumber Dude conveyed intense themes of loss and humiliation and of a victim who tries to control difficulties with limited success, mirroring some of Josh's struggles as he coped with numerous sources of stress: familial financial problems, mother's relative unavailability, sibling rivalry, domestic violence, bullies, separation of mother and stepfather, as well as loss of the biological father

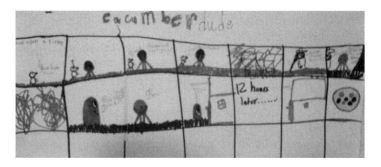

Figure 8.2 "Cucumber Dude" by Josh

during infancy. Ongoing instability affected Josh's ability to find satiation and equilibrium, which made leaving the session difficult for him.

During the sessions, Josh attempted to make sense of his anxiety, exploring the question of how to survive continuous blows that threatened to overwhelm him. This was expressed directly through his behavior and state of heightened arousal as well through the vulnerable characters depicted in his drawings. Although this was only the second session, therapeutic work was taking place as Josh engaged in organizing a flood of chaotic feelings.

FAMILY DRAWING

Family drawings can be very demanding for some children. Malchiodi (1998) observed that the children she worked with (with the exception of 4- to 6-year-olds) did not display a natural desire to draw pictures of their families. Further, she noted that well adjusted children tend to willingly comply with the request to complete this directive whereas traumatized children are more likely to avoid the task or to depict very static figures. The most common family drawing directive utilized by both psychologists and art therapists is the Kinetic Family Drawing (Burns & Kaufman, 1972), involving the directive to draw your family doing something together. Through style, form, process, placement, relative size of figures, and verbal descriptions of content, this drawing task often yields very valuable information about the child's perception and experience of family roles and relationships. Although family drawings can depict reality-based events, it is important to remember that a child's drawing does not provide a factual document but rather conveys something about the child's subjective experience of family life.

As was the case with Josh, children who experience significant family stress may refuse to draw their families. In such situations, it is often advisable to respect the child's wishes. Children frequently mobilize avoidance to cope with stress. In addition, the use of displacement through imaginative themes, rather than directly portraying life circumstances, is an age-appropriate means of coping. An alternative directive that offers a little distance (e.g., "Draw a family of animals") can meet with more success. Indirect themes have the advantage of providing safety, thus allowing for greater disclosure.

As could be expected, Josh refused to draw reality-based subjects, expressing a strong preference for drawing imaginary scenes involving aliens and robotic characters. In this way, he could exercise an additional strength: well developed drawing skill as a result of having repeatedly practiced rendering these images. Doing so reinforced his sense of mastery. The intensity of Josh's need to focus on highly charged stories supplied an effective outlet for the family-related stress he experienced.

After rejecting my invitation to draw his family, Josh agreed to draw an alien family and produced a stark drawing of "an alien mom, dad and their son" above which were diagrams depicting "special" versus "normal" alien babies (see Figure 8.3). He stated that the son had a very special type of anatomy, which was going extinct, and that he was very unusual and highly valued. In essence, this boy was an alien among aliens. The somber drawing illustrates a uniquely vulnerable creature, representing Josh's search to find the silver lining inside the dark cloud of hardship and differentness. Later during

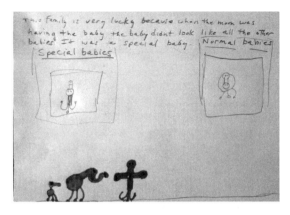

Figure 8.3 Alien family by Josh

this session, Josh spoke about feeling that it is wrong to mistreat those who are different and that "different is not worse, although many people believe this." He expressed a humane approach and identification with the underdog that conveyed both his vulnerability and his strength of character.

Reaction formation is an age-appropriate defense that was used, in this case, to channel feelings of victimization, fear, and abandonment into the more acceptable arena of compassion and advocacy. Vaillant (1993) describes this defense as one that "allows us to care for someone else when we wish to be cared for ourselves" (p. 65). This provided an opportunity for Josh to feel strong while retaining a connection to the indignation and victimization he felt.

WORKING WITH CLAY

For some children, working with clay is difficult and potentially regressive. They may smear it and become preoccupied with references to feces. In some cases, even regressed endeavors ultimately lead to more organized work—especially if the therapist gives gentle support, technical advice, and encouragement. Clay allows a child to construct something and thus to demonstrate potential strength not revealed in two-dimensional work. For example, although Josh was somewhat needy and acquisitive—he requested many pieces of colored clay—he completed very competent work (see Figure 8.4). For the first time during the sessions, he stated that he could depict a real person and produced a gentle-looking but sturdy male figure, which he described as "just a guy." While working and with my encouragement, he boasted about his own physical strength. During this session, Josh also described having been told by a judge (at a hearing regarding his abusive stepfather) that it is hurtful and against the law for children to witness parental violence. The themes he discussed while constructing a benign male figure included strength, aggression, and vulnerability. Josh had experienced the loss of his father due to a drug overdose and had witnessed his stepfather's violence, leaving him with profound questions about what it means to be a man. The work with clay evoked gentle exploration of this sensitive subject.

Figure 8.4 "Just a Guy" by Josh

Goals and Implications for Treatment

Josh had difficulty completing artworks because he was anxious and easily distracted. He seemed afraid of losing the attention he received during his art therapy sessions and talked almost constantly, apparently trying to make sense of profound losses and threats. Josh was understandably inconsistent with completing tasks expected of an 8-year-old boy, one who is normally at a developmental stage that requires confidence, adequate attention span, and the ability to navigate complex sibling and social interactions.

In considering the focus for future treatment, I had, in the back of my mind, very long-term goals. To engage successfully in love and work (E. Erikson, 1980), I wanted Josh to grow up to be an adult who could cope with stress effectively and experience trust, impulse control, and the ability to protect himself. Such goals are elusive when dealing with young children; it is necessary to have short-term goals that help children at their current levels of development and to assume that this will pave the road that leads to successful adulthood. For Josh, this would entail providing an opportunity for him to gain a sense of control within a framework designed to assist him in organizing his chaotic emotional experiences. The initial assessment period was used to evaluate the impact of a combination of structure and flexibility that served as an invitation for Josh to work hard while engaging in authentic expression. The fact that he was effectively engaged in therapeutic work during the assessment activities provided a green light to continue in this manner.

Directed and Structured Exploration

Sometimes art directives during initial sessions are designed to focus directly on presenting problems. This can provide relief and effectively establish rapport with children who are aware and open regarding their treatment problems. This approach is contraindicated for children who experience shame and confusion in relation to their presenting problems. Evocative directives are generally most successful with the support of controllable drawing materials as opposed to messy materials such as paint or wet clay.

Case Example: Directive to Address a Problem

Seven-year-old "Belinda's" mother was in recovery from addiction and had been clean and sober for 4 months. Belinda had experienced neglect and had witnessed her mother in dangerous situations since the age of 4. Currently, her mother assured her that she was on a constructive path and that she was committed to providing adequate parental care. Daily fights between mother and daughter ensued. They were caused by Belinda's refusal to attend school.

Belinda was immediately friendly and talkative with me. She reveled in attention, which made her delightful to work with but also conveyed a sense of desperate need. I was concerned that her experience of having been in the role of mother's caregiver had caused continuing anxiety, and my choice of art directive was designed to enlist related expression. My aim was to explore what was behind Belinda's school refusal based on my understanding that school refusal sometimes stems from the desire to protect a parent.

During the initial conversation about why she was seeing me, Belinda openly discussed her mother's addiction and her school refusal. I then asked Belinda to draw a picture entitled, "What worries me." Belinda drew the picture in Figure 8.5 that depicts her mother being hit by a car. Upon completing the picture, she told me that when her mother was using drugs, she would walk out in front of cars and that she could have gotten killed numerous times. Belinda shared that she was haunted by these memories. I asked if this contributed to the fear of attending school, which Belinda confirmed, stating that she wanted to make sure her mother would not use drugs or do anything dangerous. I said, "I wonder if you want to show this picture to your mother." Although somewhat nervous, she was eager to do so. The discussion with her mother about the drawing gave her mother some understanding of Belinda's level of anxiety. We developed a plan to ensure more consistent school attendance. The problem-focused theme had matched the intensity with which the child communicated and had provided initial containment of the crisis.

Figure 8.5 Mother in danger by Belinda

Although her mother was presently very committed to sobriety and to responsible behavior as a parent, Belinda remained highly anxious. However, as a result of support for her mother regarding limit setting, Belinda was able to begin attending school regularly. Still, ongoing therapeutic work was necessary. Belinda had considerable fears and insecurities. During the course of her therapy, numerous similar artworks and interactions took place. Restoring Belinda's sense of security required long-term work for which the first session merely functioned as a foot in the door.

Neutral and Mixed Themes With Case Examples

Draw a Tree

For most children, a tree is a safe and neutral subject. Drawing or painting a tree accommodates either imaginative or reality-based expression and provides opportunities for description without the burden of self-disclosure. "Kenny," a sensitive 5-year-old boy (introduced in the previous chapter), experienced performance anxiety and angry outbursts that were apparently triggered by his parents' marital discord. Much of Kenny's initial art expression consisted of paintings of trees (See Figures 8.6–9). He was assisted in this expression by his ease in manipulating paint. Kenny was very afraid of making mistakes and refused to depict most other subjects, indicating a need to avoid emotionally charged, imaginative, and technically demanding tasks. As noted previously, for Kenny to engage in any artwork, I had to offer significant encouragement by saying something along these lines, "Let's just see how it turns out, and then you can tell me if you really did not like doing it."

Kenny was pleased at his success at rendering a tree (see Figure 8.6), something he had not previously done. When encouraged to tell stories about the trees and to reflect about whether he enjoyed or disliked the process, he stated that he did not think he could do it at first but that now that he knew how to paint trees, he would like to paint more trees. Talking about his experience of the process helped Kenny to put words to his formerly nameless performance anxiety and provided some confirmation that he could be successful after all.

Figure 8.6 Tree painting by Kenny

Questions can be asked to engage children in discussing tree drawings. Examples are plentiful: Is this a real or made-up tree? How old is it? What kind of tree is it? Has it ever been hurt? Do any creatures or animals live in the tree? Is it healthy? If it is not healthy, what is wrong and what will happen? What does the tree need? Is it in any danger? Selection of questions depends on the appearance of the tree, the child's comfort level, and the child's interest in making up a story about the artwork. Whereas some children are delighted to elaborate, others experience discomfort when asked to do so. Children like Kenny whose ability to express is restricted can be gently encouraged to reflect, but their limits must be respected. The stories that children make up, either in response to questions or on their own, reveal much about their concerns, emotions, and coping styles.

Because Kenny appeared to feel put on the spot in describing his tree images, I did not initially push him to make up stories as heightening his anxiety would have been counterproductive. By the third session, however, he had become more comfortable and less anxiety ridden. Reducing performance anxiety was a primary treatment goal for Kenny, and he had taken the first tiny steps towards that goal.

Tree Before, During and After a Storm

Kenny refused to complete a painting of a person in the rain. Drawing a person is very challenging for many children; Kenny's anxiety was too high to engage in tasks perceived as overly challenging. I supported his dislike of rendering a person and asked if he could paint a tree during a storm (Miller, 1997). Subsequently, Kenny depicted two trees in slightly different states, one described as reacting to a storm of "invisible thunder stones" (see Figure 8.7) and the other as having "a bite taken out of it" (see Figure 8.8). These images seemed to mirror Kenny's experiencing escalating anger and anxiety at home. When I encouraged Kenny to tell me more about how the storm affected the trees, he did not respond verbally. Instead he drew what he later described as a "catapult tree" (see Figure 8.9). He told me that the tree had gotten angry because the storm was hurting it, and it was going to attack and explode. He told me this with demonstrative gestures and exploding noises, laughing and showing apparent pleasure all the while.

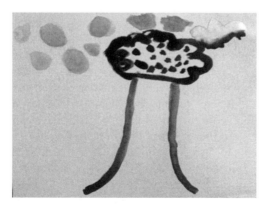

Figure 8.7 Tree with "thunder stones" by Kenny

Figure 8.8 Tree with bite out of it by Kenny

Figure 8.9 "Catapult tree" by Kenny

Kenny had not previously felt sufficiently relaxed to have fun. This was a matter of concern for his parents who acknowledged that he was so worried about winning games that he was unable to have fun. After completing the tree in the storm series, Kenny asked me if I knew ways to calm down from anger. Rather than immediately answering with my own ideas, I asked if *he* had ever found a way to calm down from anger. He said, in a somewhat mechanical voice, "Counting to 10." When I asked him if that strategy worked he said, "Not always." His parents had apparently suggested this method of anger management, but Kenny was unable to implement it because he felt besieged and alone with his angry feelings. I explained to him how hard it is to feel alone with anger, and therefore, counting to 10 may not work. I asked Kenny if his parents could help him, and he said they could not because they would get mad at him. It was hard for Kenny's parents to offer him comfort due to the stress they were under; this needed to be addressed through marital and parenting therapies. I inquired if Kenny had any nice stuffed animals and if he ever hugs them. He told me of a beloved stuffed hen named "Cluckie," explaining that sometimes he feels better when he cuddles this toy. Exploration of disruption and repair took place throughout the tree series and the discussions that followed. During the next few sessions, Kenny portrayed trees undergoing destruction and restoration. He depicted survival amid turbulence, and in doing so, created images equivalent to his feelings about parental fighting. Both Kenny and I learned about his persistent experience of vulnerability and about his need to find ways to obtain comfort and repair.

Miller (1997) attributed evocation of a patient's relationship to the crisis that precipitated treatment to the projective drawing Tree Before, During, and After a Storm. In Kenny's case, the crisis appeared to relate to anger at his parents' conflict and inability to sooth his distress. The art theme obviously stimulated association to this experience because he spontaneously discussed his anger following completion of this task.

Parental consultation sessions were interspersed with Kenny's art therapy sessions. During these meetings, I shared my understanding of Kenny's anxiety. The parents responded that they fought after Kenny was in bed and that he would seek their attention at this time. This resulted in unmanageable anger among all three parties. We discussed that he seemed to feel his parents' and his own accumulated distress as overwhelming. Subsequently, the parents decided to focus on therapy for themselves. The art therapy assessment findings suggested that reducing parental conflict would help Kenny to manage his anger and anxiety. Kenny continued for several sessions with a focus on exploring and tolerating challenges through art expression. In Kenny's short-term art therapy experience, structured neutral directives and fluid media facilitated expression of concerns. Upon discharge, his parents said that they were committed to reducing anxiety in the home environment and to providing greater support for Kenny's emotional needs.

Paint a Person in the Rain: Friend or Foe?

As noted above, some children do not like drawing people and find the directive "Draw a Person in the Rain" (Vernis, Lichtenberg, & Henrich, 1997) to be objectionable. When paint is offered, this directive offers the unique opportunity to depict a human form within a fluid environment using a less-controllable medium. The process of completing the person in the rain offers a framework for struggling with potential loss of control. Many children find this task engaging whereas others do not enjoy it and remain unengaged. The subject matter is relatively neutral, but for some, the process can be stressful because the paint may threaten to subsume the human form. Drawing (much less painting) a person is a task for which many children believe they lack skill. Although some children approach this task with a high level of flexibility, others demonstrate excessive rigidity.

Painting a Person in the Rain can provide information about coping with stress or about the capacity to engage in creative adaptation. Although this task is said to assess how a child handles stress, it is not necessarily because rain is stressful. It is perhaps equally likely that rendering people and using paint is stressful. In any case, responses should not be interpreted in a formulaic manner. As Golomb (2011) points out, singular drawings "do not lend themselves to a singular reading that has diagnostic validity" (p. 82). Children who are not skilled at drawing people may feel disinterested and incompetent and are likely to demonstrate lower levels of mastery than with other art activities; this should not automatically be interpreted as a sign of weak functional abilities.

It is always important to learn what activities are meaningful and engaging for a child as well as those that are perceived as unpleasant. This affords information to the therapist about habitual ways of coping with unpleasant experiences and offers a focus for further therapy. Undoubtedly, it is efficacious to design activities that children enjoy. Although it is not recommended to intentionally offer unpleasant activities, it is not possible to know preferences unless a variety of directives are offered. Extremely valuable therapeutic work takes place when a child can feel "heard" upon completion of a directive experienced as frustrating or unsatisfying.

"Keith" (described in chapter 3), a 12-year-old who was diagnosed with Asperger's syndrome, appeared constricted while painting a person in the rain (Figure 8.10). This picture was more rigid and less creative than his other artwork. When I asked him how it was for him to complete this directive, he said that he did not like it and that he disliked both aspects of the activity: painting and depicting real people. I conveyed interest and respect for his feelings of discomfort and his lack of interest in the subject matter.

In contrast, "Chrissy," an 8-year-old referred to art therapy because she had become increasingly fearful, angry, and critical following the divorce of her parents, responded very differently to the Paint a Person in the Rain directive. She took delight in portraying what she described as herself enjoying the rain (see Figure 8.11) and demonstrated flexibility and creativity. Although she felt victimized in her daily life, she revealed her

Figure 8.10 Paint a Person in the Rain assessment by Keith

Figure 8.11 Paint a Person in the Rain assessment by Chrissy

fun-loving and creative strengths in this painting. In the face of a fractured home life, she reinforced her strong and fun-loving side by depicting appreciation of rain and the outdoors. The self-portrait of enjoying the storm provided comfort. This reminder of happy times provided a feeling of vigor that gave her the courage to share some of her fears through artwork later in the session.

Draw a House

For many children, a house drawing is a neutral theme, but for others, it can evoke memories of a painful divorce, homelessness, experiencing abuse, or witnessing domestic violence. The request to draw a house allows a child to depict a solid structure that is real or imagined and to experience some degree of control regarding what is revealed about difficult personal or family matters. Although some children appreciate opportunities to depict direct representations of their experiences, others may become weighed down by such tasks. Some children depict real life scenes whereas others opt for the benefit of disguise afforded by imaginative work. For example, when "Cara," a frightened and anxious 8-year-old, was asked to draw a house, she drew an elaborate castle (Figure 8.12) that included threats from monsters in addition to a security system, guards, and a moat replete with crocodiles. This highly detailed, monochromatic image was completed with energy and pleasure. Her manner reflected the conversion of anxiety into a sense of purpose. She conveyed intense fears as well as the struggle to establish protective mechanisms. At home, Cara desperately clung to her parents because she was crippled by fears of kidnappers and monsters. When she was asked to discuss these fears openly, she became panicked and hysterical. The direction for her art therapy sessions emphasized gaining mastery of the frightening subjects through symbolic drawings about which she was encouraged to speak. This ultimately enabled her to discuss and master the fears in her life more comfortably.

General Guidelines for Assessing Children

Although I have offered some possibilities for art directives, it is important to find the means to elicit personally meaningful, individualized expression according to the needs and characteristics of each child. The above vignettes and suggestions are not intended as formulas but rather as food for thought. There is no replacement for an individualized approach to each child's unique vision along with respect for the need for safety that varies from one child to another. In general, there is more benefit from offering simple themes and materials that enlist a specific child's creativity and associations. In other words, art therapists need not introduce fancy or innovative art procedures as this may not elicit as much personal response from children.

There are virtually infinite possibilities for the unfolding of initial art therapy sessions. Some children are verbal and freely create imaginative stories, but clam up when the focus is more personal; others openly speak and draw about current problems. Some are uncomfortable or unable to verbalize at all. Some are bossy; others are passive or overly compliant. Some are immobilized by fear of failure; others are highly industrious but disconnected from emotions. Some insist on using rulers; others proceed with reckless abandon. There are children who are reassured by firm rules and restrictions and those

Figure 8.12 Protected castle by Cara

who become fearful when this is the case. As interpersonal and art processes unfold during initial sessions, the seeds for therapeutic focus begin to sprout.

What all children who attend therapy have in common is that they are struggling with difficulties. They need therapy in order to develop strengths to cope more effectively. Initial assessments and therapy are most effective when built on a core of strengths and personal interests. This is accomplished through attunement, fostering creativity, and developing a plan that fits. The best measurement tool of children's art therapy expressions is a sensitively attuned person who understands the language of art and developmental sequences of childhood.

Art expression is one way to be understood; it facilitates connections to others. This factor is central to both treatment and assessment in child art therapy. Whether standardized (Gantt & Tabone, 1998; Silver, 2007) or individualized methods (Kramer, 2000; Rubin, 2005) are utilized, art therapy assessments evoke unique and creative responses. Ulman (1975) quoted a colleague who stated that art-based assessment is "less scientific but more accurate, than standardized projective tests" (p. 386). The level of individualized, personal expression and style revealed through art expression is, with rare exceptions, rich and informative. The visual language of art communicates both individual and universal aspects of the human experience in both content and form.

9 Engaging and Learning From Parents

Art Therapy and the Facilitating Environment

Over three decades ago, Kramer (1977) described the role of the art therapist as supporting children in reenacting and resolving inner tensions primarily through the language of art materials and form, a powerful means of facilitating personality change. Although it is no longer possible for many art therapists to function purely in this role, it is possible to maintain this sensibility in spite of the fact that art therapists are often employed as primary therapists and have become licensed as counselors. For better or worse, many art therapists currently assume roles that were formerly held by social workers, psychologists, and even psychiatrists. This necessitates incorporating an overview of multiple factors that are part of the child's system.

Each child's system consists of a long list of people that may include parents, siblings, teachers, caseworkers, physicians, and attorneys. Often, psychotropic medication has a life of its own and, in essence, may become yet another "client" that is either helping or causing difficulties such as stunted growth, weight problems, insomnia, and so on. In spite of all these complicated factors, art expression remains a central means of communication for children that allows for clarifying and focusing on what is most important. Although it is easy to get lost in all the potentially chaotic components, it is very helpful to keep art expression in the forefront of therapy as it provides access to sincere expression of problems and a means of facilitating strengths. The art therapist is uniquely positioned to use art processes for promoting growth and bringing forth understanding of the messages that are conveyed through the child's visual language. This privileged position can also be utilized as a means of helping parents and others to support the therapeutic process. In short, the therapist can translate the symbolic language of the child to members of the child's system.

The Pitfall of Overidentification

Not only am I a champion of art and creativity but also my personal experiences and clinical work have taught me that art is a unique and highly effective means of developing individual strengths. As a child I spent many hours in school, uninterested, wishing I could be drawing and painting. I felt very much a victim of boring teachers, an experience that qualifies me to empathize with children who feel similarly. Although this identification assists in effectively engaging children in working through difficulties, it must be kept in check. Overidentification with the child client can undermine parents, the primary resource available to help children experience satisfaction and success in many areas of their lives. Further, overidentification with children is often a red flag indicative of childhood-related struggles on the part of the therapist. Awareness of such tendencies promotes both self-maturation and enhanced clinical work, offering opportunities to solidify growth on multiple fronts.

My graduate internships were structured such that I worked with the children whereas social workers were responsible for parental contact. Even within this relatively limited framework, my emotional reactions were powerful. Child art therapy expression is highly evocative and tends to elicit rescuing fantasies ("If only I were the parent for this child") that tend to go along with overidentification ("my client and I are bonded against the mean parents"). I realized the imperative to be aware of my emotional reactions and to contain them in the service of a constructive clinical focus. For a novice therapist, this can be a difficult task. Robbins (1994) points out that art therapists are faced with a tremendous challenge due to the emotionally powerful influence of nonverbal communication. It is hard not only to make sense of nonverbal modes of expression but also to tolerate upsetting imagery, particularly when abuse or disturbance is conveyed either overtly or symbolically.

The Parent–Therapist Relationship: A Delicate Territory

As a professional, most of my work with children has necessitated working with parents. In the "real world," I learned that parents are a fact of life in child therapy. This was a rude awakening in that the already challenging complexities of child-focused work became part of a larger system. However, the inclusion of parents in the work deepens the possibilities for helping children to integrate therapeutic gains in their lives. I found myself in the unique role of a translator of child art expression, a position that afforded opportunities to bridge the gap between parent and child by eliciting symbolic expression and explaining its content so as to strengthen the parent–child bond (Shore, 2000).

Of the many tasks undertaken by child art therapists, working with parents is one of the more challenging, involving as it does a potential hotbed of complex and contradictory emotions. This can be extremely difficult and requires great fortitude. K. K. Novick and Novick (2005) explain that such involvement elicits great resistance, awkwardness, avoidance and procrastination from therapists, due to the "deep and intense countertransferences to parents that we all struggle with" (p. 14). For both therapist and parent, few experiences are more distressing than the possibility of damaging a developing child. With little exception, parents of children with difficulties feel guilty and vulnerable. Feelings of fault and failure are ubiquitous. Parent–therapist relationships are complicated and require great care, due in part to the fact that the child's therapist is only peripherally able to help parents with their own personal difficulties.

The degree to which parents are interested in and able to take responsibility for their role in influencing children has a significant impact on the effectiveness of the therapy. Treatment of children is more effective when parents believe in the value of therapeutic processes and goals, and when they are able to collaborate. Each family has a culture that has evolved generationally. One must enter this culture with considerable respect, sensitivity, and a commitment to putting assumption and judgment aside. In some cases, the discomfort in working with parents is fueled by the belief that the parents have indeed harmed the child. In other cases, it may relate to the therapist's rebelliousness or own unresolved early relationships. These reactions are a natural part of engaging with clients and cannot be eliminated. Self-reflection is crucial to maintaining effective interactions with the parents of child clients.

Parental Involvement During the Initial Assessment Process

It is advisable to meet with parents alone prior to sessions with children. This affords parents an opportunity to talk freely about concerns, to provide background information, and to reveal information about the interpersonal environment in which their children exist and evolve. Paying close attention to what parents say, as well as their behaviors, other nonverbal cues, and interpersonal styles, provides substantial information about the overall context of children's lives. Schmidt Neven (2010) stated, "The first meeting contains the problem and the solution" (p. 67), meaning that families convey core difficulties through the initial contacts with the therapist, a process that may be done through an enactment of the problem that suggests the solution. For example, when parents convey high anxiety about toilet or dietary habits of children, this may signal a pervasive atmosphere of anxiety within the home. The child's problem may result, in part, from family anxiety, the impact of which can be seen as the treatment focus. The most important aspect of initial meetings with parents, then, is to observe, listen, and understand as much as possible. This goes a long way in helping parents to engage and to trust and, in addition, through absorbing the feeling of familial interpersonal styles, to glean a deep understanding of children's experience.

Although it is helpful to ask parents to extemporaneously tell about children's strengths, weaknesses, and the reasons why therapy is needed, it is also necessary to ask questions relating to areas such as early development, primary caretakers, peer relationships, medical problems, academic functioning, and personal interests. During this interview, it is a good idea to take notes or to complete an intake form. In cases of high-conflict divorce, it is often preferable to meet separately with each parent to access more constructive engagement; marital animosity often precludes focusing on what is best for the children.

Defining the Structure

Educating parents about art therapy and the process of child therapy is a crucial component of initial contact. Explaining the role of child art therapy to parents can be challenging. It demands a seemingly incompatible combination of tasks that include patiently educating about an approach that is little understood by the general public, walking gingerly through painful circumstances, delivering a sales-pitch about the value of art therapy, and providing understanding as well as sincere respect. Education about what to expect provides a sense of safety and demonstrates the level of the therapist's competence and dependability. If the parents develop trust in the therapist, the treatment can progress more smoothly. At the same time, it is important to convey the belief that the parents are the experts when it comes to their children. Throughout the treatment process, their competence, love, and sound instincts must be repeatedly recognized. To do this with sincerity, every effort must be made to empathize with parents in areas such as their struggles, vulnerability, and possible need for control.

Unlike art therapists, many parents do not believe in the power or importance of art; it is necessary, therefore, to get them to understand its therapeutic use. This is best accomplished by learning about and empathizing with their values. Only then is it possible to enlist their support regarding the benefits of giving children a voice through art therapy. It is also important to explain a little about child art therapy assessment and treatment. Although it is helpful to have a prefabricated explanation, the information should be tailored to the unique needs of each family and their existing understanding and attitudes about therapy. I generally tell parents that my approach to each child is individualized and that I begin treatment by conducting an initial assessment that takes place over the course of two or three 45 to 50 minute sessions. I go on to explain that I offer children the opportunity to use different art materials and to respond to a variety of art directives that elicit both imaginary and reality-based associations. It can be helpful to tell parents that some children prefer depicting reality-based subjects whereas others may be more comfortable with make-believe themes, both of which can reveal concerns and preferences. I also explain that my understanding of the child will likely be very similar to that of the parents and that I hope to shed some further insights about their perceptions and struggles. Parents leave the initial session with an understanding of what to expect, how to inform their child, and a plan to meet for an additional session after assessing the child.

At the second meeting with parents, which follows the initial art therapy sessions with the child, I explain what I have learned, emphasizing and validating parental concerns and struggles, and recommending a plan for ongoing art therapy if appropriate. Possible parental, familial, and school adaptations are considered. It is important to be careful about dispensing advice at this time. Although there are times when advice is helpful, particularly if solicited, most often it is better to elicit parents' ideas; they often know best about what interventions they are able to handle based on past experiences. This method helps to build parents' confidence and minimizes the possibility of imagining that the therapist has magic solutions. The utilization of self-empowerment that is part of the therapeutic approach of art therapy is also central in supporting parental competence.

If this is the beginning of ongoing treatment, parents benefit from learning that it is a process involving collaboration. The collaborative structure is based in part on what level of involvement parents desire as well as what is going to be most constructive for the child. Ideally, parents are used as a primary resource, which serves the goals not only of increasing responsiveness to their child's needs but also of helping to build parental confidence and effectiveness, all of which enhance and expedite the treatment process. Parents of a child who was treated by Winnicott stated that his reliance on their wisdom provided a safeguard against them feeling "left out in the cold and prey to feelings of rivalry and competition with the therapist" (Winnicott, 1977 p. 199).

Compassion, Respect, and Capacity for Trust

It is helpful to remember that parents were children themselves not long ago. They are often operating on instinct and responding in a manner that is based on their own experiences as children within their families of origin. Living with a child who has behavior problems can cause extreme stress and reactivity for which support is needed in order to offset the accompanying shame that is often present. The fact that parents seek help implies some desire to change established patterns, an undertaking that requires courage.

If therapy is mandated, it is likely that the parents are resentful and thus unwilling to become the therapist's ally. In these cases, it is helpful to sympathize with parents who are feeling unfairly treated by the system while being careful not to condone abuse or neglect of children. This is challenging because it can be difficult to remain compassionate towards parents who are hurting their children. The therapist must work hard to be able to see multiple perspectives and to understand that, most often, each party is feeling mistreated.

Because the child therapy process is greatly impacted by how parents feel towards the therapist, it is well worth the effort to try to earn the parents' trust. Parents who are capable of self-reflection and collaboration are an asset to the treatment process whereas those who are unable to actively engage present a substantial challenge. In these latter cases, if the treatment is sustained, the goals for the child must be scaled down. Very often the focus becomes helping the child to manage ongoing familial stress as opposed to developmental growth.

Revealing the Child–Parent Relationship

A major focus of previous chapters has been the richness inherent in viewing and understanding child art expression as a major source of information. Another valuable source for learning about the child is listening to and observing his or her parents as well as the child's reaction to them. Children may artistically describe parents in a manner that expresses life experiences such as in Figure 9.1 in which a 9-year-old boy conveyed anger about his parents' divorce. Or children may express their feeling states with a degree of disguise (Rubin, 2005), exemplified in Figure 9.2. The latter, completed by the same boy 3 months later, is an art piece that depicts the anguish of an animal that is part lion and part bird, the painful result of mismatched marital partners. Figure 9.1 conveys

Figure 9.1 Depiction of parents' divorce by 9-year-old boy

Figure 9.2 Lion and bird hybrid by 9-year-old boy

the problem in a straightforward manner, illustrating a boy's distressing experience of seeing his mother angry and his father crying at the time of the divorce.

Figure 9.2 illustrates how the parental relationship was internalized. These feelings could not be faced directly and were handily displaced through depicting a hybrid creature that utters a "roar" of pain. Parental behavior is often absorbed by children and may be expressed directly or indirectly. Similarly, parents may express descriptions of children's strengths and problems through direct or indirect communication. Examples of indirect parental communication include failure to show up for sessions, bullying the therapist, or attempting to monopolize the child's therapy time with personal demands. These interactions are very informative about the interpersonal experience of the parent–child relationship. It is helpful to examine their possible parallels to what the child may feel. In other words, when the therapist feels devalued, angry, or insecure, it may be something like what the child feels in relation to parents. When therapists strive to observe and understand reactions, this can enhance empathy and bring about heightened sensitivity towards both parents and children.

Example: The Toll of Parental Chemical Dependency

"Kali," a 10-year-old girl, experienced anxiety and low self-esteem. Her father, offering excuses about traffic or long lines at the supermarket, was repeatedly late and smelled of alcohol at the time of pick-up from sessions. During the sessions, Kali continually made hearts and flowers out of modeling clay and depicted rainbows or spelled her name with bold colored markers. Although these activities were self-soothing, it was difficult to find ways to help Kali generate new ideas or problem solving skills. We talked about her worries and disillusionment regarding her father's unpredictable arrival times. On several occasions, she mumbled in an embittered tone that her father was late because he was secretly buying beer. I noticed that I felt anxiety as sessions neared conclusion. I was worried and felt a sense of powerlessness about how to handle the awkward and potentially prolonged ending. I anticipated my guilt about leaving Kali alone in the waiting room for an unknown length of time, as well as the prospect of my next session's delay. Awareness of my reaction gave me significant insight concerning Kali's difficulties in coping with her father's alcohol-related unreliability as it was likely that my experience mirrored her feelings. This made it possible for me to be present with her resentment and resignation and enhanced my understanding regarding Kali's need to avoid challenges and to focus exclusively on safety and control. Her therapeutic needs included support, anxiety reduction, and recognition of the level of strength she demonstrated in tolerating coexisting feelings of admiration, disappointment, and abandonment towards her father.

When confronted about the lateness, Kali's father agreed to be more responsible; but it was impossible for him to alter his behaviors. I eventually changed the appointment time so that Kali's mother could pick her up. This relieved the immediate stressor and alleviated my anxieties about the ending of sessions. When children are in active distress due to parental dysfunction, the goals may be limited to helping them find ways to relieve anxiety. In Kali's case, this involved supporting her need to create artwork with repetitive themes, which allowed her to feel some internal control. The fact that she took few risks artistically does not mean that the opportunity to create controlled designs was not helpful. My role was to assist her in feeling understood in the powerlessness she experienced and to encourage her to structure her experience so as to facilitate order and safety. The father's alcoholism was a difficult reality that I, too, was powerless to change. When I spoke to either parent it was clear that they were unable to address this devastating issue at the present time.

Parental substance abuse is a powerful and difficult factor to cope with, one which invariably causes hardship and tragedy. Such conditions often result in a sense of powerlessness and despair on the part of the therapist, feelings like those of the child. Sometimes I have thought that I should run away from this type of situation, that there is no value to my work. Perhaps this is an escape fantasy based on the false notion that life is supposed to be easy. Interestingly, this way of thinking is also characteristic of substance abusers, suggesting that the family system is in some sense contagious. When strong connections are part of the therapeutic relationship, it is natural to absorb the familial patterns of coping. Self-observation on the part of the therapist regarding this material provides valuable insight. In work with Kali, this was instrumental in helping to provide a supportive treatment focus that respected her need to feel some success in coping with the demands of a painful interpersonal atmosphere.

Sharing Artwork With Parents

Children often spontaneously show their artwork to parents at the end of sessions. Over the course of time this can be planned or explored with the child, often with the emphasis on giving the child control of this decision. This provides opportunities for children to integrate the sessions with parental relationships and also allows for observation of parental attitudes towards the child, the art therapy process, and therapeutic concerns. In general, incorporating parents into the process is helpful, but there may be times when sharing art is discouraged, perhaps because it is too volatile to share at that point in time. For example, the child may be well served by being protected for periods of time from sharing artwork with a parent who only recognizes its cute or pretty aspects when the child is in need of validation and encouragement regarding deeper levels of expression.

Sharing child art therapy products is based on assessment of how well this serves the treatment goals and the capacity for parents to use this understanding constructively. There are many cases in which sharing children's art with parents serves no purpose. Frequently, the therapy is better served by gently translating the messages from the art in order to facilitate greater parental attunement regarding children's needs. Parents who tend to misinterpret communication from their children should be protected from art expression that they will not be able to understand. For example, parents who were physically abused as children sometimes overreact to a child's portrayal of a scene depicting conflict, which may trigger their own vulnerability and prevent them from being able to see the child's constructive expression of aggression. The art therapist's fluency in the language of art is a tool used for sensitively imparting the child's needs to parents.

Tolerating Disappointment

Child art therapists are very familiar with what can feel like missed opportunities. Scarcity of economic resources is a rampant factor that leads to severely compromised levels of service in most treatment settings. Additionally, working with parents can involve considerable "messiness"; and these messes are often far more uncomfortable than the messy artwork that children produce during sessions. In outpatient settings, a common impediment is lack of commitment. There are numerous possible reasons for why parents may be unable to uphold a commitment to therapy for their child including scheduling difficulties, parental unreliability, shame associated with therapy, difficulty trusting professionals, conflict between parents, inability to accept the lack of a quick fix, or ultimate inability to tolerate much change in their children. Although these disappointing experiences are commonplace, examples in the literature are scarce. The fact that most publications focus on cases that were successful serves to heighten clinicians' uncertainty and doubt. It is always important to examine whether failures to engage parents could have been prevented by heightened sensitivity or awareness on the part of the therapist. The following two cases illustrate parental disengagement that resulted in termination of therapy.

Conflict Between Mother and Father

Parental conflict creates thorny conditions for all involved. It can incite disruptive behavior in children and evoke anguish for child therapists. Frequently, the therapist's experience of being caught between parents parallels the child's struggles. Such was the case with "Brittany," a 9-year-old girl who attended therapy due to intense angry outbursts that were directed at her mother. The father, whose job was very demanding, took little responsibility for childcare, household chores, or family relationships. Mother and father blamed each other for multiple problems, including Brittany's anger and aggression. On one occasion, I opened the door to my office and heard Brittany and her mother walking up the stairs to my office. The mother was speaking angrily on her cell phone to Brittany's father; and she cursorily acknowledged me, rolling her eyes at her phone. After Brittany closed the door to my office, she said she had thought of a very good idea for a drawing while walking up the stairs. She said, "The stairs to the world are on fire," as she frantically scribbled flames and what she described as the burnt stairs. Although initially agitated, her work became more controlled as she worked, culminating in well formed lettering at the bottom of the page. Her parents' marital conflict was apparently portrayed (see Figure 9.3) in a drawing reflecting the toxicity of the intense phone conversation that she had just witnessed. The child's visual communication mirrored my experience of the parents' reaction to suggestions that their marital conflict was causing anxiety and aggression in their child. Although I could support Brittany in expression of a volatile environment, I felt helpless and vulnerable in my attempts to enlist parental empathy for their child's turmoil. The support that I provided for Brittany gave her an outlet that was comforting, but could only minimally offset the stress of living in a marital battle zone. I had to reconcile myself to modest goals that focused on helping Brittany to safely express inner turmoil so as to reduce her angry outbursts. Brittany had to work hard to conserve her energies in the face of parental conflict. Her art expression included metaphorical reference to the conflict within which she struggled to survive. The volatile image of "the stairs to the world on fire" would seem to symbolically depict not only walking up the stairs to my office but also internalization of a marital conflict that was like a bubbling cauldron.

Sadly, even after the divorce, intense parental conflict continued. My ability to help this child was very limited. When I met with either parent, attempts to discourage displays of parental conflict were not well received. Taking sides with either parent would reinforce the parental split. On the other hand, my recommendations that they protect Brittany from witnessing their conflict stirred up indignation. Each parent was convinced that the other was wrong. In the context of a no-win situation, the therapy ended without closure. I felt angry and impotent. This was not my first (or last) experience of feeling heartbroken in working with a child caught within a parental war-zone. For better or worse, my own feelings mirrored the child's experience of helpless rage and powerlessness. In working with Brittany, both her art and my understanding of it served as a container for her emotional intensity. I had to be content with therapeutic goals that focused on helping to release steam from the pressure cooker to reduce explosive tendencies. In the end, it is likely that I was also the target of blame for lack of success in eliminating the behavior problems. In essence, I felt that I was viewed as disposable, just

Figure 9.3 Stairs on fire by Brittany

as spouses and children may feel when severe discord breaks up a family (Wallerstien et al., 2000).

Losing Parental Support for Therapy

Hereditary factors, such as tendencies to be hyperactive or shy, have certain physical characteristics, or possess specific aptitudes and talents, may well be understood by biological parents who share these qualities. Biological parents may provide an understanding of hereditary and historical aspects of a child's life. This may be done explicitly through a narrative description of the child and parental roles; it may also be conveyed through parents' behaviors and interactions that the therapist observes and experiences relationally. For example, sometimes a parent is very nervous about separating from a child at the onset of the session. The quality of such anxiety can reflect the child's difficulties. It may relate to a general biological tendency towards anxiety that is shared by parent and child, a parent's fear of being alone to which the child is responsive, parental insecurity about being replaced by the therapist, fear of judgment by the therapist, distrust for the therapist's ability to help, parental reactivity in response to the child's phobias, and other possibilities. It is best to treat parental reactions with great respect and to validate concerns. Sometimes parental styles do not seem helpful to the child and may undermine therapeutic goals. In the following case, the presence of anxiety was a factor suggesting underlying relational, physiological, and hereditary origins.

It is not easy to figure out how much indulgence or comfort to provide to an anxious parent to best serve the child's treatment. The treatment of 8-year-old "Franny," who was fragile due to anxiety relating to an intestinal blockage that had been life threatening 2 years earlier, is a case in point. Her condition had resulted in severe weight loss and ongoing fears including those of foods, robbers, and strangers. Franny was often reluctant to participate in activities, which led her mother to think that her daughter would be afraid to attend the sessions. Although extremely soft-spoken, Franny attended the sessions willingly and took pleasure in the sense of empowerment inherent in art processes. When asked to draw a picture of herself, Franny depicted the experience of watching a wounded bird from her window at a bird feeder (see Figure 9.4). Whereas the bird is colorful and prominent, she portrayed herself as a tiny figure sitting in the bottom-right corner. She described the beautiful bird that was going to get better because of the water and food she had provided. In depicting the tiny, seemingly splayed image of herself and in placing central focus on the wounded bird, Franny safely conveyed her own vulnerability in a manner that allowed her to feel a sense of empowerment and control.

Another means of therapeutically gaining control took place in her use of paint that included making colorful, experimental, and contained designs (exemplified in Figure 9.5). Her process was deliberate, and we discussed her ability to be in charge of the decisions in order to reinforce her strength. When I asked Franny to draw a picture of what she wished for, she portrayed a bear that would protect her from sickness, bad foods, and robbers. She then shared her fears more openly (see Figure 9.6). After three sessions, Franny, who had been compliant and lacking in independent motivation, was a little more outspoken at home and had begun to stand up for herself. I found out that her improvement in self-activation increasingly included angry protests and negative statements about wanting more independence. Understandably, Franny's parents were upset about this, and I was

Figure 9.4 Wounded bird by Franny

Figure 9.5 Colorful painting by Franny

Figure 9.6 Protective bear by Franny

unable to convince them that although this was a difficult period, it could be a sign of improvement that would lead to a healthy resolution. The parents clearly thought I had done more harm than good. They thanked me for my time and discontinued the treatment, which surprised and confused me because I thought that it was progressing well.

When termination occurs abruptly, there is often no confirmation about what went wrong—although this creates opportunities for speculation about how interventions might have been handled differently. In this case, I wondered if I had wrongly assumed that Franny's parents would welcome her gaining a sense of power, particularly because irritability and defiance were an unexpected part of this. I may have overlooked the degree of parental worry, given the traumatic experience of Franny's medical crisis. I wondered if I had included mother in the sessions, I might have been able to gently encourage a more accepting view of the increased level of assertiveness that can come with attempts to overcome feeling threatened and vulnerable. I may have misunderstood the level of parental support that was needed. Perhaps I underestimated the mother's fear of negative expression from Franny or the traumatic impact of Franny's past medical crisis. Ultimately, I had to accept that I could not work through the difficulties with the parents.

It is very sad to feel a sense of having failed parents and child. These experiences are an inevitable part of the job. It is not always possible to help to the degree that one might wish. Although I was disappointed that the therapeutic experience was not as beneficial as I had hoped, I was able to deepen my understanding of the complexities of working with parents. In spite of the treatment ending abruptly, I hoped that Franny's art therapy experience had produced increased confidence and a sense of her capacity to believe in herself. But like many aspects of clinical work, this would remain an unanswered question. Abrupt terminations are one of the more painful experiences that child therapists deal with on a regular basis.

Increasing Interdependence Through Collaboration and Guidance

As was evident in the preceding example, the question of how much independence can be tolerated within a family is an important factor to consider. The process of growth for children involves a gradual increase of independence from parents. Although there are cultural variations regarding the degree of independence that is tolerated or encouraged, it is often difficult to pinpoint the healthiest level, given that individual families have unique styles of attachment and that there is a wide range of what can be considered healthy. It is important to assess the degree to which levels of interdependency foster growth or prohibit growth and cause stress, a process which demands cultural as well as personal sensitivity.

Ideally, there is mutual support between therapist and parents that constitutes an effective team approach to helping the child. "Ian" was a 7-year-old boy who was bullied at school and who took his anger out on his 6-year-old brother. He was withdrawn and had few friends. As I worked with him, I came to understand that he felt very resentful of his younger brother. His longstanding wish for more attention, treats, and privileges was linked to intense sibling rivalry of which his mother was unaware. During sessions, Ian was often preoccupied with wondering if his brother was getting treats, which made it difficult for him to concentrate. His hardships and feelings of deprivation caused him to experience difficulty taking risks, which was evident in his unfocused, hastily completed

Figure 9.7 Special cup cakes by Ian

efforts during sessions. For example, he made sloppy letters out of clay that spelled his mother's name, but was unable to invest in more creative work. This seemed to convey very clearly his longing and love for his mother, as well as an impoverished feeling and a wish that he could have more from her.

At home Ian did not request a lot of attention; his compliance was mistaken for placidness. When I explained to Ian's mother that he seemed to be very jealous of his brother and that he wished for special attention, she appeared deeply touched, declaring that she would make an effort to be more attentive to him. Her immediate plan was to make special cupcakes for him while he was at school and then to make sure she spent time alone with him regularly. During a subsequent session, Ian beamed as he discussed the cupcakes he had found upon arriving home from school and produced a clay sculpture of himself holding a cupcake as well as a table on which a large cupcake was displayed (see Figure 9.7). While completing this project, he accepted my technical suggestions for the first time. Although flat and somewhat haphazard, this artwork was far more solid and self-invested than previous artworks, and his preoccupation with worries about treats for his brother diminished. The parent–therapist collaboration actively facilitated his ability to invest in his efforts. The successful products reinforced his capacity to believe in himself. Ian's mother had responded well to "parental guidance" (Chethik, 1989, p. 219), which served to boost her self-esteem and provided support for child therapy treatment goals.

Strife Becomes Strength

It is commonly believed that children should be protected from adult worries, but this is often not possible. In many cases, children are preoccupied with financial, interpersonal, and other complex stressors based on the hardship their parents face, and it is unrealistic to protect them from taking on these worries. In these cases, the goals emphasize building strengths within the framework of the reality. For example, "Steven," a bright 7-year-old, was faced with the task of calling 911 when his mother, who was physically disabled, experienced a devastating fall and became unconscious. Although Steven had not been informed of the cause of death, additional preexisting stress was related to the fact that his father had died of a drug overdose when Steven was a baby. Steven's mother was overwhelmed by her physically disabling condition, which made it difficult for her to walk, and by managing her hyperactive, defiant son. In attempting to discipline Steven, she was harsh and critical, which served to fuel his negativity. Both mother and son were quite miserable when I first met them. Steven was argumentative and agitated and unable to follow rules or expectations set by his depressed and angry mother. It was heart wrenching and amazing that this small boy had saved his mother's life.

For both mother and son, there was a backlog of trauma that was only partially apparent. Due to mother's physical limitations, there was little tolerance for Steven to be out of control. But here he was in my office, darting around like a firefly while his mother sat immobilized, wounded, and critical. In spite of these difficulties, Steven did well in school and was well liked by peers and teachers. The behavioral problems were confined to his home-life, which is generally an indication of less pervasive disturbance. When I told his mother that this was an indication that she must have done something right, some of the weight of her heavily burdened existence appeared to lift.

The structure of therapy involved weekly contact with Steven's mother, sometimes through phone sessions due to her physical disabilities that made travel difficult. During his sessions, which were also weekly, Steven initially actively engaged. His first artwork was undertaken when I requested that he draw a tree (see Figure 9.8). The result was a drawing described as a "little tree," a baby whose parents had been chopped down for use as lumber by loggers. When I asked Steven how the baby tree felt about losing both parents, he said that he was happy because he was facing away from the scene and so he did not have to know that both parents were dead. "He can have fun anyway," he explained. I said that the baby tree was very brave and Steven agreed. Following this, Steven produced a precise contour drawing of a cat with black marker that he tore up, stating that it was not good.

Subsequently, perfectionism and self-deprecation prevented him from completing artworks without destroying them. For the next 3 months, Steven completed no artwork and hid in the closet, repeatedly stating that he would not do anything. As I sat alone, intermittently hearing his defiant voice, I repeatedly responded that I would wait until he was ready to try something else and that I recognized that he felt very discouraged. He willingly attended sessions, and it appeared that they were meaningful for him. Although

Figure 9.8 Baby tree by Steven

it was difficult for me to tolerate his rejection of activity, I was able to recognize that his expression of extreme negativity was necessary. I saw his behavior as a way to express and take control of the losses he had experienced and as a way to relieve his mother of dealing with his negative behavior alone.

My sessions with Steven's mother focused on her experience as a parent. I found myself frustrated by how critical she was towards her son, and I gently tried to encourage her to offer him more positive reinforcement. This was not effective because she felt frustrated, beleaguered, and self-recriminatory. I asked her about her own parents, which was a more productive direction. She described how they always criticized her as a child and led her to feel that she could do nothing right. Moreover, her parents' criticism had continued into the present and was focused on her choice of spouse, a mentally ill man who committed suicide; managing her behaviorally chaotic son; and her disability. I came to sympathize with her sorrow and repeated feelings of failure. Although I was distressed by the critical manner in which she addressed Steven, I could see that she felt victimized by him. I used my first hand knowledge of Steven's extreme reactivity as a means of understanding his mother's despair and frustration.

During parent sessions, I provided considerable support about how difficult it was to parent such a smart, anxious, and defiant boy. The more we spoke, the more she opened up about the fact that she had no idea how to be a constructive parent because she had no role models. The pain of both Steven and his mother was palpable. My job was to listen and to find ways to help them channel their resources in the service of repair. In this process, I was genuinely struck by what a caring and intelligent person the mother was, which I was gradually able to reflect to her. And as Steven deposited his pain with me, he began to behave more considerately towards his mother.

After 3 months, Steven stated that he was ready to leave the closet and that he would like to try using clay. I was delighted by his request, and I assured him that it might be best to not complete any finished products but rather just get a feel for the clay. For several months, Steven angrily destroyed faces that he formed out of clay. Increasingly, his feelings of grief and self-deprecation materialized as he described these faces as ugly, bad, and deserving of death. During these periods, I reflected the emotional quality of his expression with statements such as, "That guy feels really bad about himself." Sometimes I would say, "He feels like he is bad, but it seems like he hasn't done anything wrong." At which time Steven would mercilessly squash the face, and I would articulate grief and sadness. It was clearly helpful for Steven to repeat this process as a means of processing his stress and grief. My role was to help Steven convert his feelings of badness and unnamed dread into a structured and manageable form. When left to fester, the impact of trauma and grief is corrosive. In Steven's case this had resulted in unmanageable anxiety.

Steven's mother became increasingly able to be positive and supportive towards her son, mirroring the manner in which I had been positive with her. It would be fair to say that a dual transference was involved. Chethik's (1989) notion of "transference parenting" was operational here, incorporating a framework in which "the therapist acts and functions as a nurturing parent to the troubled adult and this 'sustenance' allows the parent to provide more adequately for his/her child" (p. 233). Similarly, when Steven deposited his toxicity with me, I became an equivalent for the parent who can survive volatility.

Previously, Steven's mother had relied on her critical mother for help with Steven, thereby perpetuating the cycle of deprecation. Based on what Steven had revealed during his sessions (regarding the innocent clay faces that were deemed bad), I told his mother that I thought it was possible that Steven believed her medical problems, and even his father's death, were his fault. Although she had never considered this, she stated that she could understand this because she habitually blamed herself. During the course of our work, she became increasingly able to find additional adults to rely on for help with her son including a neighbor who was extremely fond of Steven and who encouraged him to channel his intense energy into sports activities. This led to Steven's passionate interest in playing basketball.

As Steven became more aware of his strengths, he created a broccoli-stalk character out of clay. This character was stored and used during several sessions and was a positive male figure about whom Steven created a narrative that began with his birth followed by descriptions of hardships and victories. These involved illness and death of parents and the difficulties of trying to become a professional basketball player. The character, whom we referred to as "Broccoli," suffered many defeats but did eventually become a champion athlete. Steven created rough, undeveloped environments including Broccoli's home and basketball court. It was noteworthy that this character lived alone and was very independent, which caused me to remark about how, even as a child, Broccoli had to take care of himself. This was obviously an equivalent for Steven's circumstances that necessitated finding ways to cope with extreme loss and hardship, a task that required strengths that were beyond his years and that had placed him under enormous stress.

During final sessions, Steven expressed the desire to draw again. He chose to use oil pastels and set out to draw tropical fish, an interest of his. He was initially discouraged by the messy qualities of the medium and destroyed his work, harkening back to the self-defeating perfectionism of initial sessions and serving as a reminder of his vulnerability. Before us on the table sat many of his crumpled efforts. I gently smoothed out a crumpled paper, and started to color it in with what I said was a water background. I pointed out that the wrinkles in the paper made it look like the ocean. He was quite intrigued by this and asked me to draw a black line down the middle so that we could work side by side. He then drew a fish that I copied, which clearly pleased him as it communicated my valuing his expression. Steven proceeded to draw a smaller fish that I found very touching (see Figure 9.9). I said that the two fish together reminded me of the two of us

Figure 9.9 Fish swimming: collaborative art

Figure 9.10 Fish by Steven

working side by side and that it had meant a lot to me that he allowed me to help him during the time he and his mother had been seeing me.

During the next and final session, Steven said that he would like to do a watercolor painting of a fish, a process in which he invested great care and thoughtfulness (see Figure 9.10). Upon completion, I asked him to tell about the qualities of the fish, which he then described as swimming around on his own and sometimes meeting other fish but mostly being independent and finding food for himself. We agreed that this fish appeared very smart and capable and, in these qualities, similar to the boy who had painted him.

Steven and his mother had benefitted from a therapeutic experience that had encouraged both parties to utilize my support. Steven's art therapy expression had allowed him to discharge devastating fears and grief that ultimately served to bring forth increased self-regulation and strength. Parental involvement was a crucial component as it reinforced the possibility for a meaningful parent–child connection. Both mother and child benefitted from using the therapeutic relationship as a container for struggles involving serious self-deprecation as it facilitated a decrease in the mutual tendency to reinforce these feelings in each other. Although difficulties and unresolved areas remained at the end of therapy, the likelihood of continued growth had been initiated. At the conclusion of therapy, the torch was passed from the therapist to the parent. Although the processing of trauma and grief would likely remain an important fact of life for Steven and his mother, the progress indicated that they possessed the strength to master such difficulties when given support. This case exemplifies a situation in which conditions were far from ideal, necessitating flexibility and acceptance of tragedy. The most pressing task initially was to address significant self-hatred that resulted from intense grief. This made it possible to access the considerable strengths of parent and child. The question of telling Steven more about his father's death had yet to be addressed, raising the question of if or when it would ever be the right time to discuss this.

In theory, it would be preferable for Steven to be afforded the opportunity to be more carefree and for his mother to be physically well. Such freedom from affliction was not part of his reality. In this case, a high level of independence on the part of the child was necessary for his survival. The strife of his situation had maximized these strengths, which became important cornerstones of the treatment process.

Conclusion

Although parents are potential allies whose influence can be immeasurably beneficial, their impact is powerful and highly evocative. In the best of situations, the art therapy relationship provides opportunities for children to repair disruptions in their development while accessing parental strengths to ensure continued growth and a sense of security for the children and increased confidence on the part of parents. Regardless, the active inclusion of parents provides information that can be used to boost the child's therapeutic work. Questions regarding how to best approach each family system present themselves in unforeseen ways. Sometimes the results are gratifying and at other times, they are disappointing, making it important to value even seemingly small therapeutic gains. Although there is often the wish for a "Hollywood" happy ending, this is virtually impossible; growth, strife, and struggle continue well beyond the treatment process.

Part V

Art-Based Attunement

Facilitating Repair

10 Mentalization, Trauma, Attachment, and Art Therapy Narratives

Mentalization in Development, Therapy, and the Community

Although *mentalization* is a relatively new term, there is nothing new about the process as a component of both therapy and interpersonal experience. This psychosocial function is as ancient as human relatedness. In the 1990s, the term was applied to studies of autism and schizophrenia (Allen & Fonagy, 2006). More recently, Fonagy et al. (2004) described mentalization as an attachment-based aspect of psychosocial development that occurs in parent–child and therapeutic relationships. It involves the capacity for mutual reflection and the ability to share feeling states. Bowlby's (1988) research regarding the role of attachment in assuring self-continuity for human beings has provided the foundation for current exploration. Schore (2003) compiled research supporting the neurobiological basis for the role of parent–child interpersonal attachment experiences in self-development. Infant brain development in the context of attachment involves the expansion of the frontal lobe, a region responsible for communally oriented functioning (Fonagy et al., 2004). Relational capacities that develop early in life later become the basis for a sense of community.

Mentalization is acquired gradually during the first 6 years of life in the context of secure attachment relationships between children and their caregivers and involves the capacity to make sense of thoughts and feelings of self and others. This is the basis for both regulating emotions and engaging relationally (Bateman & Fonagy, 2006). Mentalization is transmitted generationally. Parents who are incapable of empathy or emotional regulation do not handle and respond to their infants reflectively, which perpetuates a cycle of interpersonal disconnection. The knowledge of the potential effects of this phenomenon provides the impetus for therapists to provide treatment that fosters interpersonal strengths. Ultimately, the capacity to care about and understand others helps both individuals and society.

Munich (2006) defines the sequences of the psychosocial developmental process of mentalization: the early roots of mentalization, occurring during infancy, are characterized by acting and reacting, with high levels of emotional arousal. Responsive caregivers reflect and respond to their infants in a manner that helps to foster self-awareness of reactive states. In the context of secure attachment, preschool children experience early markers of mentalization that include reflective and flexible thinking, empathy, and realistic attunement to others. Symbolic, imaginative, and interpretive thinking about self and others, in combination with representational and autobiographical agency, indicate "mentalization proper" (Munich, 2006, p. 145). Children engage in symbolic expression through play and artwork that lays the groundwork for mentalization to develop. Imaginative and symbolic processes, as well as reflection and validation of self-states from caregivers, contribute to later relational abilities such as being able to "read" others and to experience mutuality. Mentalization involves "the capacity to construct a realistic assessment of intentional mental states in self and others, but also the capacity to empathize with the emotional experience of the other" (Kernberg, 2012, p. 65).

Mentalization and the Developing Brain

As mentioned earlier in this book, Schore (2003) compiled research on brain development that highlights alternating sequences of right- and left-hemisphere brain growth such that emotion-focused experience in the right hemisphere is followed by development of cognitive understanding in the left hemisphere. During the first 10–18 months of life, this alternating process enables the child to make sense of emotional and physical experience. It is an aspect of neurological development that is relationship dependent. As the parent responds, reflects, and reinforces the need-based states expressed by the infant, the baby begins to develop the capacity to understand both his or her own mind and the mind of another person. These are critical ingredients of the self that assist in regulating affect, experiencing empathy, and negotiating interpersonal relationships. Such mentalization abilities are operational in relationships and can be facilitated by therapy.

> Psychotherapy, in all its incarnations, is about mentalizing. Psychotherapists generally (a) aim to establish an attachment relationship with the patient, (b) aim to use this relationship to create an interpersonal context where understanding of mental states becomes a focus, and (c) attempt (mostly implicitly) to recreate a situation where the patient's self is recognized as intentional and real by the therapist and is clearly perceived as occurring by the patient.
>
> (Fonagy et al., 2004, p. 368)

Many cognitively and dynamically oriented psychotherapists explicitly incorporate treatment goals and methods that emphasize mentalization (Allen & Fonagy, 2006). The concept is especially useful for treating trauma and attachment disruption because mentalizing functions are frequently compromised in these cases.

Disruptions in Mentalization

Due to the fact that early relationships are crucial in establishing secure selfhood, children who experience early attachment disruptions may not develop the capacity for coherent autobiographical narratives. Similarly, trauma disrupts self-coherence, a function that is linked to security and safety. Both trauma and disrupted attachment cause impaired ability to organize and express personal states (Schore, 1994) that are necessary to the experience of a cohesive self. Traumatic experiences and disrupted attachment serve to produce a "rigidification of self-state boundaries that transforms normal processes into pathological structure" (Bromberg, 2011, p. 47).

Severely traumatized children have often lived with damaging experiences for prolonged periods of time. Complex trauma is characterized by disorganized states that interfere with the ability to make coherent sense of experiences and relationships. This level of confusion can cause not only inappropriate and destructive behaviors but also living in an enraged, disconnected, or deflated state (van der Kolk, 2005).

Imagination as Opposed to Reality

Symbolic expression makes possible the communication of disturbing themes with a modicum of personal distance and is a useful component of treatment for children who experience anxiety and disorganization resulting from trauma or disrupted early attachment. As already noted, the ability to engage in imaginative and symbolic expression is a developmental cornerstone for the relational well being in children; it provides a training ground for understanding self and others. Therapists encourage children to link symbolic expression to important real-life experiences, but only when they are ready to tolerate such reflection as a result of reduced levels of reactivity and anxiety.

One of the earliest art therapists, Margaret Naumburg, provided case studies describing the evolution of meaningful visual narratives that illustrate mentalization as a focus in therapy. In the foreword to the first edition of Naumburg's *An Introduction to Art Therapy*, Lewis (1973) described the approach as "a way of stating mixed and poorly understood feelings in an attempt to bring them into clarity and order in the form of a composition" (p. v). Naumburg's (1973) case studies illustrate how art expression, in the context of the therapeutic relationship, is a means of reflecting and organizing reactive states so that they are gradually transformed into coherent visual narratives. This is a means of repairing the disorganization that results from developmental disruptions. The art products are representations that facilitate reflective process and provide validation of internal states upon which a shared understanding of the self can be constructed. The art and relational processes reinforce self-agency, resulting in a decrease in behavior problems in children.

Art Therapy Narratives and Mentalization

Facilitating the Course of Mentalization

Child art therapy provides the opportunity for children to make sense of confusing emotional states and incorporates a mentalization focus due to its emphasis on developmental functions, meaningful expression, and depiction of reactive states that can then be understood relationally. This process involves symbolizing previously overwhelming experiential states and gradually replacing them with coherent self-representational narratives. For children who have experienced severe trauma, therapy provides the context within which to formulate a coherent autobiographical narrative. The ability to express emotions and personal themes with increasing clarity indicates therapeutic progress. Art therapists elicit and guide meaningful expression within this process.

Creating the Beginning of a Narrative Through Art Process

The following vignette illustrates an encounter in which the focus was stabilization and the beginning of sharing traumatic stress. It exemplifies the use of media in expressing and controlling disclosure of traumatic reactions. In this case, the encounter was short term, necessitating very modest goals.

"Jacob" was a frail 7-year-old boy who had been physically abused by his stepfather for a period of several years and who now resided in foster care. His mother had not protected him from the violence. When I first met Jacob, he appeared terrified, staring off in a disconnected manner. Initially, he completed repetitive geometric shapes and dots with pencil, and he avoided making eye contact. These drawings demonstrated attempts to control and avoid intense anxiety. Jacob sadly told me that his stepfather had beaten him up and that he had been placed in foster care after several of his ribs had been broken. I asked him if he could tell me about his stepfather, to which he responded, " He has a very scary mouth and he is very big." When I asked Jacob if he would draw him, he was interested in doing so. He slowly and carefully completed Figure 10.1, describing the conditions of the abuse as he worked. He stated that he was beaten up almost every day and that he wished he could get away as he was in a constant state of fear. Jacob was unable to portray the strength of his offender, and to a large degree, he conveyed his own feelings of terror in the portrayal of the flimsy figure, infusing the drawing of the perpetrator with his own frightened and powerless state. He silently drew his stepfather's weapon, a club, repeatedly darkening it with very heavy pressure so that it appeared burnished, conveying brutality and pain. I said, "This is a terrible and wrong thing for a child to go through." Jacob said, "I wish it never happened." He turned the pencil upside down, and with the same intense pressure with which he had drawn the club, he attempted to erase it. However, he was defeated in this effort as there were too many layers of darkness. "I can't erase it. I wish I could make it go away." When the paper began to tear, he said, " It won't go away."

I asked if he thought of the beatings frequently, and he said that he was still scared and thought of them much of the time. I told Jacob that I thought that the memory would not go away but that he would stop feeling so scared after a while because he was safe now. My role was to help Jacob to begin to create a narrative to experience some organization of overwhelming memories and to educate him about ways to reestablish safety by recognizing that he was no longer in actual physical danger. As an adult, I was in a position to impart reality to this frightened child to provide the foundation for accurate referencing of self and others. This was the early stage of gaining a sense of control and establishing an autobiographical narrative.

Fonagy et al. (2004) explain that the therapist's mirroring supports the process of reflection on subjective affective states to foster the learning of affective self-regulation.

Figure 10.1 Stepfather by Jacob

As these sessions were in the context of crisis-oriented work for the purpose of helping Jacob transition to a foster home, my contact with him was limited to four sessions. To build an enduring sense of security, he would need to experience environmental safety and continued opportunities for interpersonally based understanding of his internal states.

"Stress is the enemy of mentalization," states Holmes (2006, p. 35). Often, the first goal when dealing with children who experience internalized states of terror is to reduce stress by providing opportunities for control and self-protection. Providing such opportunities fosters increased organization and serves to reduce reactivity. Controllable media can assist children in this process and serve to counteract feelings of helplessness and disorganization.

The Use of Narrative to Mentalize in the Aftermath of Trauma

The following case study provides an example of art therapy-based narrative as a tool in facilitating repair due to trauma. The creative and symbolic propensity of the client became the basis for helping her to master overwhelming states of reactivity in the aftermath of severe sexual abuse. In this case, the therapeutic process was significantly aided by the fact that the child was well supported and felt safe during the period of treatment. In addition, she had a secure attachment history and a stable personality, strengths that allowed her to face difficulties without experiencing excessive disorganization.

"Crystal" was an 8-year-old girl who received weekly art therapy for about 10 months. Her parents were divorced and she had stayed with her father for 4 weeks during the previous summer. During this period, Crystal was repeatedly raped by a 16-year-old boy, the son of her father's girlfriend. Due to the fact that she felt ashamed and had been threatened by the offender, she kept the abuse a secret for several months. Although some concerns had been raised by her sexualized behavior at school, it was not until she told her friend about the experience of being raped that the information was eventually revealed to her mother who reported it to the police.

NO LONGER CAREFREE

During my first encounter with this family, Crystal's mother and teenage sister were furious whereas Crystal appeared sad and resigned. In a melancholy tone, she explained to me that the rape had caused her to no longer feel like a carefree child and that her biggest fear was of permanently losing her relationship with her father, who had sided with the offender. He had discounted the rape although there was conclusive evidence. Crystal's mother and sister believed that father's position had been instrumental in the ensuing minimal legal consequences for the stepbrother, who was merely placed on probation and required to participate in group-based offender treatment. The intensity of their anger towards the offender and the judicial system was a powerful protective force, but it also hindered Crystal's ability to develop her own narrative.

Crystal did not appear severely disturbed. She readily engaged in art expression and had many ideas for self-generated projects, indicating that her sense of self-agency was strong in many areas. She had not suffered complex trauma, but rather a traumatic episode that took place during one month of her life. Victims of prolonged trauma demonstrate more significant impairment to global personality functioning, referred to as *developmental trauma disorder* (van der Kolk, 2005).

Early in art therapy treatment, Crystal produced a painting entitled "The Bad Man" (Figure 10.2), which she described as a dog being hurt by a man. When I asked what is happening in the picture, Crystal explained, "The dog is so scared that his ears are sticking up straight and that blood is pouring from the his body." I said, "How awful for the poor little dog. Why would anyone do such a thing to him?" The reason that Crystal provided was this, "The man is stronger than the dog and he is mean." Together we shared our anger at the man. Within the intimate interpersonal connection of the art therapy relationship, Crystal mobilized indignation for the helpless victim, who was not a realistic self-representation, but rather, a symbolic equivalent for her experience of abuse. The use of paint in this artwork allowed for fluid expression of emotional content, the runny paint mirroring the bleeding of the dog. For Crystal, this expression accomplished the task of expressing horror with a degree of distance from her own vulnerability. Her narrative was emotionally connected and well organized, a feat she was not capable of when addressing her own experience of having been raped.

Mentalization-based functions such as reflective and flexible thinking, empathy, and realistic attunement to self and other were facilitated through exploration of interpersonal content. Similar to sequences in which young children engage in reciprocal symbolic play, this could be seen as practice for later development of the capacity for a more direct personal narrative regarding states that Crystal was not yet ready to mentalize.

Unlike children with complex trauma, Crystal was not easily triggered by reminders of her traumatic experience and was able to modulate her reactions. Disconnection and numbing had allowed her to maintain distance from overwhelming emotions. Bromberg (2003) describes dissociation as a normal and potentially protective function of the mind, a defense against trauma that is enlisted "by disconnecting the mind from its capacity to perceive what is too much for selfhood and sometimes sanity to bear" (p. 561). Due to the protective impact of disconnection, Crystal's ability to function well had remained intact in most areas. In addition, although her trauma was severe, her support system and history of secure familial attachment provided significant buffers.

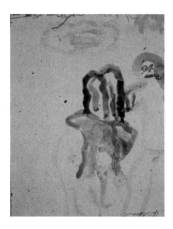

Figure 10.2 "The Bad Man" painting by Crystal

She had friends, interests, and functioned well at school. Her experience of parental divorce and low economic status, as well as being the child of a working single parent, were preexisting stressors. As a result of her mother and sister's support, she understood that she was unfairly robbed of her childhood and that she deserved better. At the same time, she felt unspeakably damaged and overwhelmed and was preoccupied with longing for her father's support, which she could not have. She stated that she had difficulty sleeping due to this worry. Perhaps her feeling of bleakness included a vague, unidentifiable, and terrifying memory of the abuse itself that felt too terrible to name.

FACILITATING THE ABILITY TO MENTALIZE

One of the activities that Crystal enjoyed was reading stories, especially scary ones. My treatment approach was to be responsive to her liking for these illustrated short stories and chapter books. This type of empathic reflection provides a facilitating environment for self-development. The first activity of this sort was to use an adaptation of Winnicott's (1971b) squiggle technique as the basis for a story. I explained the rules for this "game":

1.   We each use a different color marker and take turns closing our eyes and completing a squiggle.
2.   We pass the squiggle to the other person (who can rotate it if she chooses); she adds to it to turn it into a picture of something.
3.   We write down what it is.
4.   After we have completed a collection of pictures on a large piece of paper, we jointly write a story that includes all the images.

"The Star Person" (Figure 10.3) is an example of this technique, which helped Crystal form an illustrated narrative. The images that provided the basis for the story included two mice,

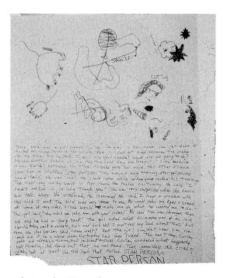

Figure 10.3 Squiggle game and story by Crystal

two snakes, some friends, two birds, a girl named Curley and a star person. The story, which she dictated as I wrote, includes several sentences that I contributed. My contributions focus on the helplessness and lack of culpability of the victim and are italicized.

> There was a girl named Curley. She started to mope because her snake died. Her dad got mad because her snake ate his bird, but he got her another snake for her birthday. Her friends gave her mice. Her other friend gave her a stuffed star person. This wasn't any ordinary star person. It could talk. It was real and it could come alive when you rubbed its tummy. The next day she went into her room and rubbed his tummy. He said, *"I haven't talked in so long. Thank you."* She was surprised when she heard him talk. When she screamed, he screamed. He said, *"I have a problem with this bird I met; he was very mean to me. He would poke my eyes and break some of my sides, and make me do what he wanted me to do."* "Why didn't you poke him with your sharp sides?" *"He was stronger than me and had a sharp beak."* Harold was the bird's name. "Hey, wait a minute, he's our bird. I'll tell my dad about that." The star person said, *"Wait a minute."* The girl couldn't hear him. He could die if he is alone after his tummy is rubbed. The next day, Curley rubbed his tummy, and he didn't answer. She wondered what happened, and finally she found out he was dead. The same day she cried and cried—but at least she still had the stuffed star person.

The process of taking disorganized images and building a coherent narrative was a satisfying activity that was in keeping with the overall process of therapy in creating a structure for managing previously disorganized states. The themes of this story include assault, betrayal, irrevocable loss, and abandonment. After we completed the story, I spoke about how sad it was for the central character, Curley, not only that she lost the star person but also that her dad could not help her. At my encouragement, we discussed how awful it was that the star person was brutalized and killed. I said that Curley must have had a lot of strength to survive this loss.

Crystal could feel compassion for the characters in the story but was very disconnected from her own emotions. I was tempted to observe that this story reminded me of her trauma, but I decided to wait because I did not want to ruin the connection to appropriate feelings of anger, sadness, and grief that had become increasingly palpable via the symbolic narrative.

The indignation expressed by her mother and sister, coupled with the abandonment, denial, and lack of validation from her father, continued to overshadow Crystal's emotions. She was concerned about how upset they were, and her disconnection served to protect herself and others from her own chaotic feelings. Once again, I was aware that the profound feelings of shame, inevitably associated with trauma, were buffered by numbness, a means of protection "from the affective flooding created by trauma—the horrifyingly unanticipated sense of oneself to oneself" (Bromberg, 2003, p. 567). Facing the horror of a traumatic incident creates extreme vulnerability and confusion. Disconnection from memory or affect creates a buffer that allows for self-survival. Expressing displaced emotions with increased coherence before encouraging integration of autobiographical themes offers the client control in modulating the uncovering process.

I provided a structure for inventing scary stories involving drawing pictures and then building a narrative around them. Inevitably, the stories that evolved expressed through metaphor the pain, terror, and shame of experiencing a rape. "The Scarecrow" (Figure

Figure 10.4 "The Scarecrow" by Crystal

10.4) is an example of this process. Crystal described this scene as an April Fool's Day prank designed to embarrass the scarecrow, who did not want to be perched on the pole. The drawing depicts a naked, detached figure pierced through the groin by a stake and declaring, "I don't like this." There is a mood of shame and humiliation. However, Crystal did not notice the bodily position and apparent nudity as the problem. Rather, she described that the scarecrow was unable to go to school due to being stuck on the post. She stated that to the scarecrow's horror, his school friends would see this spectacle. The stylized sun-face hovering above and saying "Wow!" further emphasizes the mood of exposure and ridicule.

When grappling with intense shame, it is difficult to seek connections with others. I initiated a discussion about how alone the scarecrow might feel when embarrassed and hurt, causing a "double whammy" from the combined effects of the injury and the ensuing isolation. We discussed that although it is understandable to keep a secret, this can make it feel worse. I said that it is common for people to keep secrets about abuse because they feel afraid and ashamed; they are not sure if they will get in trouble or be believed. For Crystal, the experience of trauma and loss, which inevitably produces profound feelings of shame and self-doubt (Herman, 1997), were compounded by the betrayal by her father. The narrative pictures and stories created a symbolic equivalent for the experience of rape, stimulating discharge of feelings that were previously too overwhelming to tolerate. Significantly, this was a shared interpersonal experience, offsetting the former state of isolation inherent in an extreme trauma.

MENTALIZATION OF A REENACTMENT

During one session, Crystal noticed a large roll of white paper in my office and asked if I would do a tracing of her body that she could fill in. I shared with Crystal my concern that this activity seemed too invasive, but her enthusiasm prevailed. She spread out the roll of paper and lay down on the floor. As I cautiously began to trace her arm, I noticed that she looked very scared, and I asked Crystal if this was the right thing to do. She replied that she wanted to cancel the body tracing. I felt speechless and guilty that I had allowed this activity to take place. Crystal looked pale and was trembling. I reflected that the experience must have been terrifying because this activity seemed to have made her body remember that feeling of being raped. She said that it did feel similar to the rape.

As I spoke to her, I saw the color returning to her face. I offered not only comfort but also understanding of what happens in the aftermath of trauma. I explained that often people continue to feel unsafe for a long time when they are reminded of how they were abused and that it made sense that the body tracing felt wrong. I added that being raped was way beyond what any grownup, let alone child, should ever have to go through. I said, "This time you were able to stop something that felt unsafe from happening, but with the rape, you couldn't stop it because you were overpowered." At this point, Crystal told me in more detail about the physical pain, as well as how the offender had belittled, demeaned, and threatened her. I validated how this must have terrified her to the point of remaining silent for several months but that this silence seemed to make her feel even worse. I reinforced Crystal's ability to be proactive and also validated that it was not her fault that she could not protect herself during the rape. I told her that somehow she had found the strength to cope with this experience. I talked more than I usually do during sessions, as I sensed that my explanation was being absorbed so that Crystal could begin to replace extreme terror with a coherent (mentalizing) narrative in a manner reminiscent of a mother helping a young child to make coherent sense of overwhelming distress.

The relief I observed in Crystal indicated that the experience of the attempted body tracing, which had similarities to the trauma, was used reparatively. Although I had felt guilty for allowing this activity, I ultimately realized that it created a context for a safe reenactment within a comforting and reflective relationship that enabled a sense of mastery and reintegration. I told Crystal that although the activity felt bad, she must have been somewhat ready to share her terror with me so that she could be less alone with it. This encounter, which involved mentalizing functions, also illustrated the discomfort that is a necessary part of trauma-based therapy.

Traumatized individuals may lose the ability to protect themselves and unintentionally recreate experiences during which they are victimized. My responses during this session focused on helping Crystal to build a coherent narrative as well as a belief in her own strength. Of course she would continue to face extreme challenges resulting from the experience of having been raped. However, it now appeared increasingly likely that she would be able to find ways to cope with these challenges.

Subsequently, I asked Crystal if there was a way to depict the body that felt safe. In an excited tone, she said, "I know. I'll make a book about the body." During the sessions that followed, she created full-page monochromatic drawings of isolated body parts, along with comments, that she intended to compile into a book. The body-part drawings indicated a mentalizing process and involved a shared awareness of benign physical states. The images, which included an elbow with the caption "It helps to bend the arm" and a foot with the caption "For walking, running and standing," although strong and well proportioned, were stark and disconnected. I asked Crystal about their isolation; she said, "Strange," and added that in order to teach about body parts it was necessary to take one piece at a time. She further stated that she might do full bodies when she had completed the individual parts.

Unfortunately, the stress caused by a car accident involving Crystal's mother interfered with transportation to sessions and therapy ended abruptly. Abrupt terminations are commonplace when working with children whose families are struggling to handle many pressures. In Crystal's case, significant therapeutic work had taken place. She had progressed from a state of shock and disconnection to one of increased self-agency and reflection. The therapeutic relationship and art processes laid the groundwork for continued development.

Initially, Crystal was disconnected from her emotions and bodily feelings. She, her mother, and her sister were in a state of crisis in response to which my goals included reducing anxiety for all three of these family members as well as helping Crystal gain comfort in expressing herself in a manner that was "safe, but not too safe" (Bromberg, 2011, p.104). I continually looked for indications of stress so that I could reflect these incidences back to her, a process that involved striking a balance between being protective and encouraging therapeutic risks. This was calculated to eventually lead her to gain further integration to offset the disorganization that resulted from having sustained a severe trauma.

Although Crystal had experienced severe and invasive sexual abuse that had shattered her sense of well being and had resulted in losing her relationship with her father, she had many internal and external protective factors that had been present throughout her life. During the period that she received art therapy, she was surrounded by the love and protection of several family members. These factors helped her to make good use of the therapeutic process. The fact that she was able to develop clear and personally meaningful narratives and to share her vulnerability was due to her strengths as well as the therapeutic focus on meaningful reciprocal reflection. Under optimal circumstances, the manner in which such processes unfold is individualized and based on both self-generated expression and the context of treatment. This is in keeping with the reflective processes inherent in the relationally based mentalization.

Lack of Safety and Trauma: A Distorted Narrative May Be the Best Hope for a Frame of Reference

In contrast to the preceding examples, the following vignette illustrates the impact that lack of environmental safety has on the treatment process. The degree to which a child feels safe and supported in the home environment has a profound influence on the degree of engagement in therapy. When children live in fear due to ongoing abuse or chaos within the home, organization of autobiographical narratives is less possible. These cases involve heightened anxiety states and expectations of therapy must be scaled back. Ideally, one focus of treatment is to provide increased safety within the home environment through case management, but unfortunately, such efforts are not always successful. The following case involves a child whose autobiographical narrative was subject to confusion relating to chaotic and abusive familial relationships. Although factual events were never clarified and relationships remained chaotic, the focus for therapy was on reflecting and validating the child's perceptions so as to encourage self-agency to whatever degree possible.

"Abby," a bright 4-year-old, was referred by Child Protective Services for mandated therapy due to a sexual abuse allegation that could not be confirmed. I was also informed by Child Protective Services that there was domestic violence in Abby's home perpetrated by her stepfather on her mother. Abby lived with her mother, stepfather, and infant half-brother. Her biological father claimed that during a visitation with him, she reported having been fondled by her stepfather. Her mother accompanied her to the first session. When I asked about the reason for the referral, Abby's mother asked her to explain. Abby responded, "Because my stepdaddy touched my privates." "He did?" Abby's mother incredulously replied. "No, he didn't," said Abby, looking very confused. This encounter was indicative of the murky and chaotic narrative that continued to unfold during the year of Abby's treatment.

Next, we talked about how things were going at home. Abby's mother said that she was unhappy that her husband had been required to move out because of her daughter's unconfirmed abuse allegations and explained that this was stressful given the demands on her relating to childcare. Abby and her mother also told me that their dog had recently died, which was very upsetting to both of them. Mother explained that she was sure that the sexual abuse allegation was her ex-husband's concoction and that he had convinced Abby to lie about this because he disliked her current husband. When I asked about reports that her husband had been violent towards her, she said that this was no longer a problem. Abby's mother was cooperative about bringing Abby to sessions although it was clear that she did not trust me.

During initial sessions, Abby asked to use paint to make a design. In the painting shown in Figure 10.5, she used large paintbrushes. Her excellent fine motor skills and intellectual precociousness were apparent. She took notable control of the media and the conversation. After carefully completing the well organized design, she looked me in the eye, and in a serious and pseudoadult tone she said, "I'm going to tell you a story. This is the story of a road. I was going around and around on this road with my daddy when I visited him. The road does not go anywhere. It just goes around and around and around." At this point, she picked up the paintbrush and painted over the "road" repeatedly in a circular motion. "We just kept going around and around on this road and we never got anywhere, and my dog had died. That's what we were talking about." Her tone of voice remained authoritative. "That sounds very hard and very confusing," I said. Although I did not fully understand the story, I shared my sense of the emotional experience to begin to help Abby to construct a narrative of her self-states. Her focus on the dog's death was a clear communication about grief relating to an event that we both knew was true.

I was very often unable to link Abby's descriptions to specific reality-based events. Abby did not answer any questions such as where the road was or what else happened on

Figure 10.5 The road by Abby

that day. She represented distress without revealing specific information about real life, creating metaphorical representations of danger and confusion. For example, later during the session in which she had portrayed the road, she completed Figure 10.6, which was described as a swamp filled with alligators. "Be careful," she said, "They will eat you up and you will disappear into the muck." Although I did not know the details of her situation, the symbolic expression helped me to understand her psychological state so that I could validate and reflect the affective content of the narrative. I said that a mucky swamp is a place where you could feel very frightened and lost, and she agreed.

In subsequent sessions, I offered Abby controllable media to protect her from becoming further overwhelmed. She colored and cut out numerous spiders, such as shown in Figure 10.7. She described their menacing qualities, warning me that they could lure me into danger. I asked her how scared I should be and she said, "Very scared." I uttered cries of fear, playing the role of victim, and she rescued me by capturing the spiders. Van der Kolk (2003) emphasizes that in order to begin to gain mastery of trauma, individuals need to have experiences that directly contradict the emotional helplessness inherent in trauma. Abby reduced her sense of helplessness by frightening and then rescuing me. In addition, this allowed me to understand her vulnerability and to articulate the experience back to her with clarity, a process of cocreating more coherent self-states.

At one point, Abby produced an image so reflective of sexual abuse that I called Child Protective Services—although the image included only imaginary places and people.

Figure 10.6 Swamp with alligators by Abby

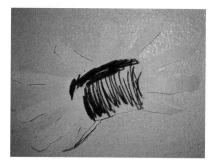

Figure 10.7 Spider by Abby

Figure 10.8 depicts "My mean cousin, Matilda," whom Abby claimed to have visited in an ugly neighborhood where a big eye loomed in the sky. She spoke in a dramatic voice, "Mean cousin Matilda has a giant tongue with a face on it, and she will lick you with it. She also has a face on her tummy." The tongue is located between the menacing figure's legs. Abby described the smaller figure as herself, victimized by both the oppressive eye in the sky and the fused, disturbing image of cousin Matilda. The image conveys a sense of psychological terror. When I asked if Matilda was real, Abby said, "Yes, but you cannot tell anyone about her because I will get in big trouble if she finds out I told anyone." I replied that when someone might be in danger I do not keep secrets. Abby did not appear upset and continued to insist that this was still private because she was going to fold it up and write in a code language on the back that only she and I could understand. She spoke in gobbledegook and wrote in mock cursive on a corner square. She then made colored "code" numbers, letters, and shapes on two of the other folded squares of the page (Figure 10.9). She asked me to keep this "private picture" folded up and to put it in a safe place, which I did.

Immediately after this session, I called both of Abby's parents and asked them about cousins and possible bullies or babysitters. My inquiries led me to find out that Abby did not have a cousin Matilda. In fact, she did not have any cousins and neither parent could think of possible suspects. I reported the content of this drawing to Child

Figure 10.8 Mean cousin by Abby

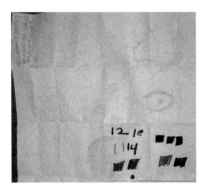

Figure 10.9 Writing in code by Abby

Protective Services, and the requirement for Abby to receive therapy was extended. During subsequent sessions, Abby continued to use codes because they appeared to provide a neutral zone with which to express her troubled and threatened state.

Figure 10.10 shows a felt-tipped pen drawing completed during the last few weeks of the therapy that terminated when Child Protective Services no longer considered Abby's case active. It is a carefully drawn image of two houses described as, "The devil's house and my house." In describing the drawing, Abby's tone was both playful and menacing. She stated that the house on the left was the devil's house and that the one on the right was her house. In a dramatic tone, such as is traditionally used for telling scary stories, she said, "Beware! The devil has traps and will get you into his lair." When I asked about the other house, she said, "My house is a safe house. Nothing bad can happen to you there." I responded by expressing relief that there is a safe place but that it is scary to know the other one is there, too. Further discussion related to Abby's vague and rapidly shifting descriptions about whether or not it was possible to avoid being entrapped in the unsafe house.

Was the depiction of the houses a metaphor for Abby's parents' different homes and her internalized experience of their conflict? Did it refer to sexual abuse or witnessing domestic violence? Was it symbolic of feelings about herself as damaged or evil? This case was characterized by numerous questions for which there were no clear answers. What was clear was that Abby benefitted from sharing internal states of fear, confusion, and powerlessness as she gained a sense of coherence and being understood. Her ability to establish a narrative that was based on reality was compromised, but communicating through symbolic equivalents for reality was an available option that was used to foster mentalization.

Although there was often a menacing quality in the art themes and narratives that Abby communicated, there was also a high level of age-appropriate play and imaginative fun that characterized our interactions. This was an important antidote to the fear and despair that she faced. Needless to say, this was a difficult case that brought up my own feelings of bewilderment and anger, along with rescue fantasies. In reviewing the case, I found it difficult to concentrate; I repeatedly missed large portions of the material, as though the memory had been sucked into a dissociative void. This is the power of traumatic narratives. During my work with traumatized children, I often had nightmares of rape and enmeshed abusive relationships. This type of powerful material

Figure 10.10 Two houses by Abby

within the treatment process can drive "nonmentalized responses" (Holmes, 2006, p. 34) within the therapist. Awareness of these reactions can enhance empathy and attunement; however, if they go unrecognized, they can interfere with the therapist's well being and effectiveness.

Mentalizing Processes in Repairing Attachment Disruption

The following case examples include children who experienced attachment disruption. As in the above vignettes, the aim was on developing autobiographical narratives to enhance coherent understanding of mental states within an interpersonal context. Whereas the examples involving trauma tended to focus on expressing danger and establishing safety, attachment-focused narratives often relate to basic trust and gratification of need.

Due to the fact that self-reflection develops in the context of parent–infant connection, children who experience early attachment disruption have difficulty in recognizing and expressing basic needs. In these cases, art therapy treatment focuses on helping children to develop narratives for expression of need-based self-states that provide a foundation for more advanced developmental tasks such as self-advocacy and empathy. The following case focuses on helping a child develop the vocabulary for expression of a basic need.

Charlie, a depressed 6-year-old, was previously introduced in chapter 3. He had experienced early and ongoing relational disruptions due to his mother's repeated psychiatric hospitalizations, instability, and severe posttraumatic stress symptoms. As mentioned in chapter 3, Charlie was severely restricted in his ability to communicate or engage in spontaneous activity. His sense of agency was undeveloped, and he seemed to be almost voiceless. Understandably, developmental functions had been hampered by repeated experiences of his mother's absences, which took place both in terms of physical separations as well as her psychological dissociative and depressive unavailability. In spite of these difficulties, Charlie's mother recognized that her son was at risk and sought treatment for him. She appeared extremely fragile but was clearly a concerned and loving mother. Charlie was the product of a casual relationship and had no contact with his father. Some of his mother's siblings provided considerable support for Charlie, particularly during his mother's absences due to hospitalization.

In chapter 3, I described Charlie's tic-tac-toe game in which animals were introduced to replace Xs and Os (see Figure 3.11). This process, which took place over several sessions, led Charlie to engage in spontaneous narrative expression involving interpersonal reciprocity. I provided patient reflection along with gentle encouragement to take small risks. We played the game repeatedly. As Charlie found the courage to emerge from his state of withdrawal, I continued to invite him to have fun and be inventive. I asked him to give names to the animals; after thinking and hesitating for a long time, he called them "Black" and "Bats." On the right side of Figure 3.11 and again as a result of my encouragement, Charlie added images of human faces that contained imaginative embellishments resembling antlers and crowns. He produced a more developed bunny that included claws, which Charlie described as helping the bunny to hop more easily. As the activity progressed, Charlie's drawings of animals were more detailed and developed. Although slow and painstaking, this was a reciprocal, enjoyable, and organizing process for Charlie. I had contributed cat, bunny and duck images (on the lower portion of the page) to invite Charlie into the realm of playful interaction, an area that had not been consistently facilitated in his developmental experience. My role was to promote what Schore (2003) describes as a "right brain to right brain" communication, intended to serve as relationally based repair. Within this framework, mentalization processes involving reflective, flexible, and symbolic thinking were facilitated.

Figure 10.11 exemplifies another collaborative experience that involved fewer contributions from me and less restrictive expression from Charlie. I incorporated some of the structure of Winnicott's (1971b) squiggle technique, but encouraged the addition of drawings that were not based on squiggles. The illustrated narrative that emerged is a chaotic scene with Charlie contributing a storm, a tidal wave with a surfer, clouds, and the "Little Caesar Pizza Man." My contributions included a tornado, added to further develop Charlie's wish to make this a bad storm. I also contributed some of the structure for the house on which we collaborated. As we viewed all the pictures, I said that it looked like they told an interesting story. In a depressed tone of voice, Charlie replied that he did not know how to tell stories. I said that all we needed to do was to look at each picture and see what it reminded us of. After a few minutes of silence, he smirked and said, "A cloud that has three butts." I said, "Do you want me to write that down?" to which he nodded. This contribution to the story implies that Charlie now felt it was permissible to be silly and babyish. Simultaneously, he exercised the cognitive and organizational abilities of acknowledging his wish to have the words written down. After I wrote "a cloud with 3 butts" above the identified cloud image, Charlie appeared troubled and said, "That could not really happen. Clouds don't have butts." I agreed and provided reassurance that we were making this up, that it did not have to be real. Charlie joined in with my comforting perspective by writing the words, "cus it is mackbeleave" [*sic*], meaning because it is make-believe.

Fonagy et al. (2004) surmise that early experiences of "playing with reality" (p. 253) constitute the basis for what later becomes the (mentalizing) ability to read the states of self and other. The adult needs to "play along so that the child can see his fantasy or idea represented in the adult's mind, reintroject this, and use it as a representation of his

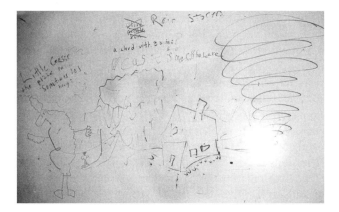

Figure 10.11 Storm: collaborative art

own thinking" (p. 266). Charlie had been deprived of opportunities for experiencing the important developmental step of "borrowing" an adult's mind. I supported engaging in fantasy to help Charlie experience greater safety and flexibility in clarifying both pretend and reality modes.

My encouragement provided permission for Charlie to continue making up the storm narrative and to request that I write some keywords at the top of the page. At the end of the process, he asked me to cross out these words. This seemed to be a means of maintaining order, an especially important experience given the level of chaos that Charlie had been subjected to. Charlie told the story in response my questions. For example, I asked, "What is happening in this storm?" Charlie stated that the storm was raging and that the house was surrounded by a huge puddle. He further responded to my inquiries about the pictures, describing that the Little Caesar Pizza man had to go to the house to deliver pizza. When I asked how the Little Caesar man felt about having to work in such a bad storm, Charlie responded that it was "very bad for him because sometimes he's hungry." After we discussed what a hard life this character had, Charlie asked me to write "Little Caesar, the pizza man. Sometimes he's hungry," as he pointed to the area above the figure. There was a moment of mutual sadness as Charlie looked at me and said, "The pizza man never gets any food but he has to go out in the storm and bring food to others all the time." Charlie shared the experience of unmet needs, and I reflected back the related feelings of longing and despair. This reciprocal process was meaningful in terms of facilitating relational sequences that had been lacking in Charlie's previous developmental processes during which he had often faced deprivation and abandonment. Our engagement in this shared experience had a satisfying and purposeful feeling in contrast to the passivity and helplessness that often characterized how Charlie presented.

Working on Basic Trust

In Part I of this book, the concept of basic trust was explored in reference to early development. Failure to achieve this foundational function can produce insurmountable difficulties in later life. Pervasive early experiences of unmet needs may result in a sustained interpersonal experience of woundedness and rage. "Eva" was a 6-year-old girl who had been adopted at 11 months and had experienced significant neglect prior to her adoption. Now in the first grade, although a bright and competitive student, she ridiculed peers and was clingy and frightened at home. Her single, well functioning adoptive mother explained that both behavioral interventions and attempts to reason with Eva had not been helpful in reducing her anger and fear. Eva's clingy behavior and inability to respect peers were problematic symptoms of attachment disruption. Although her determination and industriousness could be viewed as developmental strengths, her intense need to out-perform others appeared hostile. The sense of superiority that she displayed was a narcissistic defense that served to protect her from intense fears of abandonment and feeling unloved, states rooted in early relational neglect.

During initial sessions, Eva showed off her academic skills. She took small blocks of clay, and rather than manipulating the clay, she built structures that showcased her math skills, creating detailed, repetitive patterns. In keeping with the boastful and superior manner that had caused difficulties with peers, she described that she was "the best" in reference to these demonstrations, implying that I was stupid. Attempting to steer

Eva towards more creative work, I squished some of the unused clay while enduring resentful glances. I inquired about what could be made out of softened clay and told her that sometimes when you squeeze the clay you can get ideas because it starts to look like something. She told me haughtily that I should make something for her. On one hand, I wanted to comply with her wish because I did not want her to further devalue and reject me. On the other hand, I thought that she needed to try it and, thus, to have a successful experience of risking creative self-expression. Appealing to her narcissism, I acted as though I were too stupid to make anything. My reasoning for this was that if I acted powerless, she would trust me more because, given her early experience of neglect and abandonment, she lived in profound fear of being devalued and dumped. In acting stupid, I embodied her worst fear for herself. This enabled her to make sense of failure in a manner that was gratifying as opposed to threatening.

Eva cautiously began to make a kitten during which she appeared a bit uncertain for the first time. She formed and later painted the "tiny kitten" quite successfully. When I questioned her, she described it as "on its own." I asked about where it lives and who takes care of it, to which she responded that she did not know and appeared somewhat annoyed at the questions. But I pushed on and asked her what the kitten says about being so tiny and all alone. She then let out a little meow. I said that it probably felt sad and angry. When she did not disagree, I asked if we could do anything to help it. She replied that maybe it would like a blanket to lie on, and she carefully made a blanket out of clay. In so doing, she conveyed her internalized sense of abandonment in providing only an inanimate means of comfort.

Having explained that I thought she could help Eva develop a relational theme involving her clay kitten, I invited Eva's mother into the next session. I expressed concern to both of them about how little and alone this kitten appeared; her mother agreed. With encouragement and help from her mother, Eva set out to make a "momma with her own blanket for the kitten" (see Figure 10.12). Under my direction, Eva and her mother communicated about the momma taking care of her baby because babies need care and cannot be left alone. I encouraged discussion about ways that Eva and her mother were like the kitten and its mother, such as how Eva still needed to be cuddled, given good food, and put to bed at night. I said that maybe Eva gets scared sometimes, and her mother comforts her. Eva denied this, becoming angry and withdrawn. Her mother said that it is okay to get scared, at which time Eva sat on her mother's lap with a pout on her face.

Figure 10.12 Mother cat and kitten by Eva

This was the very beginning of finding ways to discuss and to understand difficulties relating to basic trust, and it was clear that it had to be approached with patience, given Eva's reactivity and inability to tolerate suggestions of vulnerability.

During this short-term treatment, Eva's mother was an important resource for enhancing an attachment-focused narrative with emphasis on safety and care, areas that had been compromised early in Eva's life. I conveyed my understanding to Eva's mother that much patience and empathy is demanded from a parent in this situation. It involves creating opportunities for the child to acknowledge and reflect on mental states that feel too difficult to endure. The experience of profound distrust stands in the way of self-reflection. It is a considerable challenge to create the context for tolerance of self-states. "Mentalization of affectivity" (Fonagy et al., 2004, p. 316) involves finding the vehicle for breaking intolerable experience into small, more tolerable increments that can be viewed with less reactivity.

I hoped to help Eva's mother offer this reflection of reactive states so that Eva could begin to experience the affective contents as mentalized experience. As a devoted and loving parent, it was likely that she would continue to gently reflect small increments of Eva's self-states, a task that is best done in the context of the parent–child relationship. As is often the case, it was necessary for me to tolerate an unknown outcome regarding this child's progression as I was a very small cog in the wheel of her ongoing development.

Relative Goals for Different Cases

Human beings, especially children, are always works in progress for whom therapy can serve to right the course of development in some way. In providing a mentalization-based focus for children, the goals are relative to the context of each individual. For example, in the first case, Crystal, the goals involved helping to generate mastery relating to a specific traumatic incident. In contrast, in the case of Abby, for whom an atmosphere of trauma was vague and ubiquitous, the focus was on increasing the capacity for a coherent internal narrative. The cases of Charlie and Eva focused on developing narratives for expression of need-based self-states that stemmed from early relational attachment disruptions. More advanced developmental tasks, such as self-advocacy and empathy, would not have been realistic for these children.

In sum, the above examples of mentalization-based art therapy addressed attachment disruption and traumatic stress. Autobiographical narratives involving symbolic themes, personally meaningful use of art materials, and reality-based expression constituted a means of interpersonal sharing and mutual understanding that laid the groundwork for regulating mental states. Therefore, these narratives provided a basis for more successful behavioral and interpersonal functioning.

11 Building Sturdiness

Repairing Developmental Disruptions

The Importance of Sturdiness

A sturdy structure can withstand threats whereas one with a weak foundation lacks immunity. In considering what accounts for sturdiness in human beings, the metaphor of building construction has been used. For example, *scaffolding* (Bruner, 1987, p. 74) describes the parental lending of consciousness to the child who is developing language and coping abilities. Parents instinctively and gradually remove scaffolding when the child has acquired a self-supported level of strength. Kaye (1982) describes the infant as an apprentice to the master craftsman (the parent) in a workshop where the two interact as a merged unit. The parent expects increased regulatory capabilities in concert with the infant's developmental abilities. As skills are integrated, the need for parental oversight diminishes. Similarly, within the process of art therapy treatment, the goal is always to strengthen children so that they can face challenges with heightened sturdiness. Art therapy interventions may serve as scaffolding designed to stabilize and solidify the child's personality structure.

This chapter integrates various perspectives regarding child maturation and the therapeutic process in relation to a single art therapy case. Psychosocial stages, attachment development, culture, gender, protective and risk factors, and mentalization functions are examined. Attunement to the language of art and relational states is explored in viewing the progression of treatment. This overview offers perspective on developmental, creative, and relational growth in the context of stages of therapy.

Stages of Therapy

Rubin's (2005) child art therapy model delineates a sequence of stages that assists in conceptualizing the process of long-term child art therapy. In short-term art therapy, some of the stages are evident, although the full sequence of stages are not necessarily present. The full sequence includes *testing, trusting, risking, communicating, facing, understanding, accepting, coping,* and *separating.* Although these stages may be viewed as mostly linear, Rubin emphasizes that the phases inevitably overlap, intermingle, and involve some regressions. In the following case, it is evident that the stages of therapy run parallel to the growth of the child.

"Lloyd," a 10-Year-Old Boy

Lloyd received art therapy for a period of almost 2 years, beginning when he was 10 years old. He was a kind, attractive, somewhat shy fourth grader who lived with his single mother and 12-year-old brother. His school performance was poor, and he had few friendships —although peers did not dislike him. Furthermore, his brother, with whom he spent much of his time, bullied him. Lloyd's mother reported that he had experienced abuse and neglect during his early life due to the fact that she had been a drug addict and an unfit parent. She reported not only that was she neglectful, but also that Lloyd was exposed to many unsavory individuals until he was 3 or 4 years old, including his father who was verbally and physically abusive. Lloyd's mother was a bright, caring, and vulnerable individual who had previously been living on the edge. She had been motivated to discontinue drug use when Lloyd was 4 years old due to the risk of losing custody of her children. Lloyd and his brother had sporadic contact with their father who continued to indulge in substance abuse and other high-risk behaviors.

Lloyd's mother informed me that he had low self-esteem, was depressed, was unable to stand up for himself, and that he was encopretic. He had both night- and daytime bowel "accidents," which he was embarrassed about. During initial meetings, Lloyd's mother and I discussed a plan to get help from his pediatrician regarding the encopresis. He also received an evaluation that ruled out medical causes. This was followed by medical assistance with nutritional and behavioral methods for bowel regulation.

Risk Factors

Lloyd had many strikes against him including parental substance abuse and instability, living in a single parent household, early maltreatment, poor academic functioning that likely stemmed from undiagnosed learning disabilities, economic poverty, and intergenerational patterns of abuse. During the period that I worked with Lloyd, there were numerous and ongoing economic and social stressors including living in an unsafe neighborhood, continued neglect, and contact with family members who were aggressive and involved in criminal activity and substance abuse. In contrast to his assertive brother, Lloyd was undemanding and was often a passive victim of his brother's dominance.

Protective Factors

Although Lloyd had many strikes against him, he had notable strengths including a good sense of humor and a likeable personality. His quiet demeanor had a humble and easy-going quality that made it comfortable to be around him. Poor academic functioning was apparently due to depression and learning difficulties, as opposed to lack of intelligence. Although neglectful, even while addicted to drugs, his mother continued to be loving and supportive, behavior that had instilled in Lloyd some understanding of the value of relationships. In addition, experiencing adversity may have shaped his undemanding and appreciative demeanor, which conveyed unpretentiousness and low-keyed warmth. His encopresis caused him to keep a distance between himself and other children. In this manner, he saved face but remained isolated. Although this was a form of protection, the cost was feeling ashamed and alone. As the following section describes, art therapy treatment brought Lloyd's creativity and resourcefulness to light.

Lloyd Begins to Show Himself

During the initial session, Lloyd adopted a large white board (4' × 6'). He used this to complete several highly personal works of art. The appeal of this medium was an inherent sense of power and control due to the board's large size, ability to be erased, and association with the teacher role. He conveyed appreciation for this playful venture. Lloyd's humble and fun-loving nature elicited warmth from me, which helped to establish a supportive connection within the therapy. As explored in chapter 5, protective factors such as a likable personality provide a boost to the therapeutic process.

The first drawing followed from my suggestion to a draw a scene. Lloyd explained that he was interested in depicting horrors, goblins, and ghosts, and he proceeded to draw quietly for about 25 minutes (see Figure 11.1). Because Lloyd appeared invested in the imaginative narrative stimulated by this process, I encouraged him to develop a story about the drawing. As I knew Lloyd had difficulties with writing, I asked him to dictate the story. He thoughtfully narrated the following story, playfully elaborating on gruesome themes:

Once upon a time there was this house that had ghosts and goblins and all kinds of stuff living in it. One day someone got killed there, and this ghost haunted the place forever. They buried him in their front yard right near their "dead" tree. The night was dark and there was a crescent moon, and there was thunder and lightening, and all of a sudden, they saw three ghosts, and the ghosts killed everybody in the mansion: one boy, one girl, and one hermaphrodite.

He had asked, "What is the word for someone who is born half boy and half girl?" He smiled when reminded of the correct term. Lloyd had requested that quotation marks be placed around the word *dead* because the tree was like the trees in the movie *The Wizard of Oz* in that it grabbed and taunted passers-by.

We talked about the story. I said that it was haunting, and Lloyd appeared quite pleased that he had been able to achieve this. As he was used to being passive and to being the recipient of aggression, it was a novel and empowering experience for him to

Figure 11.1 Haunted house by Lloyd

be the creator of disturbing content. When I asked him about the deceased residents of the house, he said that they were ill-advised to have moved there. I asked if they knew about the danger and he responded, "Probably not." My interest in learning more about the hermaphrodite was met with embarrassment. As the younger and less dominant male in the family, concerns about masculinity were likely. I respected the need to avoid this subject, a delicate territory, particularly given that many of the males in his life were aggressive, including his father. The drawing and story expressed themes of confusion, danger, and intergenerational destructive forces. Although such autobiographical themes would have been overwhelming if expressed directly, the symbolic format allowed for safe communication of personally relevant content.

Figure 11.2 was also completed on the erasable white board during a subsequent session. Lloyd started to draw a person, but as the picture progressed, he decided to make it a "deformed, stupid, brain-damaged guy." He described this as a "dork, with skinny, wobbling legs and messed-up clothing." Lloyd made strange noises representing the dork's distorted speech. This role-play enabled him to take control by personifying his worst fears. It revealed his identification with the victim, as well as aggression directed at the scapegoat he had created. This afforded him the unique opportunity of being able to harmlessly and playfully inhabit both the victim and perpetrator roles. I maintained a position of concern for "the dork," inquiring if anyone liked him and if he was good at anything, to which Lloyd responded that the dork was too stupid to notice his own inadequacies or ridicule from others thus sparing him considerable misery. I commented that he was quite alone, and I wondered how he coped with it. Lloyd did not respond but appeared to be considering what things were like for the imaginary character.

Later during this session, Lloyd told me that the day before, he had been hit by a car while riding his bicycle, and that he had been taken to the emergency room where he received head X-rays for a suspected concussion. In response to my questions, Lloyd revealed that he still had a headache and that he was scared. He told me that he had not been told if he had a head injury, and he was worried about this. I said that we should ask his mother, a possibility that had not occurred to him. Instead, he was accustomed to tolerating frightening experiences alone. At the end of the session, I invited his mother to join us and facilitated a discussion about the accident and the X-ray results. I did most

Figure 11.2 Picture of a dork by Lloyd

of the talking for Lloyd because even with some gentle prodding, he appeared unable to find any words. Lloyd's mother said that she thought that the doctor had explained the X-ray results to Lloyd. She comforted him and said that she was very sorry that he had not been told right away. He appeared greatly relieved when she told him that there was no suspicion of brain damage and that it was a very minor concussion.

The image of the dork embodied feeling alone, damaged, and without an intelligible means of communication. I had provided the scaffolding for Lloyd to elicit support when faced with a difficult experience. From infancy and throughout the lifespan, attachment behavior involves seeking support when in distress (Marvin & Britner, 1999). Unlike children who experience high levels of security, Lloyd was unable to seek support when feeling frightened. Early in life, Lloyd had learned to withdraw, thereby providing a means of self-soothing and protection from potentially harmful intrusions and further abandonment. He was able to connect when he did not face active distress but unable to do so when it was most needed. I could appreciate the wisdom of an avoidant inter-personal style that had developed in the context of parents who were often unavailable, unpredictable, and aggressive. A focus of the therapeutic relationship was to help Lloyd begin to shift this internal working model using the language of art as a catalyst.

The early segment of treatment was in keeping with Rubin's (2005) descriptions of initial therapeutic stages that involve processes of testing, trusting, risking, and communicating. Through his funny and creative expression of painful themes such as aberrant familial experience, danger, and self-deprecation, Lloyd could make himself known both to me and to himself. My reflection established a level of safety that had not previously been available to Lloyd and served as a foundation for more personally generated expression. This can be likened to early mentalization involving affect mirroring that provides the basis for further maturation of self-reflective and communicative abilities (Fonagy et al., 2004).

Facing Damage and Despair

Following the early sessions during which Lloyd used more readily controlled media to depict themes of isolation, danger, and disturbance, he expressed an interest in using paint on large paper (30" × 42"). Painting provided opportunities for soothing and playful exploration as well as experimentation. Figure 11.3 began as an enchanted forest that contained fluid green and purple foliage and the suggestion of a pleasant environment.

Figure 11.3 Enchanted forest by Lloyd

As Lloyd worked, the paint colors became increasingly murky, which intrigued Lloyd. He said, "I'll just go with it and let the brown take over," as he experimented with losing the bright colors and shapes that had been suggestive of plants, flowers, and birds. This experimentation was clearly soothing; it was a process reminiscent of his bowel incontinence in that it trod the fine line between maintaining and losing control. Unlike encopresis, the painting was a neutral zone that was neither private nor shameful and could be shared.

It was uncomfortable to be privy to Lloyd's impending obliteration of the images. I felt a sense of dread at the potential for sinking into a brown mess and attempted to help Lloyd save the forms. "Is there a way to save the forest?" I asked and recommended that we step back from the large painting and take a look at it. He said that the beautiful enchanted forest had begun to be taken over by mud. I suggested giving the painting a title that would describe the mood it conveyed. He responded, "Droopy," and wrote "dropy." He then said, "Droppy and ploppy and dreary." When I asked what he thought of the painting, he said that it was sad to lose the forest but that he thought he had done a good job of creating a "dreary mood-piece." This process involved the sharing of a significant physical and emotional state that calls to mind Robbins' (2000a) contention that a therapeutic holding environment offers opportunities to symbolically revisit early battles and experience a different outcome.

After doing this painting, Lloyd was no longer encopretic. This is not to say that the painting process provided a cure, but rather, it was part of a bigger picture. Lloyd's capacity for self-regulation was also apparently improving in response to care from his mother and medical attention from his pediatrician, which set the physiological and behavioral wheels in motion. The painting was a sensory and physical experience during which Lloyd could feel supported in expressing messiness, despair, and varied levels of control, thus creating an equivalent for bowel functions. When he wrote the word "dropy," he was taking decisive action and electing to articulate the experience as opposed to submitting to loss of control. The painting process encompassed a sense of damage due to loss of control as well as recovery through heightened self-agency.

Thus far, Lloyd's artwork had an impermanent quality, having been completed on an erasable board and involving primarily experimental use of paint. The themes had remained playful, although highly charged, whereas the actual subject matter did not explore personal experience directly. This allowed for a sense of control and offered protection from becoming overwhelmed. Gradually, more active risk-taking and facing of distress became possible, and the use of disguise and playful experimentation could be suspended. His initial activities had established a base for facing greater challenges. With this more sturdy foundation in place, Lloyd had increased ability to be his own agent. Consequently, he was less passive, withdrawn, and avoidant, as was evidenced by his choice to spend less time with his brother and his increased ability to ask for help when faced with difficulties. This increase in facing, communicating, and understanding difficulties mirrors Rubin's (2005) description of middle stages of child art therapy.

The treatment period that followed incorporated Rubin's (2005) later stages identified as accepting, coping, and separating. These processes do not often occur in short-term therapy or with children experiencing extreme distress. They indicate both progression of therapy and developmental gains of the individual. Previously, Lloyd's work had emphasized formulating thoughts and ideas through narrative expression

(Figures 11.1 and 11.2) and contrasting active control with submission and loss of control (Figure 11.3).

Themes Relating to Real Life Experiences

Lloyd became interested in completing pastel drawings on 18" × 24" paper. Figure 11.4 was completed in a state of quiet absorption and was followed by his inquiring about whether I could tell what the image represented. I said that I was not sure, but I thought it looked like broken glass and blood. Lloyd appeared to feel validated by my accurate perception and explained that this was a picture of what it looked like after someone had been pushed out of a window. "The guy was all cut up." I asked if he had ever seen anything like that, and he explained that he had seen it on a television show involving medical and crime scenes. He then told me that he stayed up late watching television and that he had been unable to fall asleep because he was frightened. After validating that such imagery is powerful and can really scare people, I asked if he thought it would be a good idea to avoid watching such shows. He said that he wanted me to speak with his mother about helping him with this.

Lloyd then told me that he was sometimes afraid of his father (whom he saw about one time per month) as he was threatening and rough. During subsequent sessions, Lloyd shared some early memories of physical abuse and degrading treatment from his father. I was aware that there were intergenerational patterns of abusive and high-risk behaviors in this family. Lloyd had not developed the ability to find protection from danger, which served to confirm experiences of victimization. It had not occurred to him that he had a choice about whether to watch scary television shows. Nor had it occurred to his mother that she should protect him as neglect and lack of protection permeated the family culture.

The "Haunted Tree," Figure 11.5, was also completed in silence. When I asked about it, Lloyd said that it was a spooky tree with an owl living in it on a cold, dreary night. He then added that the scene takes place after Halloween. "It's the night of my birthday. It is rainy and cold so nobody can come to my birthday party." I said that the drawing certainly conveyed a lonely mood. When I asked what he thought of this picture, Lloyd

Figure 11.4 Broken glass by Lloyd

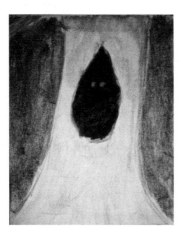

Figure 11.5 "Haunted Tree" by Lloyd

said that he liked it because it was mysterious and looked haunted and that it captured the mood he was trying to express. Ironically, the act of creating and sharing a representation of feeling alone and abandoned is an antidote to feeling helpless and isolated. The image looks like a close-up of the dead tree depicted in the first drawing completed (Figure 11.1). The personal development reflected in this later art piece illustrates what is possible as the process of art therapy deepens over time. Increased tolerance for turmoil and articulation of experiential states indicates an enriched level of interpersonal development. As was explored in the previous chapter, self-reflection and the increasingly coherent ability to represent and communicate affective states is indicative of mentalization capacities.

Lifting of Despair

Lloyd completed a charcoal drawing with a clear intention of portraying two figures (see Figure 2.1). As described in chapter 2, he requested that I hold my arms outward so that he could use me as a model for this portrayal. When I observed that this looked like a gesture drawing intended to capture a pose quickly, he responded that a school lesson about Matisse had inspired him and added that an art piece can convey a sense of harmony. I asked if he had intended to portray specific people or if the subject matter was impersonal. Lloyd stated that the drawing symbolized his relationship with me. We discussed the importance of feeling supported by others as he did in our relationship. This was the first time that Lloyd portrayed positive feelings in his art, a shift from previous themes involving fears and abandonment. I shared my observation that in addition to using his therapy to experience support, he had become increasingly able to rely on his mother, who met with me regularly and who had become more supportive as a parent. She had recently begun to advocate for an educational evaluation to determine if Lloyd had learning disabilities. My interest in and support of Lloyd's creative vision and relational states—as well as his mother's increased capacity to extend a protective influence—had reduced Lloyd's despair. The drawing of the two of us suggested not only increased trust in me but also increased trust in himself. Further, he was showing a newfound ability to make use of resources, as evidenced by the integration of the art lesson at school.

An Image of Tranquility

Lloyd more frequently spoke about his familial, social, and school experiences during sessions, although he was often quiet and withdrawn. Figure 11.6 was completed in the context of describing discomfort within his family. He verbalized feeling overwhelmed by his brother's "rowdiness." This was a stressor in Lloyd's life because he was intimidated as well as afraid of getting pulled into trouble; he constantly faced coercion from his brother to join in questionable acts such as stealing a supermarket-shopping cart. Moreover, he discussed that there was tension within his extended family because there was a lot of substance abuse, resentment, and blaming. He spoke of a family drive to the country during which he felt very oppressed due to tension among family members. He said that he felt really bad, but further explained that he saw a beautiful sunset and a large strong tree from the car window. He said, "If you see something very beautiful, it can make you feel better."

After confidently drawing the aforementioned scene, he jumped up and went out to the waiting room. Upon returning quickly, he drew a dove in the sky that was based on a Picasso print displayed in the waiting room. He returned to this print several times during the course of completing the image. Lloyd was very satisfied with this drawing and stated that he would remember the image of both the scenery and the dove as a way to feel better at times when he felt " bad." I reflected that it takes strength to create such a vision and to be able to anticipate the need for comfort from distress.

My approach emphasized utilizing the art and relational processes for reflecting and validating Lloyd's experiential states so that he could increasingly develop a sense of solidity. When Lloyd began therapy, he already possessed the ability to self-sooth through withdrawal and self-reliance. The process of therapy had reduced the gloom of

Figure 11.6 Tranquil scene by Lloyd

facing difficulties alone. He was now more able to share his experiences, which led to expression of positive affect and a belief that he could make choices about his manner of coping. Having gained increased ability to communicate and connect with others, Lloyd established a connection with his mother's younger brother, one of the better functioning family members.

Separation and Facing Impending Loss

Termination of therapy occurred because I was leaving the agency for a new job. The level of intimacy that occurs during art therapy encounters, in which both pain and beauty are transformed into meaningful expression, is profound. Therefore, it stands to reason that termination invariably evokes strong feelings of loss for both therapists and clients. It is important to honor these relationally based experiences by calling attention to the powerful impact of ending the therapy. The termination stage provides a unique opportunity to actively address the closure and to foster a healthy experience of separation. J. Novick and Novick (2006) emphasize that a conscious approach to termination increases the likelihood of satisfaction with therapy and contributes to the likelihood for the patient to feel equipped to continue on a path of growth and adaptation to challenges throughout life. Nucho (2003) points out that the termination stage has been underemphasized in the literature; and this fact jeopardizes the possibility for art therapists to utilize the inherent experience of both mourning and accomplishment in the service of therapeutic growth. In long-term treatment, it is especially important to anticipate strong reactions and to seize opportunities for fostering therapeutic work during this stage of therapy. Rubin (2011) emphasizes the potential for the albeit painful ending of therapy to be used for potential learning and reworking of separation-related feelings. In this case, my initiation of the ending was not an ideal circumstance, as Lloyd would have benefitted from further therapeutic work.

My approach to termination was to actively acknowledge the ending and to look for reactions. When I told Lloyd that I would be leaving the agency in 2 months, I said it was going to be hard for me to leave him as I valued his work and our relationship very much. We talked about the fact that endings can be hard. After we discussed this, I asked Lloyd if he would like to do a picture relating to this theme of ending. He quickly completed Figure 11.7, which depicts an ungrounded, festively colored "pot o' gold" at the end of

Figure 11.7 "Pot o' Gold" by Lloyd

a rainbow. When I asked Lloyd to tell me how this related to the ending of his therapy with me, he said that it might relate to this theme because the pot o' gold represented that he felt a lot better now than he used to feel. Bear in mind that although there was certainly truth to his perception of self-improvement, termination often evokes avoidance reactions as a means of protection. Furthermore, Lloyd's internal working model involved retreating when faced with distress in response to neglect, an effective means of self-protection from experiencing feelings of abandonment. It made sense that when faced with a significant loss, his immediate reaction was to avoid sharing distress. The price that Lloyd had paid for this coping strategy was isolation and implosive anxiety. Therefore, it was important that I challenge his attempt to put a dismissive and positive light on the termination. I said that while I agreed that he had shown much growth, I would understand if he also felt some anger or unhappiness about my leaving because it is hard when an important relationship ends.

My comments suggested that it is possible to have several different responses. I asked Lloyd if he would like to do another drawing about this ending. In response he drew Figure 11.8, an image depicting his vision of my new location, portrayed as a stark building bearing my name positioned on the edge of a cliff. When I viewed this quickly drawn image, I commented that this might not be a safe place and asked Lloyd what he thought. He stated that perhaps the impending loss felt like being dropped from a cliff.

Termination is very evocative and tends to elicit not only feelings related to the ending of the meaningful therapeutic relationship but also previous painful losses. Temporary regression is a common and understandable reaction to the therapist's departure. The anticipation of loss can stir up fears that the former symptoms will return. The loss of a trusting relationship is always painful and the fact that I was initiating the separation exacerbated the situation, implying as it did a loss of control and a sense of rejection. I told him that it would be natural for him to question the wisdom of having placed his trust in me at this point. I made considerable effort to actively elicit and to validate reactions to my departure.

During a subsequent session, Lloyd and I discussed how he had changed during the last 2 years. He said that he did not allow himself to be bullied as much and that he did not feel as scared or sad as he used to. He said that he now wanted to be an artist when he grows up because doing artwork feels very satisfying. I commented that although he still faced challenges, he had learned how to cope with them better by standing up for

Figure 11.8 Termination image by Lloyd

himself, expressing his worries through talking and art, and getting others to notice and help him more readily. I suggested that Lloyd draw a continuation (see Figure 11.9) of the previous depiction involving the cliff (Figure 11.8) to represent where he felt himself to be regarding his treatment goals. Although the diagram-like image depicts progress and was described as "half-way" towards his goals, it also implies an unsafe and precarious state. We discussed the experience of feeling precarious, as well as a plan for Lloyd to transition to another therapist. During final sessions we reviewed Lloyd's artwork. This provided an opportunity to reflect on his struggles, creativity, and growth. The ongoing challenges in his life included family stress, poverty, and academic difficulties. Although he had been diagnosed with a learning disorder, there was a discouraging scarcity of services available.

During the final session, Lloyd spontaneously completed a drawing of a hand waving good-bye (see Figure 11.10), an image that concretely confirmed the reality of an important ending. The simple drawing conveys both strength and a sense of loneliness. Although significant growth had taken place, there were many difficulties still to be faced. Looked at from another perspective, I was powerless to stop the tide of poverty and intergenerational familial patterns, yet it was apparent that Lloyd had gained sturdiness in his ability to cope with difficulties. His response to termination indicated that he had developed an ability to grieve, a potentially protective factor.

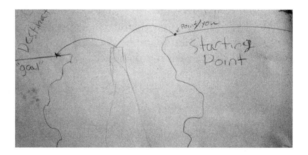

Figure 11.9 Progress toward treatment goals by Lloyd

Figure 11.10 "Good-Bye" by Lloyd

Fraley and Shaver (1999) examined Bowlby's findings on the link between attachment disruption, inability to grieve losses, and psychopathology. They concluded that disconnection from feelings of loss and the inability to recover from loss poses psychological and physical risks whereas the ability to mourn predicts more positive psychological adjustment. Vaillant (1985) maintains that coping with loss is a metaphor for attachment style. "Psychopathology is not caused by separation and loss of those loved but, rather, is caused by the failure to internalize those loved" (p. 59).

In the most ideal circumstances, termination is initiated by the child after dissipation of presenting problems. However, the ideal rarely occurs, and unlike the above case example, many terminations are abrupt or unplanned. Nonetheless, opportunities for planned termination allow for review of treatment goals, consolidation of growth, and successful mourning.

An Overview of the Therapeutic Process

Developmental Shifts

Somatic and depressive symptoms were present when Lloyd began art therapy treatment. Isolation and disconnection offered protection from feelings of fear, abandonment, and defeat. Lloyd did not seek comfort from attachment figures when in distress and avoided both facing conflict and undertaking challenges. The encopresis was related to a somatically based conflict involving the opposing forces of surrender and control that were rooted in early development.

Defenses are developed as a means of self-preservation. During infancy, withdrawal and inhibition of impulses are physiological responses to perceived danger. The structure of Lloyd's personality incorporated infantile stress-based reactions such as motor inhibition (Kestenberg, as cited in Levick, 1983); "numbing, avoidance, compliance, and restricted affect" (Schore, 1994, p. 124); and freezing (Fraiberg, 1987). The protective and adaptive nature of such coping patterns cannot be overemphasized.

Such defenses offer a form of protection that allows many personality strengths to survive intact, providing a buffer against states that threaten to overwhelm the self. Letting go of such protection is not desirable or possible until an increased feeling of sturdiness has developed. Although there is a value in sharing traumatic memories, "the need to forget" (Alvarez, 1992, p. 151) is also part of the process of integration for children. Periods of retreat from painful content were necessary in establishing a basis for building strength through playful narratives and controlled line drawings. This served as a foundation for later engaging in higher levels of self-exposure.

During the course of art therapy treatment, Lloyd was able to use the language of art to take a more active stance. Defensive maturation was evident as he funneled disturbing and previously unnamed states into comprehensible artistic equivalents. This increasingly brought forth Lloyd's cognitive understanding of affective states and the ability to see himself as having choices about how to cope. Although he developed the flexibility to utilize higher-level defenses, including displacement, intellectualization, sublimation, and anticipation; states of disconnection involving avoidance and numbing continued. The increased range of defensive functions, including some that are considered more mature, indicates healthier coping.

Methodology

Media and Themes

Media and themes can promote building or uncovering (Robbins, 1994). Building processes reinforce strength whereas uncovering fosters greater risks, such as decrease of control and increased self-disclosure. Lloyd used controllable media and large-scale line drawings as a means of gaining equilibrium and building strengths. I saw this as an equivalent of the young child's developmental experience of learning to stand and balance on his or her own two feet, a prerequisite for further exploration. When I suggested themes, media, and directives, they were derived from attunement to Lloyd so that he could feel himself as the active and creative force behind the art therapy expression. Both his personal interests and level of readiness regarding the need for strengthening versus risk-taking were taken into account.

The need for disguise (Rubin, 2005) was supported when difficult processes or themes were in the forefront. The use of uncontrollable media (large-scale, messy painting) was counterbalanced by nonthreatening themes. This promoted safe experimentation, a developmental experience that had been lacking in Lloyd's early life. Subsequently, Lloyd was able to channel emotional content through modulating the opposing forces of control and emotional expression. I encouraged direct representation of personal reality-based themes only after Lloyd had established a stable foundation in both self-development and the language of art processes. Art expression served as the foundation for growth and provided the basis for integration of positive and negative states.

Art as Therapy

Lloyd simultaneously progressed in terms of artistic and personality development. Art increasingly became a meaningful language for transforming the experience of passivity and despair into forms that established balance and integrated opposing emotions. Within this framework, Lloyd safely engaged in a level of experimentation, risk-taking, and self-representation that had previously been out of his reach. In the course of life, developmental gains are forged through an effective struggle to master conflicts and challenges, a process involving balancing rather than removing threats and difficulties (E. Erikson, 1950). Indeed, art therapy affords clients a unique opportunity for growth through the experience of artistic sublimation. "The harmony of art is attained through the integration and balance of tensions, never through simple elimination of dissonance" (Kramer, 1993, p. 67). The art therapist injects an element of hope as she or he takes on the multiple roles of audience, assistant, and container. This comprised "speaking to the child in the language of the medium, respecting the specific problems that arise in the making of a piece of work, empathizing with the child's style, bearing with him until the work is completed" (p. 120).

Art Alone is not Enough

As the primary therapist, my responsibility involved using the art as a bridge for building relational strengths. Art processes fostered self-agency, providing a context for personally generated statements. Increasingly, my role included helping Lloyd to integrate "art as therapy" gains into the reality of his social, familial, and academic experiences. The therapeutic relationship was of primary importance and was used to help Lloyd tolerate increasing levels of risk so as to gently learn to reap the rewards of self-agency and interpersonal connection. Parental involvement as well as artistic and verbal expression of life experiences boosted opportunities for generalizing developmental gains.

The Quality of Sessions

Considerable periods of time during art therapy sessions are often spent in silence, requiring that the art therapist wait patiently. This is an activity that can appear pointless, but the value of which should not be underestimated. Waiting and observing can reflect concern and attunement, a powerful therapeutic force. Although verbal expression and behavioral change may promote and indicate successful therapy, silent periods of creative work during relational attunement can also be instrumental in facilitating growth. Art therapists face the challenge of balancing the amount of nonverbal and verbal interaction, a situation for which there is often no obvious guidepost. In such cases, the therapist is well advised to be a follower who gently supports the child to take the lead. Awareness of treatment goals and attunement to the child's expression informs the therapist regarding when to offer reflection or active intervention.

   With Lloyd, it was all too easy for me to sink into a passive, silent state. His quiet disconnection had a soothing quality. Although Lloyd had not used drugs, I was reminded of the substance-abusing culture of his family and the pull of that culture, which includes escape through insulation. I had to work to keep from letting the therapeutic ship sink into numbness. I frequently struggled to extract myself out from under what felt like a heavy blanket to find the words that would create an interpersonal connection. The ability to recognize the powerful pull of interpersonal states is a tool that assists in both understanding and responding therapeutically to children.

Mentalization and Resilience

As explored in chapter 10, mentalization is an important interpersonal developmental function that involves capacity for self-reflection, self-agency, self-representation, and mutually based interpersonal reflection. During the course of art therapy treatment, Lloyd shared previously overwhelming affective states and, thus, shaped coherent representations that could be viewed, contemplated, and changed. As he gained a sense of comfort with his own subjective experience, his sense of self-agency and capacity for regulating emotion increased. "Affectivity of this sort has the aim of promoting positive affect, but it should also help us to be able to accept and cope with negative affect" (Fonagy et al., 2004, p. 436). The therapeutic process facilitated the ability to handle internal and external experiences while maintaining engagement with self and others. These attachment-based functions are protective factors associated with higher levels of resilience in children (Sroufe et al., 2005). As was explored in chapter 5, internal protective factors, such as internal locus of control and ability to engage with and elicit help from trustworthy adults, boost the likelihood of successful maturation.

What it Means to Be a Boy

Some of the factors salient to this art therapy case are gender-specific—although it is dangerous to generalize, given the levels of individual variation inherent for both boys and girls. Nonetheless, it is important to acknowledge both the strengths and challenges that were part of Lloyd's maleness (Haen, 2011). Many of the art-based themes related to the question of what it means to be a boy. An obvious example of this was Lloyd's reference to a hermaphrodite early in treatment. The fact that Lloyd had few positive male role models weighed heavily on him. It was a struggle for him to internalize a positive male image, and the longing for a loving father created an irreparable void that took the form of despair and self-doubt. Although he began to explore such gender-related questions, this was a likely focus for further treatment for which the current therapy had attempted to plant seeds.

The Culture of Multigenerational Substance Abuse and Poverty

The culture of a family is a powerful structure with deep roots that are woven over the course of many generations. It is within this framework that a child develops. When he created a symbolic equivalent early in treatment, I caught the drift of Lloyd's family culture. Describing his drawing of a haunted house (see Figure 11.1), Lloyd stated, "This house … had ghosts and goblins and all kinds of stuff living in it" and was "haunted forever." I had a sense that this portrayal was no exaggeration of the level of terror and brutality that was part of the family culture. There was multigenerational abuse and addiction that was seated in a pervasive culture of poverty. Low economic status often carries enormous biological, legal and social risk factors. These vulnerabilities begin prenatally and may later permeate the lives of children. Within this climate, areas such as proper medical attention and supervision of television, recreational, educational and social activities fall by the wayside (Brown, 2012; Widom & Nikulina, 2012). In the course of therapy, I helped Lloyd and his mother to begin to address some of the above factors as they were brought to light through the art therapy process.

The Growth Process

The ability to feel good and to develop resources is adversely affected by intergenerational poverty. Conger et al. (2012) found that interventions designed to strengthen personal attributes in youngsters helped to shift familial patterns and to influence positive outcomes in later development. Malchiodi, Steele, and Kuban (2008) point out the value of creative interventions that develop strengths that are needed to cope with adversity. Both the triumphs and threats to survival that were expressed in artwork were recognized as related to the tenacity that is part of coping with difficulties. Lloyd's mother's active struggle to refrain from drug use and abusive relationships initiated a positive shift in the family culture towards an increase in protective factors. Lloyd developed the ability to begin to recognize the downward pull of his family's culture and to consider ways to be more proactive. No doubt, he would need continued support to navigate through life constructively, as a culture of defeat significantly contributed to his makeup.

Shifts in intergenerational coping patterns evolve slowly, particularly when minimal community and school-based resources are available. The treatment focus, in the above case, emphasized building constructive propensities, both in the developing child and in the family's capacity to cope with adversity. Creativity and art-based communication helped to facilitate a kind of sturdiness that enhanced self-agency and relational strengths. The ability to engage in constructive activity and self-advocacy is a major accomplishment for children who have learned to expect defeat. Although external factors remained far from ideal, the treatment enhanced both a sense of actuality and interrelatedness with others, qualities of healthy development that E. Erikson (1950) described as contributing to the capacity for mutual engagement with society throughout the life cycle.

12 Creativity, Containment, and the Therapist's Use of Self

This chapter is about the art therapist's use of self in providing containment for children as they embark upon the struggle to overcome distress. The practitioner is charged with the task of navigating through verbal and nonverbal communication, sensory experiences, and areas of mutual vulnerability within the therapeutic relationship. Therapists participate in this active and absorbing interface during which the demands to think on one's feet require creativity, self-awareness, and courage.

The Therapist's Relational Style

Regardless of theoretical orientation, the quality of child art therapy treatment is largely determined by the relational style of the therapist. It is fascinating to observe how variations in therapists' personalities influence treatment choices. Each treatment relationship is unique, involving a process that is based on the interface of client and therapist personality styles (Robbins, 2000a, 2000b). The therapist's cultural and socioeconomic background, as well as familial and early relational experiences, strongly influences the choices that are made at every step of treatment. In what can feel like a perilous journey, each therapist struggles to become skilled in an approach that is both personal and grounded.

Qualities such as empathy, patience, kindness, tolerance for ambiguity, and passion for creative art processes are obvious job requirements. It is also advantageous to be interested in dealing with challenging relational experiences, a territory where the basic personality of the practitioner is revealed, sometimes uncovering previously unrecognized aspects. A perk of the job is that opportunities to learn about oneself are almost constant. Although these are not *always* welcome at the end of a long day, they provide the context for developing both clinical skill and personal growth.

Absorption of Pain

Caring and wanting to help can increase vulnerability to suffering, an insidious occupational hazard. The therapist's emotional reactions often parallel a client's distress. When this happens, it is necessary for the therapist to recognize that the client's distress is temporarily deposited in him or her and that professional survival depends on actively managing this condition without being overwhelmed by it. Indeed, strong reactions are almost inevitable as it is tragic to witness children who are faced with extreme despair.

Paradoxically, surviving these experiences leads to restoration, a process during which the therapist gains strength and thereby bolsters the child's clinical progress by example.

Therapists' tools for effective self-restoration are as individualized as is treatment of clients. Nonetheless, the first step generally involves acknowledging the level of pain that has taken hold. The danger of ignoring this is that it can lead to anxiety and depression thus causing diminished ability to tolerate the client's pain and disrupting treatment. Professional well being is dependent on the active struggle to find antidotes. Whereas athletes gain endurance by physical conditioning, child art therapists gain meaning and personal strength by tolerating and working through the impact of disturbing clinical states. Supervision and personal therapy are often needed to assist here.

Allowing Children to Struggle

Whether to offer assistance and how much to control art processes are ever-present questions for child art therapists. Although children are dependent on adults for help, they also need to learn to trust themselves. The amount of control or assistance to offer is often unclear. In determining the best answer, it is necessary to evaluate how the assistance, or lack thereof, affects the treatment process. Some practitioners must work hard not to take over for clients whereas others are more comfortable allowing struggle. These inclinations are influenced by innate personality characteristics modulated by early experience. There are advantages and disadvantages to having either an active or a passive relational style. Those therapists who are able to freely tolerate process tend to be better at facilitating creative activity, and those who are more active tend to be better at providing supportive structure when it is needed. What is most important is to be intimately familiar with one's own interpersonal style, as this creates the context for learning to make adjustments that support the individual needs of clients.

Attitudes About Art Materials

As a child I did not have many art supplies. I was content to draw on discarded paper with ballpoint pens and to make paper dolls out of the cardboard that came inside pantyhose packages. Subsequently, I have an appreciation for simple art materials. However, some clients do not share this propensity, and I have found it most helpful to use materials that match their unique preferences rather than my own. Fortunately, in studying art, I had experience with a wide variety of media, and I use this familiarity as a means of understanding a spectrum of client preferences.

For this reason, it is important that art therapists have personal experience with varied art processes. Intervention methods are most effective when clients feel that the creative work came from within, as opposed to having been superimposed by an outside authority. A combination of familiarity with various art media and methods and self-awareness facilitates filtering out one's own tendencies and makes room for the unique needs, responses, and associations of each child. "The art therapist's approach and goal varies with each individual. He substitutes his knowledge and deliberate acts in any area where the individual is unable to function fully" (Kramer, 1977, p. 7). In practice, this requires that the therapist possess clinical knowledge and the ability to self-observe both as an artist and a relational being.

Reflecting on Choice of Materials

Seemingly insignificant preferences can lead to significant insight. For example, I experienced personal insight while teaching a graduate art therapy class. I was writing on the chalkboard with a tiny scrap of chalk when a student handed me a shiny new stick of chalk that had been sitting right before my eyes. Although I was appreciative, I noticed that I felt ashamed in response to the student's gesture, perhaps because I had been unaware of my tendency to use old scraps. I wondered, then, why a new stick of chalk was better. I let my mind wander in order to analyze my reaction and came up with the following questions: Was there something wrong with me for using a scrap of chalk? If new and shiny is better, does this mean that I am inadequate in some way? Is it not okay to feel conflicted in response to a kind gesture? Having made some sense of my fleeting reaction, I could point out to the class the strong influence of personality, early environment, and culture on preferences, including the preference for specific art materials. Differences in preferences can result in failed communication between therapist and client. Ideally, during art therapy sessions, the therapist's heightened awareness minimizes the possibilities for misunderstandings.

Therapists' habitual relationships to materials produce the conditions for unknowingly imposing their own preferences on clients. Sensitivity about art materials is a means of providing containment and organization. Respecting the unique properties of the child's personal preferences relating to art materials deepens the therapeutic process. Occurrences such as the manner in which children respond to accidentally breaking an oil pastel stick, how much paper they feel entitled to use, or likings for the new and shiny versus the old and familiar materials provide opportunities for validation of preferences. Accurate reflection fosters a sense of security in children, thereby establishing groundwork for making it possible for them to face challenges.

Relational and Material-Based Containment of Distress

Sometimes very young (and occasionally older) children do not relate as well to art supplies as to everyday objects. A 3-year-old boy, who had witnessed domestic violence, was drawn to boxes of facial tissues as opposed to art supplies. With passion, he pulled tissues from the box, described them as monsters, and threw them onto the table. The spongy pliability of the material conveyed a feeling of unpredictability—an apparent equivalent for his experience of instability within the home. While growling menacingly, he enacted a conflict with the tissue-monsters to determine whether they would disobey him.

When he commanded ownership of the box of tissues, I struggled with the question of whether to prohibit this and thought, "Is this allowed? These tissues are not art supplies. What if he uses all my tissues?" I was not sure about whether restriction or permissiveness was needed with this child. He had experienced many disruptions and, subsequently, enacted his fear through bossiness and aggression. I decided to give him the box of tissues for use during his sessions and clarified that the other tissue boxes in the room were not his. I told him that this would be his very own box and offered him a bigger box to store it in. On the box, at his request, I helped him draw a monster to protect the supplies from invaders. I gratified his request to help him draw a scary monster because, due to his early developmental level, he was frustrated by his inability to draw in a representational manner. I knew that in a period of months he would gain this ability. The use of his chosen materials along with my assistance served to emphasize both self-protection and containment of fear and aggression. The box contained the tissue monsters he sought to control whereas the monster drawing offered protection from invasion. This process captured the very essence of his struggles to master fears.

Similarly, an 8-year-old girl who experienced distress relating to previous maltreatment, used a box as an artwork, a storage container for other artworks, and a means of organizing drawings about significant people in her life. The outside lid of the box was an ever-changing layered drawing that incorporated her name; the inside included a stove on which she symbolically enacted her need to be in charge through cooking (see Figure 12.1). Both in her life and during sessions, she needed to take active control due to unsafe and unpredictable experiences that she had sustained. Her ongoing process of using and reconfiguring the container provided opportunities for me to reflect to her the anxiety and organizational self-nurturing propensities that she had developed to survive difficulties.

In the previous chapter, the notion of scaffolding, an attachment-based function, was mentioned. Therapeutic scaffolding encompasses relational, environmental, and physical factors. Materials may be seen as an extension of the scaffolding that art therapists provide. Children absorb these influences in the service of growth. They make use of available supplies and take ownership of the therapeutic environment. With the help of the therapist, children invest in meaningful and creative use of resources, an important aspect of interpersonal development.

Provision of supplies that fit a child's yet unknown vision provides a fertile ground for therapeutic work. Selection of art materials involves a partnership and nonverbal understanding between the child and the therapist. Meeting the unique treatment needs of children through suitable art media is a result of creativity and attunement on the part of the therapist. In the above examples, the materials were influential in helping the children to grasp the notion of safety and organization as a means of repairing ruptures. The children used the materials to enhance their creative and relational growth.

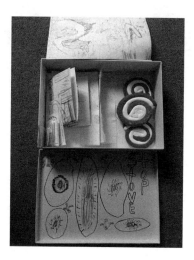

Figure 12.1 Box by 8-year-old girl

Restricted Art Expression as a Form of Containment

Restricted creativity can be helpful for children who experience internal and external chaos. They gain a sense of equilibrium and control through creating repetitive patterns or stereotypical imagery that is seemingly devoid of content or originality. Although such artwork can be uninspiring, it is necessary to remember that for children who experience distress, maintaining a semblance of stability is like walking a tightrope during which the risk of deviating from a narrow line of vision is perilous. In such cases, imaginative or innovative processes and exploring difficulties may be off limits. Rather, efforts at achieving stability are the priority, with the knowledge that increased solidity leads to a decrease in rigidity. This involves recognizing the value of seemingly uncreative efforts, which Kramer described as "art in the service of defense" (1993, p. 121). Rigid defenses allow for anxiety reduction, the basis for later growth.

For example, "Marie," a 10-year-old whose parents were divorcing, drew repetitive, tiny rows of flowers and crosses (see Figure 12.2). She attended a fundamentalist Christian school and said, when asked about her parents' situation, that God did not approve of divorce. Then she quickly said that it would be fine and appeared to feel ashamed that she had made a negative statement. I felt helpless to assist in bringing order to her chaotic experience concerning the clashing values of her religion and her parents' infidelity. Marie selected purple, red, and pink pens and immersed herself in a repetitive pattern of hearts and crosses. Intense marital conflict prevented her parents from providing support or explanation about their divorce and extramarital affairs. I hoped to be able to influence them to see the value of finding ways to explain their complex situation to Marie. In the meantime, I had to accept a significant level of restriction that helped Marie to feel more stable. She was taking initial steps towards finding equilibrium through producing a repetitive pattern.

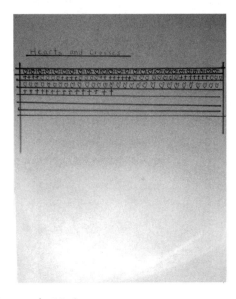

Figure 12.2 Hearts and crosses by Marie

Other Relational Issues

Relational Containment of Boundary Violations

Boundary violations from children create feelings of vulnerability, aggression, and doubt in the therapist. In these cases, the therapist's awareness of reactions can inform interpersonal and art-based interventions. Creating an atmosphere of psychological safety for both therapist and client is the first priority. Often this can be done only after feelings of danger are experienced and recognized.

Since the age of 3, 7-year-old "Savannah" had experienced severe trauma that included sexual abuse from several of her mother's boyfriends. She had also been moved frequently and exposed to domestic violence. She was transferred to me because her therapist was leaving the agency, and I anticipated that she would experience difficulties accepting a replacement. Very often, the replacement therapist bears the brunt of the child's anger at perceived abandonment. With this in mind, I asked Savannah to draw a picture of her previous therapist, as I thought helping to process this loss would ease the transition. To my surprise, Savannah told me that she had always hated this therapist and ignored my directive. Instead she drew a picture of me (Figure 12.3) floating next to a heart on which was written, "Annette is my favorite." The image of my body was drawn with an outline that suggested nudity with transparent clothes added on top. Savannah then told me that she loved me best, gave me a hug, and tried to sit in my lap. As she was about to kiss me on the lips, I instinctively pushed her away. In a state of shock, I had protected myself from an overture that felt disturbingly invasive. I was frightened by my primitive reaction and then worried that I was being hurtful to an already hurt child. At the same time, a small part of me felt flattered that I was the favorite.

In cases involving deep disturbance, the therapist's emotions are often indicators of the diagnostic picture (Kernberg, 2012). My strong response of disgust, shame, and violation was quite likely a mirror of Savannah's chronic state. As I observed her drawing an unclothed representation of me and reacted to the ensuing physical contact, I came to uncomfortably understand Savannah "from the inside out" (Bromberg, 1998, p. 127). She had permeated me with her own perpetual feelings of contamination. *Projective identification,* a concept first developed by Klein (1946), is a two-person process that involves transmission of unconscious states from one person to another. As an interpersonal (perhaps instinctive) developmental process, projective identification occurs

Figure 12.3 Drawing of therapist by Savannah

during infancy, at which time the mother can feel what the infant feels, information that is used to inform responsive care. Throughout life, projective identification is operational in relationships.

Disturbed children elicit especially strong reactions because they (unconsciously) "deposit" intolerable feelings within the therapist, which ultimately provides opportunities for containment and reflection. This allows children to develop the awareness necessary to make choices about the way they relate to others. Constructive therapeutic use of projective identification requires tolerating and decoding these distressing imprints of human relatedness. Thomas (2001) aptly describes what I had experienced with Savannah. Projective identification with children who have severe disturbance resulting from sexual abuse involves "putting into therapists, the fundamental fear that closeness leads to loss of sexual control" (p. 22).

Having collected myself, I told Savannah that physical contact is not allowed in my job as her art therapist. I quickly made up this rule as a way to protect myself. Her facial expression indicated a combination of shame and relief at the boundary clarification. Sensing her shame, I added that she did not know that these were the rules until now; therefore, she could not be faulted for breaking rules. Further, it is a natural response to feel unsafe or confused before you know the rules. I was telling her something about what I had felt during our previous interaction, unsafe and confused. Although she did not respond verbally, she appeared more settled.

When asked to tell more about her drawing of me, Savannah replied that she really liked hearts and that purple was her favorite color. I said that it was good for me to hear her favorite things because this was my first time meeting her, and I wanted to get to know her. I strove to let her know that I respected interpersonal boundaries and valued her preferences. I told Savannah that she was just getting to know me so I would expect that her opinion of me would be evolving for a while and that I knew that her former therapist thought well of her. I added that I could understand how it can be hard to forgive someone when they leave, and I asked if this might produce a feeling of hatred. Although Savannah seemed to consider this, she did not say anything more. Her next drawing provided further explanation as it depicted feelings of excruciating abandonment that had dominated her life—as well as her reaction to the therapist's departure.

Savannah was very engaged in my suggestion that she draw a house. She immediately selected a yellow marker and worked with concentration on the image seen in Figure 12.4. She explained that this is a house that has four rooms and that you could see them all from the outside. In response to inquiry, she said that the figure on the upper left is a 7-year-old girl on the bed in her room. She is "all alone, locked in, and nobody likes her." I asked why the girl is lying on the bed, and Savannah explained that she is bored, feels really bad, and is hungry. From the kitchen, the smell of yummy burgers wafts up to her room, but she is not allowed to have them. I asked who cooked the burgers, and Savannah replied that the girl's mother cooked them, but then left to go to Antarctica. The burgers were intended for relatives, who may stop by but who will not make contact with the girl. When I said that is a very sad story about a hungry girl who has no one to take care of her, Savannah punctuated the hopeless message with the words "The End" on the roof of the house. This tragic story conveyed Savannah's emotional state of extreme abandonment and helplessness. Naming this state served to take the edge off the solitary confinement that was represented symbolically.

Figure 12.4 House with abandoned girl by Savannah (Image enhanced from original pale yellow drawing)

This was a disturbing encounter during which I had extricated myself from what felt like a parasitic attack; I had preserved my own psychological safety and left Savannah with the suggestion that I valued her well being. Her sense of extreme vulnerability had led to a relational feeling of victimization. After I tolerated and redirected this feeling, Savannah was better able to engage in meaningful expression through symbolic art. Although she had initially related to me with sexualized ingratiation, my redirection helped her to tolerate her own emotional state so that safer interpersonal communication was possible. When a child behaves manipulatively or menacingly, it can be overwhelming and difficult to provide relationally based reflection. The therapeutic intervention of redirecting projection and establishing containment involved protecting myself both physically and cognitively, which served to establish a boundary that had been threatened.

Savannah continued to relate through disorganized and distressing expression during art therapy treatment that lasted 4 months. It was abruptly terminated due to another in a long series of family moves. During sessions, my focus was to help Savannah tolerate expression and to begin to integrate her fragmented states of being. Her inability to integrate self-states caused her to see relationships as either completely loving or hateful. Very often her drawings depicted extreme victimization as well as the reverse, total gratification. Her defensive structure relied heavily on the use of splitting, that is, experiencing all-good and all-bad states with no middle ground. For example, Figure 12.5 depicts

Figure 12.5 Crushed girl and birthday girl by Savannah

on the left a girl who is sad because she is in a pit and being crushed by rocks. On the right side is a girl who is happy because it is her birthday. She is blowing out candles on a fancy cake and has received a special balloon. This artwork depicts extreme states that reflected Savannah's unstable personality and chaotic life experiences.

During final sessions, I encouraged Savannah to experiment with developing further the theme of clay flower faces, an activity that she had "invented." As she worked with the clay she discovered that the faces could shift from happy to sad and from frightened to calm. Figure 12.6 shows one such example, a flower face to which Savannah attributed both an emotion and a wish, "Worried, but hoping for ice cream." In this art expression, she continued to convey states of deprivation and victimization versus gratification, but the medium allowed the possibility of controlling, modifying, and integrating these extremes.

The termination took place by way of a phone message stating that Savannah was moving out of state and could not attend sessions anymore. The above case, including the abrupt termination, elicited strong countertransference reactions in me. The termination saddened me because it appeared to be a repetition of negligence and abandonment that was so familiar to Savannah. Once again, I sought to use my reactions to understand the context in a logical manner. My therapeutic interventions had focused on providing psychological safety within the relationship. The feeling of danger was so strong that I frequently (illogically) felt that my very survival was threatened as I came to experience feelings of extreme abandonment, shame, and flight-or-fight impulses.

The Child Art Therapist's Use of Self Through Countertransference

Countertransference was initially defined by Freud as analysts' feelings towards patients that were caused by their own unresolved conflicts and served as an impediment to therapeutic progress. In recent years, the field of psychology has reformulated this assumption and acknowledged the existence of a two-person relationship. Thus, countertransference is now viewed as a window through which the therapist's reactions may contain useful information about a client's interpersonal functioning. Racker's (1988) study was instrumental in promoting the shift from viewing the therapeutic relationship as a one-sided experience to the more multifaceted view of a two-person construct.

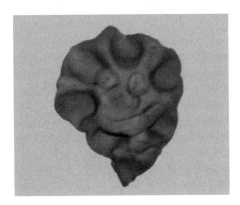

Figure 12.6 Flower face by Savannah

In suggesting that therapist reactions informed about patients' interpersonal styles, Racker (1988) identified three types of countertransference: *concordant, complementary,* and *secondary.* Concordant countertransference involves ordinary empathy and a positive identification. Children and parents who are not severely disturbed are more likely to engender this less complicated reaction. Although overidentification is a danger of concordant countertransference, it is often indicative of a positive and successful working relationship.

Complementary countertransference is generally more disturbing, as it involves the presence of projective identification during which the therapist feels almost unbearable aspects of the client's internal experience. When complementary countertransference is at play, the therapist, as the frontline recipient of the client's relational disturbances, experiences reactions such as aggression, retaliation, and fear. These reactions are informative because they often provide a picture of clients' relational issues in everyday life. The above vignette, describing Savannah, illustrated complementary countertransference.

Secondary countertransference, on the other hand, involves perceived expectations and pressures on the therapist that are brought on by the influence of a third party. Often, supervisors and graduate programs engender strong secondary countertransference reactions in students. For example, children may want to take artwork home, but the art therapist retains it for supervision purposes or a school assignment. Graduate programs may insist that student therapists retain client artwork, causing students to feel conflicted if this does not seem to be in the child's best interest. This can engender feelings of victimization in students, which causes them to overidentify with wounded clients.

Insurance companies supply ample material for secondary countertransference. For example, they may promote a financially based treatment agenda that devalues longer-term therapies or art therapy, which can cause self-doubt on the part of the therapist thus negatively affecting the treatment process. For child art therapists, parents are often another contributor to secondary countertransference. As described in chapter 9, parents can engender strong reactions such as fantasies about adopting child clients or feeling devalued.

Art-Based Challenges to Provision of Containment

Art therapists are subject to unique reactions due to the role of providing art directives, supplying materials, storing artwork, and witnessing the power of art expression. For beginning art therapists, a child's refusal to do artwork may stir up secondary countertransference relating to worries about accumulating required hours of art therapy contact. When children discard or resist completing artwork, it can bring up feelings of failure regarding professional identity.

Sending artwork home with children who reside in chaotic households raises questions about how much to elevate the safety of artworks. Clients' insistence on bringing home potentially inflammatory or highly personal artwork raises considerable discomfort for therapists and requires snap decisions regarding the best therapeutic intervention. Restrictions protect but they may be met with protest and damage client trust of the therapist. Children may wish to use art therapy products for school homework assignments, which demands that the therapist weigh whether the child needs permissiveness in this area or an explanation about the value of privacy and the difference between school and therapy. Regardless of the content, when faced with challenges to maintaining the protection of artwork, it is most useful to understand the reasons behind children's desires and demands. In addition, exploring the roots of one's own reactions helps to clear the path towards the most appropriate intervention.

The Therapist as Protector of Artwork

Protecting artwork is often viewed as metaphorically safeguarding a client's self or self-regard. Therefore, it can be stressful and painful for the therapist when children wish to destroy or treat artwork casually. At the same time, children are the owners of their artwork and need to feel in control. The appropriate fate of an artwork at the end of a session or at the end of treatment is highly individualized. Sometimes it is helpful to insist that art products be left behind. At other times, the cost of losing the child's trust it too great, even though releasing the artwork could result in consequences such as ridicule, exposure, or damage to art products. Very often, children do not take many of their artworks at the conclusion of therapy because they have no interest in holding onto them. The therapist is then faced with the question (for which there is no clear answer) of what to do with these very private objects after client terminations. My storage cabinets house a veritable bone yard of child therapy artifacts. I have difficulty discarding these creative and meaningful artworks not just because I value them. In some cases, children later return to therapy, and these objects can be used as way to help children to gain perspective on earlier growth and struggles. If the artworks are considered part of the medical record, as is the case in some settings, then they should be retained (at least photographically) for a legally required period of years.

Containment Through Behavior Management

Behavior Management, Depriving Children, and Being Mean

Although some practitioners are already skilled in managing groups and individuals, saying "no," setting limits, and providing consequences is not what most child art therapists signed up for. Restrictions, rules, and consequences may appear to fly in the face of what art therapists are most devoted to, that is, inviting creativity and building trust. However, many children fall apart in the absence of external controls.

Example of a Child Needing Restriction

Upon entering my office and before I could take a breath, "Lilly," a 9-year-old girl, opened all my cabinets and began to unload and claim massive amounts of art supplies as her own. After I convinced her to let go of fabric, ribbons, and boxes of paint, she started to open a cabinet containing other children's artwork. This time I firmly stated (in fact, practically growled) that there were some rules that we needed to discuss. I pictured myself as a large bear as I said, "Children may not open these cabinets. They are private. This is how I keep things safe here."

Immediately, I thought that if someone had spoken to me like that when I was 9, I would have held back my tears and trembled with fear. This is because I had strong internal behavioral controls and very much wished to be seen as a helpful person. Lilly, however, did not have strong internal controls, and due to the fact that her basic needs had not been met, she did not have the luxury of wanting to be a good person. She stood tall and said, "But I need a lot of stuff! I want it all." My mind flashed to her history. Although, currently residing in a supportive foster home, she had been homeless for several years before her mother's custody had been terminated. Her life had been characterized not only by extreme hardship but also by lack of positive reinforcement for prosocial behavior. She felt very deprived and had not learned basic manners. On the one hand, my knowledge of her impoverished experience made me want to give her things, whereas on the other hand, I knew that her feelings of need would not be satisfied. The safety of rules and accountability was needed to provide a structure necessary for self-regulation. If I allowed her to have any extra supplies, this would reinforce her demanding and overbearing behavior. Even though with many children an atmosphere of permissiveness is helpful, the opposite was true for Lilly.

Children who lack internal controls feel safer when limits are provided. Lilly sought to fill the void produced by being homeless and motherless; but this was a void that could not be filled. Limits were needed so that Lilly could begin to build distress tolerance. After I gently instructed her to sit down, I presented colored pencils, markers, and paper. I reassured her that she could do much better work now that she was seated. In doing so, I lent support to offset her fragile ability to regulate desperate feelings of need.

Lilly produced a colorful drawing of a "kitten princess" (Figure 12.7), the focus of which was a soothing fantasy. She told a story of the princess who lived in a castle with a kitten prince who had kissed her and rescued her from danger. My support had enabled her to move from destructive and agitated behaviors to the use of displacement and fantasy, a process of representing rather than enacting her wish to be gratified. Although frequent use of fantasy (that I later became familiar with) was yet another form of escape from her state of anguish, it was a notable improvement over the initial impulsive and devouring behavior.

The Need for Correction

Children who are very needy or destructive force therapists to face the fact that no creative work can take place without first managing behaviors. This is especially pressing

Figure 12.7 Kitten princess by Lilly

in group art therapy. Group leaders must sink or swim when faced with children who lack internal behavioral controls. Much to the consternation of many beginning art therapists, completion of artwork, let alone civilized behavior, depends on restriction of materials and freedoms. Behavior management is a necessary skill that is often difficult for sensitive individuals to learn. Surviving one or two groups in which children's behaviors escalate to the point of grabbing, throwing, standing on tables, and destroying each others' artwork generally provides incentive to learn methods of behavioral intervention. These include defining and enforcing clear rules, issuing warnings, offering predictable rewards, sometimes ignoring minor attention seeking provocations, developing contracts with children, utilizing time-outs, and working with other staff to coordinate consistent approaches to each child.

Even well adjusted children need behavioral modification in order to manage demands such as bedtimes, homework, and turning off electronic devices. Intense, unregulated behavior patterns generally signal deeply entrenched internal chaos for which the therapist can provide external correction. Just as Kramer (2000) denoted the "third hand" as skillfully attuned technical assistance with art ensuring increased competence in self-expression, Redl and Wineman (1965) designated effective behavior management as "antiseptic" behavioral correction upon which children can build increasingly constructive activity.

Behavioral limits and restrictions are most effective when accompanied by encouragement and support that convey a belief in the child's strengths and in the value of prosocial behavior. The message to children is one of acceptance of who they are as well as a belief in their capacity to develop increasingly age-appropriate behaviors. Their need for help is respectfully acknowledged and addressed. Supporting and manipulating external behaviors provides a context for building internal strengths and offers relief for children because it prevents them from being seen as too much to handle.

Containing Impoverishment

The following case explores relational containment of impoverishment in facilitating creativity and growth. When faced with a child who presented with what felt like a void, lending hope and containing feelings of deprivation were necessary.

"Ian," a 7-year-old who was introduced in chapter 9, experienced poverty, neglect, and scarcity of adult supervision in addition to continual attacks from family members and peers. Within the family, there was a scarcity of financial and caretaking resources and intense rivalry among siblings who were close in age. The theme of impoverishment was pervasive Ian's life. As Davies (2005) and Fontes (2005) both point out, economic poverty is a risk factor that can lead to lower levels of resilience in developing children. The culture of poverty involves considerable stress on parents and children such that feelings of deprivation may surface in many areas. Ian's impoverishment extended to his sense of self-agency and his ability to put forth effort. He appeared extremely sad and lacking in thought content and motivation. Poor motor control and difficulty sticking with tasks were additional concerns.

Ian, a chubby boy who conveyed a feeling of insatiable hunger, often brought snacks, and food was a frequent topic of conversation during our sessions. While eating, he took large mouthfuls, thoroughly enjoying the apple or box of crackerjacks. When he finished eating, he often said he wished there was more. Initially, our moments of strongest connection took place as I watched him eat. When I asked him to name some things he liked, he could not think of anything except a variety of foods.

During the first session, the mood felt heavy as I engaged Ian in drawing a picture of his family, which he completed reluctantly and quickly. As the drawing was rough and undeveloped, I attempted to enlist more investment. I asked about pets, which Ian quickly added. He appeared baffled when I inquired about the content of his drawing as though interest from another person was disturbing and foreign. His artworks were all completed quickly and with a sense of failure and confusion. For example, while discussing his hurriedly completed family drawing (Figure 12.8), he did not articulate a grasp of separate households although his parents had been divorced for 4 years. Due to the pervasive lack of effort, I thought that perhaps Ian was cognitively impaired and that he did not like art or coming to see me, but none of these speculations were accurate. It was as though he lived in a fog that had resulted from being lost in the shuffle of poverty, neglect, and physical and emotional attacks. It seemed as if his existence involved no sense of order or explanation—as though nothing (including himself) mattered.

At the end of the first session, Ian noticed a tiny action figure on a shelf and asked if he could have it. I replied that I would not be able to give him the toy but that I could see his longing and disappointment. I said that it would stay on that shelf and be there when he returned next week. During subsequent sessions, he hid the toy in his pocket several times and looked as though he intended to steal it. However, when he saw me watching, he returned it to the shelf. I struggled with the possibility of giving the toy to Ian, but I decided against this because I wanted to help him to find ways to cope with the difficulty of longing for something that he could not have. I had doubts about whether this was the right choice, a common experience for therapists when children convey impoverishment. If I gave him the toy, I would have been agreeing with his feeling that he must be fed as opposed to maintaining hope that his inner resources could be developed to fill the void. I would have felt better if I had given him the toy, as I did not especially want it. However,

Figure 12.8 Family drawing by Ian

relieving my own discomfort about not wanting to feel stingy would not have served Ian's needs in the long run. While many child therapists do give children "prizes," the idea of creating one's own prize is something to cherish. Most often, the results of the treatment process later confirm that withholding immediate gratification is not harmful.

During the following months, I "fed" Ian in a way that helped him to complete drawings and three-dimensional art products. Without considerable encouragement, his work was extremely lacking in investment and form. At first, he made rough and sometimes unrecognizable letters that spelled his and my names out of colored clay. My gentle attempts to encourage more developed personal themes were met with discomfort and avoidance, which helped me to see that he was not yet ready for more advanced art development. As his interest in words and letters increased, we developed a routine in which Ian instructed me to make word-search grids that included words he dictated to me while he doodled and scribbled on a very large sheet of paper (exemplified in Figure 12.9). He came up with themes for the word-search, such as "animals," "cars," and "birthdays," and I contributed treatment-oriented themes, such as "comforting things" (Figure 12.10) and "things you don't like about school." It was an accomplishment for Ian to articulate his experience through listing words to fit the themes of each grid. His accompanying large scribbled designs were counterbalanced by the task he had designed for me (i.e., to "feed" him a highly structured grid of letters containing hidden words).

Figure 12.9 Doodles and scribbles on large paper by Ian

Figure 12.10 Word-Search game involving Ian

During this early period of treatment, Ian had become a good student who liked reading. Increasingly, he told me that he liked school, but that he did not like that he was bullied there as well as at home. Much of his conversation related to combative interactions with siblings or bullies and the unfairness of others not getting into trouble for wrongdoings.

After several months Ian began to respond to my invitations that he form animals or people, as opposed to letters, out of clay. Figure 12.11 is one example that was intended to be a rhinoceros. Although the figures were rough, distorted, and often barely recognizable, he valued them very much. When they were completed, he took them home after we carefully wrapped them in tissue paper. He was unable to wrap items independently, just as he could not identify the right location for legs or facial features on animal figures without my assistance. These areas of delay seemed to be, in part, related to neglect and deprivation. Ian began to bring his favorite blanket to sessions and lay wrapped in it on the floor while he thought of what to make out of clay. I commented on how important it is to feel comforted.

Gradually, the idea of attributing meaning to artworks became more acceptable to Ian. At first the themes were unpleasant. For example, Ian depicted a baby who had been dropped, was hungry, and was crying because his mother hated him (see Figure 12.12),

Figure 12.11 Rhinoceros by Ian

Figure 12.12 Drawing of a hated baby by Ian

and a monster who peed on his monster brother. This subject matter reflected feelings of abandonment and anger. As Ian expressed increasingly personal themes through artwork, he seemed to be releasing a previously buried and pervasive sense of deprivation and deprecation.

I helped Ian to make several puppets, as he often mentioned to me that he really liked puppets. This interest had developed because he had briefly seen a play therapist who had very nice puppets. Ian made puppets out of fabric and several other materials. After the puppets were completed, Ian enacted dialogues with me. They portrayed someone being rejected, deprecated, or abandoned.

During one session, with my help, Ian formed finger puppets and a larger hand puppet out of model magic (see Figure 12.13). He described the puppet characters as various types of ghosts and enacted a scene that involved a baby and a child ghost running away from their father, whom they told they did not need any more. They said they were leaving because he was always mean to them. "We like this nice ghost," the small puppets said of the larger puppet. They cuddled against the bigger puppet and made noises of comfort. Then they climbed inside of the large puppet while yelling, "We are staying here. We like the big puppet. It is safe here." The ability to develop themes and to find safety had apparently been accomplished as a result of the containing relational and art processes. My role had been to tolerate unformed expression for long periods while very gently encouraging growth. With time, Ian became able to create his own sense of order, containment, and symbolic representations, which eased his disconnection and abandonment. Ian increasingly came to believe that his expression mattered. It was necessary for me to convey a strong belief in the value of his expression so that he could learn how to relate to and rely on both himself and others.

Navigating Demands for Self-Disclosure

Therapist self-disclosure has an impact on children. When utilized thoughtfully, it may heighten trust and increase feelings of intimacy within the relationship. Because self-disclosure can evoke strong emotional reactions in clients, it is important to consider

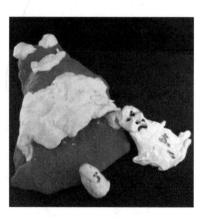

Figure 12.13 Puppets by Ian

its possible impact. I tend to limit use of self-disclosure because I am concerned about interfering with clients' imaginative processes and feelings of ownership of the content of sessions.

Ian asked personal questions with increasing frequency, which was in keeping with his need to be filled up. "Do you play sports?" "Do you have children?" "Where do you buy these supplies?" I responded by saying in a very nurturing tone, "You are very interested in me." Instead of answering questions, I attempted to find out what they meant for him. I asked if he wished I did or did not have children. He replied that he wished that I did not have children and shyly admitted that this was because he wished I could come to his birthday party and my own children would compete with my ability to do this. When it was difficult not to answer the questions, I struggled with how to best support the therapeutic process. What therapeutic good would it do to answer the questions? At one point, I told Ian that when I did not answer his questions it was because I wanted his sessions to be focused only on him although I valued his interest in me very much. He appeared very comforted and relieved to hear that I would not allow him to be neglected or abandoned. This intervention served to educate him about the exclusively client-centered function of therapy and to reinforce the notion that he mattered. It also opened the door for exploration of the disappointment he felt at having therapy only for 1 hour a week.

Representations of impoverishment may relate to economic, cognitive, interpersonal, and emotional conditions experienced by children. Often there is an interplay of factors that lead to a child's experience of longing and emptiness. Impoverishment implies that there are not enough resources. Behavioral problems may ensue as a result of the experience of wanting more than can be provided. Resulting symptoms often include stealing, provocation, feelings of hopelessness, and lack of effort. Impoverished art images manifest minimal effort, restricted imagination, low levels of graphic development, and sparseness of composition. Impoverishment may be demonstrated during sessions as lack of initiative, minimal spontaneous verbal or art expression, and lack of investment. For the therapist, this can be difficult to tolerate, evoking feelings of failure and despair. Frequently, the therapist's inclination is to fill in the void created by the child's lack of resources. Whereas providing significant support is necessary, it is prudent to avoid acting on the desire to extend indiscriminate generosity. It can be helpful to remember that children who lack internal resources are increasingly at risk for developing substance abuse, psychiatric disorders, and criminal behaviors; this provides incentive to encourage children to develop tolerance for distress and mobilize strengths rather than simply seek gratification.

Mystery, Ambiguity, and Growth

Children are works in progress. Their experience in art therapy is a blip on the screen of their overall development. During sessions it is sometimes hard to see where the process is leading. Due to numerous pressures and societal attitudes of discomfort with ambiguity and negative emotions, there may be pressure to try to force outcomes, such as encouraging children whose therapeutic need is to explore grief and despair to verbalize positive statements. It requires strength and struggle to maintain a vision of what constitutes genuine support of the client's self in treatment. As there is sometimes pressure to produce quick solutions, it is especially important to remember that when children build self-agency, they become increasingly able to behave prosocially. This reminder helps to insure that the mystery and uniquely individual properties of creative processes be protected and utilized as agents within therapy.

Both the demands and rewards of work as a child art therapist include conditions that are sometimes suspenseful, often stressful, and never boring. Actively facing and surviving the challenges of immersion in this dramatic world is taxing and requires concerted effort. Fostering creativity and relational growth in children involves facing numerous threats, such as those from children's out-of-control behaviors caused by states of deprivation, intergenerational patterns of abuse, and the larger society's inhumanity. This chapter and the book as a whole have focused on a tapestry of themes relating to an art therapist's interface with challenging, ambiguous, and meaningful processes. These experiences hold the seeds for therapeutic growth for children as well as for professional and personal learning for the therapist.

References

Ainsworth, M. D. S. (1969). Object relations, dependency and attachment: A theoretical review of the infant–mother relationship. *Child Development, 40,* 969–1025.

Allen, J. G., & Fonagy, P. (2006). Preface. In J. G. Allen & P. Fonagy (Eds.), *Handbook of mentalization-based treatment* (pp. x–xxi). Chichester, England: Wiley.

Alvarez, A. (1992). *Live company: Psychoanalytic psychotherapy with autistic, borderline, deprived and abused children.* London, England: Tavistock/Routledge.

American Psychiatric Association. (2000). *Diagnostic and statistical manual of mental disorders* (4th ed., text rev.). Washington, DC: APA.

Bateman, A., & Fonagy, P. (2006). Mentalizing and borderline personality disorder. In J. G. Allen & P. Fonagy (Eds.), *Handbook of mentalization-based treatment* (pp. 185–200). Chichester, England: Wiley.

Bowlby, J. (1982). *Attachment and loss: Vol. 1. Attachment.* New York, NY: Basic Books.

Bowlby, J. (1988). *A secure base.* New York, NY: Basic Books.

Bromberg, P. M. (1998). *Standing in the spaces: Essays on clinical process, trauma, and dissociation.* Hillsdale, NJ: Analytic Press.

Bromberg, P. M. (2003). Something wicked this way comes: Trauma, dissociation, and conflict: The space where psychoanalysis, cognitive science, and neuroscience overlap. *Psychoanalytic Psychology, 20*(3), 558–574.

Bromberg, P. M. (2011). *In the shadow of the tsunami and the growth of the relational mind.* New York, NY: Routledge.

Brown, S. (2012). Poverty status and the effects of family structure on child well-being. In V. Malholmes & R. B. King (Eds.), *The Oxford handbook of poverty and child development* (pp. 54–67). New York, NY: Oxford University Press.

Bruner, J. (1987). *Actual minds, possible worlds.* Cambridge, MA: Harvard University Press.

Burns, R. C., & Kaufman, F. A. (1972). Actions, styles and symbols in Kinetic Family Drawings (K-F-D): An interpretive manual. New York, NY: Brunner-Routledge.

Canino, I. A., & Spurlock, J. (1994). *Culturally diverse children and adolescents: Assessment, diagnosis and treatment.* New York, NY: Guilford Books.

Chethik, M. (1989). *Techniques of child therapy: Psychodyanamic strategies.* New York, NY: Guilford Press.

Conger, K. J., Martin, M. J., Reeb, B. T., Little, W. M., Craine, J. L., Shibloski, B., & Conger, R. D. (2012). Economic hardship and its consequences across generations. In V. Malholmes & R. B. King (Eds.), *The Oxford handbook of poverty and child development* (pp. 37–53). New York, NY: Oxford University Press.

Cox, M. V. (2005). *The pictorial world of the child.* Cambridge, England: Cambridge University Press.

Davies, D. (2005). *Child development: A practitioner's guide.* New York, NY: Guilford Press.

Di Leo, J. H. (1977). *Child development: Analysis and synthesis.* New York, NY: Brunner-Mazel.

Edgcumbe, R. (2000). *Anna Freud: A view of development, disturbance and therapeutic techniques.* London, England: Routledge.

Erikson, E. (1950). *Childhood and society.* New York, NY: Norton.

Erikson, E. (1968). *Identity, youth and crisis.* New York, NY: Norton.

Erikson, E. (1980). *Identity and the life cycle.* New York, NY: Norton.

Erikson, E., Erikson, J., & Kivnick, H. (1986). *Vital involvement in old age.* New York, NY: Norton.

Erikson, J. M. (1988). Wisdom and the senses. New York, NY: Norton.

Fonagy, P., Gergely, G., Jurist, E. L., & Target, M. (2004). *Affect regulation, mentalization, and the development of self.* New York, NY: Other Press.

Fontes, L. A. (2005). *Child abuse and culture: Working with diverse families.* New York, NY: Guilford Press.

Fraiberg, S. M. (1955). *The magic years: Understanding and handling the problems of early childhood.* New York, NY: Scribner.

Fraiberg, S. (1987). Pathological defenses in Infancy. In L. Fraiberg (Ed.), *Selected writings of Selma Fraiberg* (pp. 100–136). Columbus: Ohio State University Press.

Fraley, R. C., & Shaver, P. R. (1999). Loss and bereavement attachment theory and recent controversies concerning "grief work" and the nature of detachment. In J. Cassidy & P. R. Shaver (Eds.), *Handbook of attachment: Theory, research and clinical applications* (pp. 735–759). New York, NY: Guilford Press.

Freud, A. (1939). *The ego and the mechanisms of defence.* New York, NY: International Universities Press.

Freud, A. (1946). *Psychoanalytical treatment of children.* London, England: Imago.

Freud, S. (1938). *The basic writings of Sigmund Freud* (A. A. Brill, Ed. & Trans.). New York, NY: Random House.

Friedman, L. (1999) *Identity's architect: A biography of Erik Erikson.* New York, NY: Scribner.

Gantt, L., & Tabone, C. (1998). *The Formal Elements Art Therapy Scale: The rating manual.* Morgantown, WV: Gargoyle Press.

Garrity, C. B., & Barris, M. A. (1997). *Caught in the middle: Protecting children of high-conflict divorce.* San Francisco, CA: Jossey-Bass.

Golomb, C. (2003). *The child's creation of a pictorial world* (2nd ed.). Hove, England: Psychology Press.

Golomb, C. (2011). *The creation of imaginary worlds: The role of art magic and dreams in child development.* London, England: Jessica Kingsley.

Haen, C. (2011). Boys and therapy: The need for creative reformulation. In C. Haen (Ed.), *Engaging boys in treatment: Creative approaches to the therapy process* (pp. 3–40). New York, NY: Routledge.

Herman, J. (1997). *Trauma and recovery: The aftermath of violence—From domestic abuse to political terror.* New York, NY: Basic Books.

Holmes, J. (2006). Mentalizing from a psychoanalytic perspective: What's new? In J. G. Allen & P. Fonagy (Eds.). *Handbook of mentalization-based treatment* (pp. 31–50). Chichester, England: Wiley.

Hughs, D. (1997). *Facilitating developmental attachment.* Northvale, NJ: Jason Aronson.

Kaye, K. (1982). *The mental and social life of babies: How parents create persons.* Chicago, IL: Chicago University Press.

Kellogg, R. (1970). *Analyzing children's art.* Palo Alto, CA : Mayfield.

Kernberg, O. F. (2012). *The inseparable nature of love and aggression: Clinical and theoretical perspectives.* Arlington, VA: American Psychiatric.

Klein, M. (1946). Notes on some schizoid mechanisms. *International Journal of Psychoanalysis, 27*, 99–110.

Klorer, P. G. (2008). Expressive therapy for severe maltreatment and attachment disorders: A neuroscience framework. In C. A. Malchiodi (Ed.), *Creative interventions with traumatized children* (pp. 43–61). New York, NY: Guilford Press.

Koppitz, E. (1968). *Psychological evaluation of children's figure drawings.* New York, NY: Grune & Stratton.

Kramer, E. (1977). *Art therapy in a children's community.* New York: Schocken Books.

Kramer, E. (1993). *Art as therapy with children.* Chicago, IL: Magnolia Street.

Kramer, E. (2000). *Art as therapy: Collected papers* (L.A. Gerity, Ed.). London, England: Jessica Kingsley.

Levick, M. (1983). *They could not talk and so they drew: Children's styles of coping and thinking.* Springfield, IL: Charles C Thomas.

Levick, M., Safran, D. S., & Levine, A. J. (1990). Art therapists as expert witnesses: A judge delivers a precedent-setting decision. *The Arts in Psychotherapy, 17*(1), 49–53.

Lewis, N. D. C. (1973). Foreword to the first edition in Naumburg, M. *An introduction to art therapy: Studies of the "free" art expression of behavior problem children and adolescents as a means of diagnosis and therapy* (pp. v–vi). New York, NY: Teachers College Press.

Lindstrom, M. (1970). *Children's art.* Berkeley, CA: University of California Press.

Lowenfeld, V., & Brittain, L. (1987). *Creative and mental growth.* Upper Saddle River, NJ: Prentice Hall.

Mahler, M., Pine, F., & Bergman, A. (1975). *The psychological birth of the human infant—Symbiosis and individuation.* New York, NY: Basic Books.

Malchiodi, C. A. (1998). *Understanding children's drawings.* New York, NY: Guilford Books.

Malchiodi, C. A., Steele, W., & Kuban, C. (2008). Resilience and growth in traumatized children. In C. A. Malchiodi (Ed.), *Creative interventions with traumatized children* (pp. 285–301). New York, NY: Guilford Press.

Marvin, R. S., & Britner, P. A. (1999) Normative development: The ontogeny of attachment. In J. Cassidy & P. R. Shaver (Eds.), *Handbook of attachment: theory, research and clinical applications* (pp. 44–67). New York, NY: Guilford Press.

Masterson, J. (2000). *The personality disorders: A new look at the developmental self and object relations approach.* Redding, CT: Zeig, Tucker & Theisen.

McWilliams, N. (1994). *Psychoanalytic diagnosis: Understanding personality structure in clinical process.* New York, NY: Guilford Press.

Miller, M. J. (1997). Crisis assessment: The projective tree drawing, before, during and after a storm. In E. Hammer (Ed.), *The clinical application of projective drawings* (pp. 153–188). Springfield, IL: Charles C Thomas.

Munich, R. L. (2006). Integrating mentalization-based treatment and traditional psychotherapy to cultivate a common ground and promote agency. In J. G. Allen & P. Fonagy (Eds.), *Handbook of mentalization-based treatment* (pp. 143–156). Chichester, England: Wiley.

Naumburg, M. (1973). *An introduction to art therapy: Studies of the "free" art expression of behavior problem children and adolescents as a means of diagnosis and therapy.* New York, NY: Teachers College Press.

Novick, J., & Novick, K. K. (2006). *Good goodbyes: Knowing how to end in psychotherapy and psychoanalysis.* Lanham, MD: Rowman & Littlefeld.

Novick, K. K., & Novick, J. (2005). *Working with parents makes therapy work.* Lanham, MD: Rowman & Littlefeld.

Nucho, A. O. (2003). *Psychocybernetic model of art therapy* (2nd ed.). Springfield, IL: Charles C Thomas.

Racker, H. (1988). *Transference and countertransference.* London, England: Karnac Books.

Redl, F., & Wineman, P. (1965). Controls from within: Techniques for the treatment of the aggressive child. New York, NY: Free Press.

Robbins, A. (1994). A multi-modal approach to creative art therapy. London, England: Jessica Kingsley.

Robbins, A. (2000a). *The artist as therapist* (2nd ed.). London, England: Jessica Kingsley.

Robbins, A. (2000b). *Between therapists.* London, England: Jessica Kingsley.

Rubin, J. A. (2005). *Child art therapy.* New York, NY: Wiley.

Rubin, J. A. (2011). *The art of art therapy: What every art therapist needs to know.* New York, NY: Routledge.

Sameroff, A. J., & Emde, R.N. (Eds.) (1989). *Relationship disturbances in early childhood: A developmental approach.* New York, NY: Basic Books.

Schmidt Neven, R. (2010). *Core principles of assessment and therapeutic communication with children, parents and families: Towards the promotion of child and family wellbeing.* New York, NY: Routledge.

Schore, A. N. (1994). *Affect regulation and the origin of the self.* Mahwah, NJ: Erlbaum.

Schore, A. N. (2003). *Affect regulation and the repair of the self.* New York, NY: Norton.

Shore, A. (2000). Child art therapy and parent consultation: Facilitating child development and parent strengths. *Art Therapy: Journal of the American Art Therapy Association, 17*(1), 14–23.

Siegel, D. J. (1999). *The developing mind: Toward an interpersonal neurobiology of experience.* New York, NY: Guilford Press.

Silver, R. (2002). *Three art assessments.* New York, NY: Routledge.

Silver, R. (2007). *The Silver Drawing Test and Draw a Story.* New York, NY: Routledge.

Sroufe, L. A., Egeland, B., Carlson, E. A., & Collins, W. A. (2005). *The development of the person: The Minnesota study of risk and adaptation from birth to adulthood.* New York, NY: Guilford Press.

Sroufe, A., & Siegel, D. (2011, March/April). The verdict is in: The case for attachment theory. *Psychotherapy Networker: Your Source for Community, Learning and Excellence.* Retrieved from http://www.psychotherapynetworker.org/component/content/article/301-2011-marchapril/1271- (accessed 15 January 2013).

Stern, D. (1985). *The interpersonal world of the infant: A view from psychoanalysis and developmental psychology.* New York, NY: Basic Books.

Thomas, L. (2001). Containing the bad object: Observations and thoughts on the generation of bad feelings between people in an organization, a professional network, a therapist, and a child attending individual art therapy. In J. Murphy (Ed.), *Art therapy with young survivors of sexual abuse: Lost for words* (pp. 19–35). Hove, England: Routledge.

Ulman, E. (1975). The new use of art in psychiatric analysis. In E. Ulman & P. Dachinger (Eds.), *Art therapy in theory and practice* (pp. 361–386). New York, NY: Schocken Books.

Vaillant, G. E. (1985). Loss as a metaphor for attachment. *The American Journal of Psychoanalysis, 45*(1), 59–67.

Vaillant, G. (1993). *The wisdom of the ego.* Cambridge, MA: Harvard University Press.

van der Kolk, B. (2003). Posttraumatic stress disorder and the nature of trauma. In M. F. Solomon & D. J. Siegel (Eds.). *Healing trauma* (pp. 168–195). New York, NY: Norton.

van der Kolk, B. (2005). Developmental trauma disorder: Toward a rational diagnosis for children with complex trauma histories. *Psychiatric Annals, 35*(5), 401–408.

van IJzendoorn, M. H. (1990). Developments in cross cultural research on attachment: Some methodological notes. *Human Development, 33,* 3–9.

Vernis, J. S., Lichtenberg, E. F., & Henrich, L. (1997). The-Draw-a-Person-in-the-Rain: Its relation to diagnostic category. In E. Hammer (Ed.), *The clinical application of projective drawing* (pp. 335–345). Springfield, IL: Charles C Thomas.

Wallerstien, J., Lewis, J., & Blakeslee, S. (2000). *The unexpected legacy of divorce: A 25 year landmark study.* New York, NY: Hyperion.

Werner, E. E., & Smith, R. S. (2001). *Journeys from childhood to midlife: Risk, resilience, and recovery.* Ithaca, NY: Cornell University Press.

Widom, C. S., & Nikulina, V. (2012). Long-term consequences of child neglect in low income families. In V. Malholmes & R. B. King (Eds.), *The Oxford handbook of poverty and child development* (pp. 68–85). New York, NY: Oxford University Press.

Winnicott, D. W. (1965). *The family and individual development.* London, England: Tavistock.

Winnicott, D. W. (1971a). *Playing and reality.* New York, NY: Routledge.

Winnicott, D. W. (1971b). *Therapeutic consultations in child psychiatry.* New York: Basic Books.

Winnicott, D. W. (1977). *The piggle.* Madison, CT: International Universities Press.

Winnicott, D. W. (1990). *Maturational processes and the facilitating environment: Studies in the theory of emotional development.* London, England: Karnac Books.

Yalom, I. (2000). *The gift of therapy.* New York, NY: Harper Collins.

Index

Note: *Case examples* in the index are in *italics*.